"'Follow the money' isn't just sound advice for people tracing political corruption or criminal activity. Brennan and Surprenant persuasively demonstrate that understanding financial incentives and how institutions are held accountable is critical for checking the dynamics that lead to mass incarceration and excessive criminalization. This insightful book offers countless examples of the ways in which perverse incentives lead to excessive punishment without bringing public safety or other benefits. If we want to take a more rational approach to criminal justice policy making, analyzing the incentives of institutional actors is the key place to start, as this book shows."

—**Rachel Elise Barkow, author of** *Prisoners of Politics: Breaking the Cycle of Mass Incarceration*

"The authors say interesting and at times provocative things about a number of important topics, and they do so in a clear, accessible, and engaging manner. They make good use of both specific examples and more general statistics and they strike a nice balance between the concrete and the theoretical. I highly recommend this book to anyone who is interested in thinking critically about our criminal justice system."

—**David Boonin, University of Colorado, Boulder**

D1177108

INJUSTICE FOR ALL

American criminal justice is a dysfunctional mess. Cops are too violent, the punishments are too punitive, and the so-called Land of the Free imprisons more people than any other country in the world. Understanding why means focusing on color—not only on black or white (which already has been studied extensively), but also on green.

The problem is that nearly everyone involved in criminal justice—including district attorneys, elected judges, the police, voters, and politicians—faces bad incentives. Local towns often would rather send people to prison on someone else's dime than pay for more effective policing themselves. Local police forces can enrich themselves by turning into warrior cops who steal from innocent civilians. Voters have very little incentive to understand the basic facts about crime or how to fix it—and they vote accordingly. And politicians have every incentive to cater to voters' worst biases.

Injustice for All systematically diagnoses why and where American criminal justice goes wrong, and offers functional proposals for reform. By changing who pays for what, how people are appointed, how people are punished, and which things are criminalized, we can make the US a country which guarantees justice for all.

Key Features:

- Shows how bad incentives, not "bad apples," cause the dysfunction in American criminal justice
- Focuses not only on overincarceration, but also on *overcriminalization* and other failures of the criminal justice system

- Provides a philosophical and practical defense of reducing the scope of what's considered criminal activity
- Crosses ideological lines, highlighting both the weaknesses and strengths of liberal, conservative, and libertarian agendas
- Fully integrates tools from philosophy and social science, making this stand out from the many philosophy books on punishment, on the one hand, and the solely empirical studies from sociology and criminal science, on the other
- Avoids disciplinary jargon, broadening the book's suitability for students and researchers in many different fields and for an interested general readership
- Offers plausible reforms that realign specific incentives with the public good.

Chris W. Surprenant is Professor of Philosophy at the University of New Orleans, where he directs the University Honors Program and is the founding director of the Urban Entrepreneurship and Policy Institute. He is the author of *Kant and the Cultivation of Virtue* (2014), and editor or co-editor of *The Value and Limits of Academic Speech* (2018), *Rethinking Punishment in the Era of Mass Incarceration* (2017), *Kant and the Scottish Enlightenment* (2017), and *Kant and Education: Interpretations and Commentary* (2011).

Jason Brennan is the Robert J. and Elizabeth Flanagan Family Professor of Strategy, Economics, Ethics, and Public Policy at Georgetown University. He is the author of ten books, including *Cracks in the Ivory Tower: The Moral Mess of Higher Education* (2019) and *Against Democracy* (2016).

INJUSTICE FOR ALL

How Financial Incentives
Corrupted and Can Fix the US
Criminal Justice System

Chris W. Surprenant and Jason Brennan

 Routledge
Taylor & Francis Group

NEW YORK AND LONDON

First published 2020
by Routledge
52 Vanderbilt Avenue, New York, NY 10017

and by Routledge
2 Park Square, Milton Park, Abingdon, Oxon, OX14 4RN

Routledge is an imprint of the Taylor & Francis Group, an informa business

© 2020 Taylor & Francis

Library of Congress Cataloging-in-Publication Data
A catalog record for this title has been requested

ISBN: 978-1-138-33880-7 (hbk)
ISBN: 978-1-138-33882-1 (pbk)
ISBN: 978-0-367-85544-4 (ebk)

Typeset in Bembo
by Swales & Willis, Exeter, Devon, UK

CONTENTS

ACKNOWLEDGMENTS

We both want to thank the editors at Routledge, especially Andy Beck, for their help bringing this book to press, including finding a non-anonymous reviewer, who offered helpful feedback on previous versions. We also want to thank David Boonin, a non-anonymous review, whose comments were especially helpful.

Chris's work on this project was supported by grants from the Louisiana Board of Regents (ATLAS—LEQSF(2018-19)-RD-ATL-09), the Charles Koch Foundation, and the King's College Center for the Study of Human Flourishing. He also thanks the faculty, students, and community members at the following organizations for their helpful questions and feedback on some of this material when it was presented to them: Arizona State University, Austin Institute, Ball State University, Bridgewater State University, California State University—Sacramento, Center for the Study of Liberty, Dillard University, Georgia State University, Institute for Humane Studies, Jackson State University, Law Firm of Ferguson Braswell Fraser Kubasta, Louisiana State University—Baton Rouge, Morehouse College, Quincy University, Southern Methodist University, University of Dallas, University of Illinois Springfield, University of North Carolina—Greensboro, University of Texas—Austin, Wake Forest University, Wellesley College, and West Virginia University.

Jason wishes to thank Robert and Elizabeth Flanagan for their continued support for his research.

Parts of Chapter 4 were previously published by Jason Brennan as "Corporal Punishment as an Alternative to Incarceration," in *Rethinking Punishment in the Era of Mass Incarceration*, ed. Chris Surprenant (New York: Routledge Press, 2017), 294–308.

An earlier version of Chapter 5, "Crime Doesn't Pay, Unless You're the State," was published by Chris Surprenant as "Policing and Punishment for Profit" in the *Journal of Business Ethics* (2019), 159(1).

1

IT'S WORSE THAN YOU THINK

If you're reading this book, then it's likely you already believe that the US criminal justice system is broken. You may also believe that there are two justice systems—one for the haves and one for the have-nots—and that an individual's ability to receive justice, either when accusing someone of bad behavior or when being accused, depends more on the characteristics of the individuals involved rather than the merits of the case.

Maybe you don't believe these things, but you can see why people might. Hardly a day goes by without hearing a story of a police officer shooting an unarmed citizen, a judge or prosecutor imposing an unreasonable punishment, a small town raising money by aggressively policing moving violations, or county sheriffs seizing cash and goods from people doing nothing more than driving on the interstate. Police are too aggressive, too violent, and can violate our rights with virtual impunity. On YouTube you can watch cops play high-stakes games of Simon Says with civilians, and then watch those cops murder or tase the civilians when they can't follow contradictory directions. Police are rarely punished for excessive force, even when they murder civilians. After incarcerated people serve their time, they return to society as second-class citizens who often cannot vote and have no hope of securing good long-term employment.

The vast majority of the people negatively affected by these policies are poor and black. High profile books such as Michelle Alexander's *The New Jim Crow* demonstrate the racial disparities in our justice system: Black Americans are disproportionately and excessively fined by police[1] and are arrested at disproportionately higher rates for non-violent offenses like marijuana possession.[2] Black men receive longer sentences than white men for the same crimes.[3] Perhaps most disturbing, while one in nine American men will spend part of their life in prison, when sorted by race that number changes to one in three black men as compared to one in 17 white.[4] These numbers suggest that the answer to our criminal justice woes may lie in underlying issues of race and racism: Racist laws, put in place by racist politicians, policed by racist cops, and enforced by racist judges.

But the story is not as simple as it seems. Legal scholars John Pfaff [5] and James Forman, Jr.[6] have questioned this straightforward and intuitively persuasive story about race and racism. Pfaff argues that dramatic changes in prosecutors' behavior during the early and mid-1990s is more responsible for mass incarceration than the War on Drugs or draconian sentencing laws that disproportionately target black Americans. Forman goes further. He argues that it was many black mayors, judges, police chiefs, and community leaders—not just their white counterparts— who embraced tough-on-crime principles as a response to surging violence and drug abuse in black communities. This approach by black leaders to addressing problems within their own communities led to many of the racial disparities we see in the criminal justice system today.

We believe the fundamental story is different from what Alexander, Pfaff, Forman, and others describe. When it comes to the color of justice in America, follow the money. What matters even more than black and white is *green*.

Financial incentives, and people responding rationally to those incentives, are responsible for most, if not all, of the dramatic changes we observed in US criminal justice over the last 50 years.

The incarceration statistics are the most dramatic. The so-called Land of the Free is also the Land of the Imprisoned. At the beginning of 2018, approximately 2.3 million people were incarcerated in the US. That's about one in 100 citizens. The US has 5% of the world's population but 25% of the world's prison population.

In the US, 27% of all people incarcerated, including 60% of all females incarcerated, have not been convicted of a crime. They're sitting in local jails awaiting their day in court, either too poor to come up with bail or denied bail, often because of technical parole violations. The US incarcerates women —who commit most crimes far less often than men—at a higher rate than most other rich, democratic countries incarcerate men. As a result, about 1.5 million children have at least one parent behind bars.[7]

The problem isn't just that we throw too many people in jail for too long. While nearly 1% of the population is locked up in cages, an additional 4.6 million people, or an additional 2% of the population, are currently under state control through probation or parole. In total, over 7 million people, or nearly 2.5% of the population of the United States, are under some form of "carceral supervision"—that is, incarcerated, on parole, or on probation.[8]

So much for the "Land of the Free". That label was false in 1814, when about 13% of the country was enslaved, and it remains false today thanks to our overly punitive and harsh criminal justice system.

Let's be clear: The US is not normal. No other country on earth—even communist states or dictatorships—throws so many of its citizens in jail so readily and for so long.[9] Only 11 US states incarcerate citizens at a lower rate than the Russian Federation,[10] and 35 US states, including overwhelmingly white states like Wyoming and Montana, put people in prison at a higher rate than repressive, authoritarian Cuba.[11] The US is a modern, rich, liberal, republican democracy, just like Canada, Switzerland, Germany, Norway, the United Kingdom, France, or Australia. But our criminal justice system looks little like theirs.

It wasn't always like this. In the 1950s, the US criminal justice system looked more or less like Canada's or the other liberal democracies in Western Europe. We had slightly higher crime and a slightly harsher and more punitive system, but we were not *unusual*. Even as late as 1971, Finland, Belgium, France, Germany, and the United Kingdom had an incarceration rate of about 100 prisoners for every 100,000 people, while the United States was about 150 for every 100,000. We were at the high end of the cluster, but we were in the cluster. Fast forward to today, and the incarceration rate in those other countries hasn't changed much—they're all still at about 100 prisoners for every 100,000 people. (The UK has jumped up to 150/100,000, making it as punitive as 1950s America.) But the US incarceration rate has skyrocketed to about 700 prisoners for every 100,000 people.[12]

And who profits from mass incarceration? Nearly everyone involved, except the prisoners themselves. The so-called prison industrial complex in the United States is a $182 billion (yes, billion) industry.[13] While many people who want to express their outrage seem to focus on private prisons, private prisons represent only a small fraction of the money flowing in—$4.3 billion, less than 2%. Public corrections agencies (prisons, jails, parole, and probation), courts and other legal costs, policing, and public administrative employees consume the bulk of this funding. All of these people have a personal stake in preventing the types of reform that would make their jobs go away. Beyond the people involved in the justice system directly, service providers also have the most to lose. Companies that provide health care, food, utilities, and other services (e.g., bail bondsmen) all have their livelihoods to lose if reform efforts lead to a smaller criminal justice footprint.

Politicians benefit from mass incarceration as well. While we may not be surprised to learn that politicians in some states benefit from being seen as tough on crime or because they have brought financial gains to their constituents by housing prisoners in their district, they also benefit in unexpected and surprising ways. For example, the US Census counts incarcerated persons as residents of the jail or prison, not the town they lived in before being incarcerated. In Connecticut, this so-called prison gerrymandering is responsible for creating nine state representative districts that would not meet federal minimum population requirements if not for counting their prison populations. Even worse, seven of these districts are majority-white and exist because of the majority-black prison population, a population who cannot vote and are otherwise not represented.[14]

And our problems with mass incarceration aren't even the half of it. As you'll soon see, the entire US legal system is broken at the local, state, and federal levels. That it is broken is not a coincidence or accident, nor is it the result of a few nefarious actors. Fixing it requires us to understand why it's broken and how financial incentives drive bad policy.

The Faces Behind the Numbers

There's a famous quotation often attributed to Soviet leader Joseph Stalin: "The death of one man is a tragedy, while the death of millions are mere statistics."[15] While Stalin himself probably never said that, whoever did knew something deep about human nature. Our brains are designed to understand stories, not numbers. We empathize easily with one person; our eyes gloss over when we hear about millions. But one problem affecting criminal justice in the United States is that horrible stories about injustices and lives being unnecessary destroyed emerge nearly every single day. Open a calendar, close your eyes, pick a week, and you can look through local newspapers to find a handful of stories demonstrating the injustice of our justice system.

To prove this point: We've written the first draft of this section during the week of August 12, 2018. What sorts of injustices came to light during this same week last month, July 9–13, 2018? As it turns out, quite a few. That such stories are occurring with such frequency and across the country should convince us that something has gone terribly, terribly wrong. Below are some of the most egregious, one from each day of that week.

July 9, 2018—New Orleans, Louisiana

What would you do if you received a letter from your local district attorney ordering you to appear at a certain date and time to testify against someone who has been accused of committing a crime? What would you do if that letter was labeled "SUBPOENA" in big, bold, red letters at the top, and came with the threat of jail time if you didn't comply? While it is not unusual for a district attorney to have judges issue subpoenas to witnesses, especially those who might be reluctant to testify, it is highly unusual—if not unprecedented—for a district attorney's office to issue *fake* subpoenas, that is, subpoenas (or letters that look like subpoenas) that were never signed off on by a judge. While forging official documents would be bad enough, the Orleans Parish District Attorney went further and ordered the police to arrest citizens when they failed to comply with these fake subpoenas.

On July 9, 2018, *The Lens* reported that the district attorney's office issued 249 fake subpoenas over a three-year period. For at least 50 of these cases, there were "court filings seeking to arrest crime victims and witnesses for allegedly failing to cooperate. Almost all of those were granted; 16 people were arrested."[16] But it wasn't just the Orleans Parish District Attorney who was issuing fake subpoenas. District attorneys in neighboring Jefferson and St. Tammany Parishes also issued similar looking documents, with Jefferson Parish going so far as to issue one fake subpoena to an 11-year-old.[17]

July 10, 2018—El Paso, Texas

Almost daily in the US, there are multiple credible news stories of police officers or other government agents using, or threatening to use, an inappropriate amount of force to resolve a problem that they themselves created. July 10, 2018, was just another day.[18] Perhaps the most egregious reported incident of excessive force on that day was in El Paso, Texas, where a police officer, responding to a trespassing call in the area, came across a group of children—all around 12 or 13 years old—playing in a street.

What happened next is under investigation, but by the time the mobile phone cameras started rolling the officer had pinned the head of one of the children against a stone wall with his knee, and was shouting at the others to back up before pulling a gun on them.[19] Then, after another officer forcefully grabs the pinned child and throws him on the ground, the original officer goes to grab his gun again, thinks better of it, and pulls out his baton instead and starts pointing it at the children. If that wasn't bad enough, the officer then approaches one of the children recording, attempts to grab the phone to stop the recording, and when the child gives the phone to another person to continue recording, the officer grabs him, forcefully pins him against a police car, and cuffs him, all for doing nothing besides recording what was happening (which is perfectly legal). At the end, to top it off, the officer is heard telling the kids, "Somebody's going to end up dead one of these days."

Many people in the US who read this story likely will have a reaction along the lines of, "Yeah, that's terrible, but it happens all the time. At least no one was killed." Yes, no children were killed in El Paso, but police did kill people on July 10, 2018, in Casper, WY;[20] Phoenix, AZ;[21] and Garland, TX.[22] In only one of these cases (Casper, WY) was the person shot thought to be carrying a gun, and even in that case it wasn't clear whether he was even holding the gun when he was shot. The shooting on July 10 was the third officer-involved shooting in Casper in 2018, a town of less than 60,000 residents.[23]

July 11, 2018—Michigan

While many abuses happen at the local level, sometimes state-level policies create incentives for law enforcement agencies to behave badly. One such example is civil asset forfeiture, or the process by which the police are allowed to seize assets from an individual who is suspected of a crime—even if they have little to no evidence to support this suspicion and that individual is never charged. A news article released on July 11 finds that in Michigan during 2017, police seized the property of close to 1000 people—more than $13 million in cash and assets—without those people ever being convicted of crimes.[24] Although Michigan state police *claimed* that these assets were mainly those of drug traffickers and that forfeitures were motivated by their interest in stopping criminal activity, that explanation seems implausible based on what was seized in 2017, data that took over six months to be released.[25]

A more likely explanation is that Michigan is taking advantage of asset forfeiture laws to raise additional revenue for county and municipal expenses. Here, Michigan is not alone. Between 2014 and 2017, the United States government, with the assistance of state law enforcement agencies, seized over $9 billion in assets (yes billion, with a "b"),[26] an amount higher than all reported property theft throughout the US in that same period. In short, without due process and with only the thinnest pretense of reasonable suspicion, American governmental entities steal more from their citizens than all burglars, muggers, and thieves combined. Cops can simply state they're suspicious of you, and that's good enough. They don't have to have good evidence and don't have to prove their suspicions. Due process here amounts to little more than police fiat.

The government has a clear motivation to seize assets under such questionable circumstances: Police departments and municipal governments around the country rely on seized assets, whether cash directly or property that can be sold for cash, to help pay for operations and programs that they otherwise could not afford. Cops can't put seized money into their paychecks, but they can use it to fund their precincts, which means nicer amenities and more money in the budget for pay raises. The law gives police a positive incentive to fleece you, and police take the bait.

July 12, 2018—Biscayne Park, FL

Each of the stories we identified during this week are egregious, but this story out of Biscayne Park, Florida, a small suburb of Miami, likely wins as being the most egregious. On July 12, 2018, Raimundo Atesiano, the former police chief of Biscayne Park, was indicted for pressuring his officers into targeting random black men and women to pin crimes on in order to clear their cases. According to police officers working under Atesiano, they were directed as follows:

> If you have burglaries that are open cases that are not solved yet, if you see anybody black walking through our streets and they have somewhat of a record, arrest them so we can pin them for all the burglaries.[27]

One of the people arrested under these orders was 36-year-old Clarens Desrouleaux, a Haitian immigrant, father of two children, and resident of Biscayne Park who had lived legally in the US for more than 20 years.[28] Although Desrouleaux was discovered in possession of a check stolen from a house that had been burglarized, there was no evidence to suggest he was the person who broke into the house. But instead of dropping the case, the prosecutor pressed forward because two police officers, Charles Dayoub and Guillermo Ravelo, testified that Desrouleaux had admitted to them that he had broken into the house, something which both Dayoub and Ravelo later admitted never happened. The district attorney threatened to charge him as a habitual offender if he didn't take a plea, which would have meant a prison sentence of up to 30 years if convicted, so, instead, Desrouleaux pled guilty to the burglary and was sentenced to five years in prison.[29]

This story has a somewhat happy ending, at least for everyone but Desrouleaux. Former chief Atesiano was sentenced to three years in prison after pleading guilty to conspiring to deprive individuals of their civil rights.[30] Guillermo Ravelo and Charles Dayoub both pled guilty to their roles in these activities and were sentenced respectively to 27 months in prison[31] and 12 months in prison. All of the arrests made by Atesiano and his officers were expunged.

But this investigation did not come soon enough for Desrouleaux. Not only did he serve the five-year sentence for a robbery he didn't commit—nearly two years longer than the combined sentences of Ravelo and Dayoub, the men who framed him and betrayed the public's trust—but he was also deported back to his native Haiti when he was released from prison in April 2017.[32] Although Desrouleaux has filed a federal civil rights lawsuit seeking an unspecified amount in monetary damages, he is still unable to return to the US to be united with his family and two children, and will never get back those five years behind bars.

July 13, 2018—Brooklyn, NY

Clarens Desrouleaux's story of being falsely accused of a crime and serving time as a result is unfortunately neither unique nor all that uncommon. On July 13, 2018, 44-year-old Shawn Williams left a New York prison as a free man after serving just under 25 years in prison for a murder he almost certainly didn't commit. Williams was convicted based on the testimony of one witness who later claimed that New York Detective Louis Scarcella intimidated her into identifying Williams.[33] The witness claimed that she did not recognize Williams but that detectives told her that he was the killer, briefly imprisoned her when she was unwilling to testify, and then forced her to return to New York from Georgia to testify falsely against him.

It gets worse. Detective Scarcella was aware that Williams was actually in Reading, PA during the days before and after the murder. Williams was arrested in Reading on July 2 for drinking beer in public and received documented medical treatment at a Reading hospital on July 11. There was no evidence suggesting that he had returned to Brooklyn during this period or that he was in Brooklyn on July 9 when the murder was committed. Detective Scarcella was aware—or should have been aware (since Williams told him)—of both the July 2 arrest and July 11 hospital stay, yet he proceeded with the case anyway.

Williams was one of 14 people wrongfully convicted after "shady investigations involving tainted evidence, misleading testimony or forced confessions" by Scarcella.[34] These 14 men served a combined total of 245 years behind bars. Looking for a happy ending or justice served? You won't find it here. Not only did the Brooklyn District Attorney's Office continue to defend Scarcella's work as convictions continued to be vacated,[35] but also there are currently no plans to pursue a case against Scarcella. In fact, he was recently honored by New York Police Department's retired detectives association.[36]

These stories are outrageous. But they are somewhat tame by comparison to others that have come out over the last few years—some of which we'll bring to your attention throughout this book. It just so happens that these occurred during this one week we selected at random. If you want to be disgusted, you can play this game as well. Select a week at random from the calendar. It won't take you long to find similar stories that broke on each and every day.

The Three Blind Men

The small bit of good news is that something is changing. Criminal justice reform is no longer a partisan issue. People on both the Left and Right, both Democrats and Republicans, agree that the American criminal justice system must change. But they don't always agree on why it's a mess or what exactly we should do.

To fix the criminal justice system, we need to work together, across political divides. Still, our different political affiliations help us see some problems but blind us to others.

The philosopher Robert Nozick once joked, "Normative sociology, the study of what the causes of problems ought to be, greatly fascinates us all."[37] Nozick means that when most of us notice a social problem—too much crime, too much obesity, too many fatherless children, too much ethnic segregation, or whatnot—we already know who or what we want to blame. We're ready to point the finger at our favorite villains without ever taking a serious look at the evidence. We're like doctors who stand ready to diagnose the disease before we've reviewed the patient's symptoms.

The economist Arnold Kling says Americans divide into three major political tribes: Conservatives, progressives, and libertarians. These three tribes see the world differently and speak different languages.[38] Thus, they can barely talk to each other. Each walks away from conversations convinced the other two tribes are full of evil idiots. Even when they agree that there is a new problem, they immediately conclude they already know the cause—and it turns out to be pretty much the same cause for every new problem. That's normative sociology for you.

Progressives want to stand up against oppression and inequality. No surprise, then, that when they examine the US criminal justice system, they conclude the underlying causes are racism, poverty, and inequality. We'd fix things by overcoming racism, funding better schools, and offering better welfare programs for the poor.

Conservatives want to stand up for moral values and the Western tradition. No surprise, then, that when they see our problems, they conclude there is a breakdown of moral virtue and community spirit. We have a criminal justice problem because we have a *crime* problem. No wonder we have so much crime, they say. Too many kids are being raised by neglectful or overworked unwed moms, with dads nowhere around. People don't take pride in their communities and don't pitch in. Law and order need to be enforced. When violent crime engulfs our cities and drugs flood our villages, we need to protect society.

Libertarians want to stand up for individual rights against encroaching governments. No surprise, then, that when they see our problems, they blame it on the Drug War. The era of mass incarceration, they note, began exactly at the same time Nixon declared a War on Drugs. They say that the Drug War has—as microeconomics would predict—ghettoized inner cities and created violent black markets in drugs and all the associated gang violence. It has turned normal people into criminals and police into "warrior cops."[39]

In this case, everybody's partly right and partly wrong. They're a bit like the proverbial blind men feeling different parts of an elephant—one feels the side and thinks the elephant is a wall, one feels the trunk and thinks it's a snake, one feels the leg and thinks it's a tree. Progressives, conservatives, and libertarians have each diagnosed a piece of the problem. But they are also too quick to think they know the whole animal. Since they only see a piece of the problem, their proposed solutions are at best incomplete.

Progressives are right that poverty and crime go together. They are right that racism partly fuels the aggressive and punitive way laws are enforced. They are right that black Americans are treated much worse than whites. For instance, black Americans do not use or sell illicit drugs at higher rates than whites, but they are arrested, convicted, and imprisoned at much higher rates.[40]

But the progressive story doesn't quite work. Remember, until the early 1970s, the US criminal justice system was only somewhat more punitive or harsh than Europe's. Then over the last four decades, we started incarcerating people at a rate that makes China, Russia, and even Saddam Hussein's Iraq look *soft*. It's not as though that in 1970s and 1980s, Americans suddenly became *more racist* than they were in the era of Jim Crow, in the era when you could openly say racist things without any backlash. We're not saying racism disappeared, but the criminal justice system became more punitive as racism waned—and yes, it has waned, if not been eradicated. Further, over-whelmingly white states, such as Wyoming, are more punitive toward their white criminals than other countries are to their citizens.

Moreover, poverty cannot easily explain why crime rose. Crime rose even as poverty rates dropped. For instance, consider black Americans. Their inci-dence of crime rose between the 1950s and 1980s, even though the poverty rate for black families more or less steadily dropped from over 50% in 1960 to between 30–35% throughout the 1970s and 1980s.[41] The percentage of indi-vidual black Americans in poverty faced a similar drop. Yet as they got richer, the government also become more, not less, punitive toward them.[42] Poverty has not vanished from the US, but even the poor are in absolute terms gener-ally better off today than in the past, and yet incarceration rates rose.

Beyond that, what we call "poverty" today is different from what we called poverty in the past. If you compared the standard of living of US households at the poverty line today, they in many ways are on par with or superior to average or middle-class households in the 1970s.[43]

In short, the progressive story can't quite be right. Racism and poverty had a downward trend while mass incarceration had an upward trend. That's the opposite of what their story predicts.

The conservative story also gets something right. Conservatives are correct that violent criminals tend to come from one-parent households. The break-down of families partly explains the rise in crime.[44] They are also right that part of the reason the US has more prisoners is that we have more crime; we have more violent police at least in part because we have more violent criminals.

But their story doesn't quite work either. Yes, the US has higher crime, but not enough to explain or justify why the US puts so many people in jail for so long. In other words, our higher incarceration rates are not proportional to our higher crime rates, and our higher sentence lengths are not proportional to our worse crime. (Also, while US crime rates are higher, oddly, *victimization* rates in the US may not be much higher than elsewhere.[45])

Starting in 1994, violent and other forms of crime started to drop in the US; as of 2014, violent crime fell to 1950s levels. It wasn't as though all those single moms got and stayed married. Criminologists left and right have studied why crime dropped. Everyone agrees that increased policing helped, but they also agree it can explain only a fraction of the drop. We don't really know why crime rose in the 1960s through 1980s, and we don't know why it has fallen since.[46] Nevertheless, even when violent crime disappeared, our criminal system has become ever more punitive and aggressive.

Libertarians are in the same boat. The War on Drugs indeed explains why the US police are trained to deploy military tactics against civilians, why they use SWAT teams too much, and why the Pentagon unloads excess military equipment—such as machine guns and armored cars—onto police stations even in rural, low-crime towns.[47] They are right that just as alcohol prohibition caused mob violence in the 1920s, so drug prohibition causes gang violence today.

But even if the War on Drugs ended tomorrow and the jails released all the prisoners convicted or accused only of drug offenses, the US would still have far more prisoners than any other country, would still incarcerate at a higher rate than almost any other country, and would still impose longer sentences and harsher punishments.[48] Only about one in five US prisoners are there *only* for drug crimes.[49] Some of the non-drug crimes result from conditions created by the Drug War—just as alcohol prohibition led to increased gang violence in the 1920s—but eliminating the Drug War wouldn't solve the problem on its own. There are too many other crimes not connected, even indirectly, to conditions created by the Drug War.

Bad Incentives, Not Bad Apples

People of different Ideologies blame the problem on different villains. But one thing we all share is a built-in bias to blame bad things on bad intentions.

We are social primates. Our brains are designed *to read other minds*. We quickly ascertain what other people want, how they feel, and whether we can trust them.

But the problem is that we use this mind-reading technology everywhere, even when there are not minds to read. Look at how ancient people around the world tended to believe a spirit lived in every tree, field, or brook. Even today, when some tornado hits, people wonder if God is trying to teach them a lesson. Or whenever the election goes the wrong way—that is, the other side wins—they assume Russian hackers or deliberate voter fraud carried the day. People have a hard time understanding how bad changes could occur unless some bad man is directing everything from behind the curtain. We want to blame bad things on bad guys with bad intentions.

But what social scientists have discovered is that big social changes usually result from human *action* but not human *intention*. There is usually no mastermind pulling levers, no ghost haunting the house, no evil belief system running the show. It's usually something else. Social trends *emerge* from individual behavior, as people react to one another, not because someone decided to create that trend.

Economists often say that when we want to explain behavior, we should start by looking at the incentives people face. When people get rewarded for doing something, they do more of it. When they get punished for doing something, they do less. If they can do something destructive which benefits them and push the costs onto others, they do more of it. When they themselves bear the costs of their bad behavior, they do less. If we see lots of people doing something bad, it's probably not because they are a bunch of bad apples, or bad people with bad intentions. The problem is not bad apples, it's that we're putting normal apples in a bad barrel. It's the incentives they face that are messed up.

In turn, we can explain the incentives people face by looking at the rules people live under, as they are enforced. Big trends emerge from individual behavior without anyone running the show. Rules create incentives, and incentives determine behavior. That's basic economics.

To illustrate, imagine you sign up for a class. On the first day, you walk into the lecture hall filled with 300 students. The professor says:

> I believe we should all be equal. So, I will not assign you individual grades based on individual performance. Instead, we will have a final exam 14 weeks from now, worth 100% of your grade. I will average all final exams together, and every student will receive that same average grade.

If a professor did that, he'd more or less guarantee the final grade would be an F. Hardly anyone would study. When that happens, it would be silly to complain that "Kids today are lazy," that the students are incompetent, that their parents didn't teach them well, or that they don't care about learning for learning's sake. The problem is with the rules, not the students. Under these bad rules, studying still takes time and effort, but brings no reward. Studying hard just leads students to be suckered by their peers. Regardless of whether the student works her butt off or spends the semester watching Netflix, she'll get the same grade. The students can't even use peer pressure to ensure the other students study; there are too many of them in the class for that to work. (Later, we'll show you that this metaphor explains why voters are misinformed about crime and how to reduce it.)

Back to criminal justice: Over the past 40 years, the US criminal justice system went nuts. It can't be that all of a sudden, in 1971, all the judges' and prosecutors' hearts became two sizes too small. It's not that they became even more racist right at the time when racism became a bad word. Politicians made many mistakes, including some stupid mistakes, but it's not as though over the past 40 years our politicians became even more crooked, conniving, and stupid. Much as you might want to blame it on a few badly motivated individuals, you don't get a system this messed up without the cooperation of almost everyone involved.

Criminal Justice without Romance

There were a few shocks to the system in the 1970s and 1980s. This caused people to change some of the rules, which in turn caused problems that made people act badly. American hearts didn't turn cold in 1971. No one is sabotaging the system.

We are hard-wired, it seems, to prefer romantic stories about why things happen. But social science has no time for romance.

One romantic view holds that since criminal justice is about justice, the kinds of people who work in criminal justice must have especially noble and public-spirited motivations. After all, the purpose of criminal justice is to keep law and order, punish the guilty, exonerate the innocent, make people pay their debts to society, right the wrongs, and, perhaps, get the guilty back on their feet for a second chance.

Maybe these are good *ideals*. But beware. Even if criminal justice *should* promote such ideals, it doesn't follow that it will.

There's no guarantee or reason to believe that the kinds of people who work in criminal justice are motivated solely or even predominantly by such ideals. They are likely to be regular people, with their own private and selfish concerns. Many will just pay lip service to these ideals, perhaps convince themselves their hearts are in the right place, but then act like normal people.[50]

Sure, the people who want to work in criminal justice—or in government— may be somewhat different from the kinds of people who want to become used car salespeople, business executives, or nurses. But people are people. The system isn't full of saints.

A slightly different romantic view sees the problems of criminal justice as the result of a battle between the forces of good and evil. *Law and Order* and all your favorite cop movies show gritty do-gooders fighting for justice. That means taking on the crooked DAs and the dirty cops; once you clean up the dirt, the system returns to normal and dispenses justice as the Constitution intended.

On this romantic view, there are good guys and bad guys. Bad things happen when the bad people are in charge; good things happen when the good people are in charge. On this romantic view, when something bad happens, you try to change *who* rules, not *the* rules.

In 1986, James Buchanan won the Nobel Prize in Economics in part for pointing out how silly this mode of thinking is. Before Buchanan's time, social scientists would often just pretend that government agents must be competent and motivated to do the right thing. So it was a puzzle why governments so often passed bad laws or passed dumb rules that made thing worse, not better. Buchanan's apparently earth-shaking idea—an idea which seems obvious in retrospect—was that government officials, from lawmakers to the police, are just like everyone else. Handing someone a gun, giving him a baton, or empowering him to make laws, won't make him an angel. The power to do good is also the power to dispense favors and rig the system for your own benefit. Once you create that power, you can expect people to compete for the chance to control, use, and abuse it.

Criminal justice without romance looks different. When you see bad behavior, you ask:

- What incentives do the rules create?
- Who bears the costs of people's actions and choices?
- Who benefits?
- Why are the rules the way they are?

When you ask those sorts of questions, you'll find you rarely have to blame things on bad apples sabotaging the system. Bad rules create bad incentives which induce normal people to act badly.

What do we know about people? Your commonsense stereotypes are pretty accurate. Most people are mostly—but not entirely—selfish. That is, they tend to care about themselves more than other people, though they may love a select few friends, children, family members, or a spouse more than themselves. We don't usually sacrifice our self-interest for the greater good. We aren't sociopaths—we really do care about morality and justice for their own sake. But we're neither devils nor angels. We tend only to see what's right in front of us. We tend to measure things by our good intentions and often have no idea how to figure out whether the things we do—like pass certain laws, or change certain criminal codes—actually work. We aren't lazy, but we aren't worker ants either. We'll put in the effort to fix a problem—or even to be aware of it or learn how to fix it—only if the expected benefits to ourselves exceed the expected costs. When other people suffer the costs of our actions and we reap the benefits, we'll tend to do more of those things.

Sure, people vary a bit; we're not all the same. Some people are more racist than others, some are more virtuous, some are harder working. But the moral problems facing criminal justice didn't arise because our good will vanished. It's something else.

Many people recognize the system is bad, but, as we said before, they offer facile diagnoses as to what has gone wrong and thus offer facile solutions. They blame a few bad apples or bad ideologies. Libertarians blame racism, police militarization, and the Drug War. Liberals and so-called progressives blame racism and inequality. Conservatives blame the moral breakdown of society and the collapse of the family. They are all partially right, but only partially right.

Our distinctive contribution to the debate is to insist that we should *follow the money*. The reason the system is dysfunctional is because the key players in the system—from voters to politicians, town aldermen to state legislatures, local police to prison guards, prosecutors to district attorneys to public defenders, face dysfunctional incentives.

Voters make bad choices because democracy incentivizes them to be misinformed and to vote symbolically. Local jurisdictions strapped for cash can make money by demanding fines for every small infraction—and by expanding the number of things that count as infractions. Local jurisdictions can save money by hiring fewer police and sending more people to state prisons. Prosecutors, district attorneys, and politicians win elections from misinformed voters by saying they are tough on crime and tough on criminals, not by defending more humane—or more *effective*—approaches to criminal justice. State legislators have every incentive to keep jails and prisons open in their home districts. The key players have a *monetary* and power-based stake in keeping things going as is, but hardly anyone has a stake in fixing the system. The benefits of bad behaviors are concentrated among the few while the costs are diffused among the many; so the few act badly and the many do nothing. (We'll explain this further in Chapter 2.)

Why Should *I* Care?

If you've read this far, you probably already care about fixing American criminal justice. But perhaps you wonder if you *should* care. Or perhaps you know many people who don't care, who think that caring about criminal justice means you're a namby-pamby bleeding heart liberal, a pie-in-the-sky Christian do-gooder, or some sort of anarchist. We've heard people—including our own family members— say, "I'm not a criminal. I'm a law-abiding citizen. Who cares?"

Well, for one, you should care because we should do the right thing. Yes, even wrongdoers have rights. Vlad the Impaler wasn't soft on crime, but neither was he a role model. Punishments are supposed to be proportional to the crime. You take an eye for an eye and a tooth for tooth; you don't punish people more than they deserve, and you don't punish innocent people. We know you don't ground your kids for six months each time they tell a lie. If you did, you'd be a bad parent. Well, similarly, we shouldn't overpunish criminals—we should give them no worse a punishment than they deserve.

Now ask yourself, was Eisenhower's 1950s Republican-led America full of bleeding-heart softies who underpunished its criminals? Is it really that now, in 2020, we've finally figured out the right amount of punishment? Is the US—with much longer sentences than other countries—the only country punishing its criminals the right amount, while the other free countries—plus the unfree countries like China and Russia—are far too lenient?

Second, you should care because you're paying for this system. In 2010 alone, the US federal government, 50 US States, and local jurisdictions spent approximately $80 billion on incarceration, including "expenditures [to] fund the supervision, confinement, and rehabilitation of adults and juveniles ... and confinement of persons awaiting trial and adjudication."[51] California spends over $75,000 a year per prisoner housing each of its 130,000 prisoners.[52] (That's more than the full sticker price at Georgetown University, the posh private school where one of us authors works.) Criminal justice isn't cheap. And we the innocent are the ones who pay for it through our taxes. Every dollar spent on prisons could have been spent on your children's schools, on fixing your roads, on serving our wounded veterans—or left in your paycheck to spend how *you* see fit.

There are hidden costs, too. For instance, of the 2.2 million people in jail right now, about 1.2 million are there for something other than violent crime.[53] Many of the people there for violent crime have arguably been there too long; they've paid their debt to society and it's time to give them a real second chance. Imagine those 1.2 million people were out working full-time at meager *minimum wage* jobs. That's at least $18 billion in services they could be providing the rest of us instead of rotting away in cells, cut off from families, surrounded by, learning from, and befriending other criminals. $18 billion is a low-ball estimate, of course. Further, wages don't capture their entire possible value to others.

You should care because the real costs are higher even than *that*. As we'll explain in Chapter 3, some of the things people get punished for shouldn't be crimes *at all*. And, as we'll explain in Chapter 4, many times there are far better ways to deal with crimes than by *punishing* people—in particular, we should make many criminals *undo* or pay for the harm they've done rather than sit in jail. In England 1000 years ago, if you hurt someone, you were made to pay them back and make them whole, not sit in a jail cell doing nothing. Maybe it's time to revisit this better functioning system.

Conservatives are (rightly) concerned about families and civil society breaking down. But our system pours fuel on the flames. Think about it: What happens if someone gets incarcerated for a minor crime? We put the criminal in a camp with other criminals, where he therefore makes friends with criminals or must adopt a tough, alpha male mindset to survive, all while breaking him off from civil society and the family and community ties that give him a stake in behaving nicely. This is a counterproductive strategy for rehabilitation; it's not a good way to turn a criminal into a productive, law-abiding citizen. After the criminal serves his time, we make it hard, if not quite impossible, for him to get a job or an apartment. Repeat this same story for one out of three black men in America, and what you get are whole neighborhoods full of kids growing up with missing fathers. That's a recipe for generation after generation growing up desperate and ready to commit crime.

The American founders understood that the state is a dangerous servant and a fearful master. When the criminal justice system becomes more aggressive, we all bear the consequences. Turn on the news and you'll hear a horror story about a SWAT team smashing through the wrong house. (Oh, as for the "right house": Statistically speaking, the typical SWAT team deployment was called in only to find a small amount of drugs.[54]) If the police are trained to treat every encounter with civilians as a deadly threat, then *you* are in danger every time you get pulled over.

You should also care because, though you don't realize it, *you probably are a criminal.* Law professor Doug Husak estimates that at least 70% of American adults have committed a crime that could put them in prison for a year.[55] More dramatically, leading criminal law attorney Harvey Silvergate estimates that the various federal laws, regulations, and technical prohibitions have become so vast and open-ended that the average American commits—without knowing it—about three felonies a day.[56]

Oh, and the fact you don't know you're committing something like three felonies a day doesn't protect you. As Husak points out, the government has imposed "strict liability" rules on a large number of these rules and regulations.[57] This means that, for many offenses, the government no longer has to prove you had a guilty mind/criminal intent, or even that you could possibly have known about the offense or regulation.

By the way, good luck learning what these rules are—the *Code of Federal Regulations* is about 175,000 pages long, and there isn't a person alive who knows more than a fraction of those rules. There are about 300,000 federal regulations which can be enforced with criminal punishment. Statistically speaking, the reason you aren't in jail right now isn't because you are a law-abiding citizen. Rather, you are technically a criminal, but the government chooses not to prosecute you. At its discretion, it could.

On the Interstate Highways, speed limits are too low. The result: Everyone speeds, driving 80mph instead of 65. But then this means cops can pretty much pull over anyone at any time. Turns out your whole life is like the Interstate, except that with most things, the speed limits are hidden from you in 175,000 pages of dense and vague legalese, the meaning of which is up to the people in charge.

Finally, you should care because the American ideal of a free people is an ideal worth realizing. We have strayed too far from that ideal.

The Basic Problems and the Basic Solutions

Reform in the US must focus on four major areas:

1. *Fix bad incentives.* We have to change how prisons are financed, in part by making local jurisdictions pay a good portion of the costs of sending people to prison. But even more dramatic reforms are needed to ensure that governments and government agents cannot profit from prison.

2. *Reduce the scope of criminal justice.* The problem is *overcriminalization*, not just overincarceration. Too many things are criminalized in the first place. We must reduce the number and scope of laws which create civil and criminal violations. We have too much crime in part because we make too many things crimes. Branding people criminals tends to ruin their lives, incentivize them to engage in more serious criminal behavior, and spoil the communities in which they live. Overcriminalizing small infractions leads to increased *big* crimes.

3. *Changing the punishments.* We should reduce the use of incarceration as a punishment for bad behavior. We should look for alternatives, such as requiring criminal convicts to pay restitution to victims or to a broad range of charities of their choice (within certain limits). We argue that corporal punishment—yes, caning—is more *humane* and effective than imprisonment in most cases. That does not mean that we should return to corporal punishment, but rather that this fact should lead us to think twice about our current approach.

4. *Eliminating the causes of crime.* The US has a crime problem, and so any good solution must address the causes of crime. We argue that a great deal—though not all—of crime results from problems stemming from poverty and a lack of opportunity, and offer positive solutions to reduce poverty.

We think bad incentives explain why the criminal justice system in the US is so badly dysfunctional. To be clear, we regard all the last three items on the list partly as instances of the first. We need to reduce the scope of criminal justice, change the kinds of punishments people receive, and eliminate some of the causes of crime in part because that's what it takes to fix the bad incentives different actors face. For instance, we'll argue that the way *public* prisons are funded incentivizes local municipalities to substitute less effective incarceration for more effective policing—because that saves them money and allows them to externalize the costs of local law enforcement onto other taxpayers in the state. Later in the book we'll discuss possible changes to tax rules to fix this problem. However, a better solution, we think, in light of various other perverse incentives other agents face, is to dispense with incarceration in many cases and instead use alternative forms of punishment.

Further, one reason why we should reduce the scope of criminal justice is that in many cases this is the best way to fix the incentives. If people have perverse incentives which cause them to misuse power, you might try leaving them that power but incentivize them to use it better, but sometimes the best response is simply to *take the power away*. Sometimes what seems like the more obvious first response—leave them the power but change the incentives—is too impractical or difficult.

In short, even when we're not talking about simple changes in the rules, we're still talking about fixing bad incentives. With that in mind, here's a general outline.

In *Chapter 2*, we'll discuss the bad incentives every actor in the criminal justice system, from voters to agents to politicians, face. These incentives explain why such actors act stupidly, irrationally, selfishly, and/or malevolently at various times. Fixing the problem means fixing the incentives.

In *Chapter 3*, we'll argue that part of the problem is overcriminalization—too many things are subject to criminal penalties which should either be entirely legal or instead dealt with via torts and other civil actions. We will argue there are good independent reasons to restrict the scope of criminalization but also that one reason to reduce the scope of criminal justice is that tort and civil justice systems have better internal incentives.

In *Chapter 4*, we'll argue that incarceration—both pre- and post-conviction—should be used only in special circumstances, when a person represents a clear and immediate danger or threat to others. In most cases, other forms of punishment would be superior. To illustrate this, we'll defend at length why caning or flogging is both more effective and more humane than incarceration. We do so not because we're convinced corporal punishment is best, but instead to show you just how awful and misguided incarceration usually is. Whatever horror you have at caning, you should have far more at incarceration.

Again, we think there are independent reasons to accept this conclusion, apart from the issue of bad incentives. However, one major reason to substitute corporal punishment for incarceration is that doing so will eliminate or reduce some of the incentive problems which explain overincarceration. Many public and private actors profit from overincarceration in ways they could not under alternative punishment schemes.

In *Chapter 5*, we'll examine at length the problems of fines and civil forfeiture, and how various police departments and municipalities "profit" from crime. This leads police to abuse citizens and lead towns to deploy police in search of easy money rather than to stop important crimes. We need to eliminate or reduce such fines and civil forfeitures because they incentivize localities to use criminal justice not to keep peace, but to raise revenue for themselves.

In *Chapter 6*, we'll discuss the empirical work on the connection between poverty and crime. Reducing poverty could partly reduce the incidence of crime and is justifiable for its own sake. We issue a number of recommended reforms which could reduce crime, especially in blighted rural towns or "inner cities". The connection to incentives should be clear: Increasing prosperity reduces the incentive to turn to crime as an alternative.

In *Chapter 7*, we'll defend a grab bag of possible reforms, each of which is meant to change the incentives agents face or to put some sort of check on others' bad behaviors. These reforms are practical in the sense that to make them work doesn't require any fundamental change in human nature; they do not require people to become more just or moral. The downside, though, is that there is no political will right now to implement these reforms, and we don't know how to create such a will. We hope this book will help.

Notes

1 Alexander 2010. Sances and You 2017.
2 Drug Policy Alliance 2018.
3 United States Sentencing Commission 2017.
4 Howard 2017, 3.
5 Pfaff 2017.
6 Forman 2018.
7 Prison Policy Initiative 2019a.
8 Prison Policy Initiative 2019b.
9 At least according to their official numbers. There is good reason to believe that the official incarceration numbers reported by Russia, China, and other similar nations are not accurate. See, for example, Doman et al. 2018.
10 Prison Policy Initiative 2017a; BBC 2019.
11 Prison Policy Initiative 2017a.
12 Howard 2017, 12.
13 Prison Policy Initiative 2017b.
14 Wagner 2014.
15 The quotation is probably apocryphal.
16 Maldonado 2018a.
17 Maldonado 2018b.
18 Eliahou and Zdanowicz 2018.
19 Eagle Pass News Leader 2018.
20 City of Casper 2018.
21 Rapanut 2018.
22 Heinz 2018.
23 Sanderson 2018.
24 Shackford 2018.
25 Gentert 2018.
26 US Department of Justice 2017b.
27 Ovalle, Rabin, and Weaver 2018.
28 Flynn 2018.
29 Weaver 2018a.
30 Ovalle and Weaver 2018.
31 Weaver 2018b.
32 Innocence Staff 2018.
33 Possley 2018.
34 Marcius and Fanelli 2018.
35 Feuer 2017.
36 Barshad 2017.
37 Nozick 1974, 247.
38 Kling 2017.
39 Balko 2013.
40 Hamilton Project 2019.
41 US Census Bureau 2018, Historical Poverty Table 2, 2010 Census.
42 US Department of Education 1998; US Census Bureau 2018.

43 Sheffield and Rector 2011.
44 Harper and McLanahan 2004
45 Farrington, Langan, and Tonry 2004; Lappi-Seppälä and Lehti 2015.
46 Lind and Lopez 2015.
47 Balko 2013.
48 Pfaff 2017, 21–50.
49 Prison Policy Initiative 2019b.
50 Simler and Hanson 2018.
51 Kearney and Harris 2014.
52 Associated Press 2017.
53 Prison Policy Project 2019b.
54 Balko 2013.
55 Husak 2009, 24.
56 Silverglate 2009.
57 Husak 2009, 30–6.

2

IT'S ALL FOR-PROFIT

Here's a true story we got from economists Tyler Cowen and Alex Tabarrok.[1] As you know, the British once used Australia as a penal colony. The government shipped prisoners from the British Isles to Australia—a long, dangerous journey. They had a big problem: In the early years (the late 1700s), roughly a third of prisoners died en route. The survivors arrived in bad shape; sick, starved, scurvy-ridden, barely able to work. The reason: the ship captains and crew treated the prisoners badly. They beat them and kept them in awful conditions. Instead of feeding the prisoners, they hoarded the government-provided food and then sold it upon arrival.

A-ha!, you might think. Bad captains and crew! Just hire better people. Well, the British tried that, and it didn't work. Well, you think, they just need better regulations. Require ships to bring along a doctor. Require they feed the prisoners better and give them citrus. Have inspectors check for regulator compliance. Good ideas, but they tried that, and those ideas didn't work either.

Finally, an economist offered a new solution: Instead of paying captains for each prisoner they accept *on board*, pay them instead for each prisoner they *successfully deliver to Australia*. In 1793, Parliament adopted the rule, and the survival rate jumped to over 99%. Not only that, but also the survivors arrived much healthier and ready to work.

The economist didn't change the captains' hearts. But he changed the rules, which changed their incentives, which changed their behavior. The economist recognized there is no reserve army of saintly sea captains out there. He recognized that regulations, though well-meaning, were too hard and costly to enforce. So, he figured out a way to align the captains' self-interest with the public good. Problem solved. (Or at least 99% solved.)

Profit: It's the *How*, Not the *What*

Most people have a split view of human nature. They think that in business or as consumers, we act selfishly most of the time. But when we act as church elders, teachers, doctors, NGO employees, police officers, or prosecutors, suddenly we transform into selfless do-gooders motivated overwhelmingly by a sense of justice.[2] If you have such a romantic view of human nature, then of course when you see a church, a "non-profit", or a government agency act badly, you'll tend to assume it's being sabotaged either by some malevolent special interests on the sidelines or infected with bad apples.

It's true that there are for-profit and not-for-profit enterprises. But there is no such thing as not-for-profit *people*. Most people are selfish most of the time. Most people have a limited degree of altruistic concern for strangers; they are on occasion willing to sacrifice their self-interest for the greater good. Fellow citizens who work for federal, state, or local governmental agencies or entities, or who work for not-for-profit entities including charities and universities, are all individually working *for-profit*. They are not volunteers. They work to make money for themselves and their families so they can pursue their hobbies, buy cool consumer goods, take fun vacations, and live in comfort. Like you and everyone else you know, they are motivated not just by money, but to gain status, prestige, power, and influence among their peers.

"Profit" sounds like a dirty word to most people. But all "profit" means is that you value what you get more than what you give. The police officer values his labor less than the money the police force pays him; the state values his labor more than the money they pay. Both sides make a profit, even if though we call the state a "non-profit entity."

Profit-seeking is neither inherently good nor inherently bad. It's *how* we make profit that matters. Adam Smith—the "father" of modern economics—understood this well. People are always looking to profit. Whether that drive leads individuals to do good or evil depends on the background rules and conditions. If you live in a feudal system where the only way to make a profit is to murder your neighbors and take their land, that's what people will do. If you live in a corrupt banana republic—or a communist state or a crony capitalist regime—where the best way to make a profit is to capture government agencies and exploit the citizens, that's what you'll do. If the way you make a profit is by providing a service others want more than the money they'd have to pay you to provide it, then you'll do that.

The point isn't whether people work for profit or not. Everyone works for profit. Rather, the question is whether the background rules induce them to seek profit in ways that serve others or to hurt them instead. Bad rules create bad incentives which produce bad behaviors and bad outcomes. Good rules create good incentives which produce good behaviors and good outcomes. If you want to change the outcomes, change the rules.

The Central Incentive Problem of Government

Adam Smith saw that markets had a simple logic. Two people will make a trade if and only if they both expect to profit from the trade, and by that Smith means that they each see themselves as better off after the exchange than before. You value what I have more than what you have and vice versa. When people make a mistake—if you learn that new burrito place isn't worth the $6 you spent—they at least tend to learn from those mistakes and not repeat them.

For markets to work, you don't need people to be fully free or autonomous. Even desperate captives in a prisoner of war camp are better off when markets are introduced.[3] All that's required is that people are not literally forced to trade, in the minimal and weak sense that the offer to trade *adds* a new option but doesn't take away other options. You'll then only take that trade if it's better than all your other options, however good or bad the other options may be. That's why trade is almost always what economists call a "positive-sum game," that is, an interaction in which both parties are made better off.

The magic of the modern market economy is that it puts selfishness to work for others; selfish traders can generally promote their own interests only by helping others. Even then, real-life markets are far from perfect. Sometimes agents make systematic mistakes and don't learn from their errors—like when too many people smoke cigarettes and don't quit early enough, or when people pretend vaccines are dangerous in order to win status among their stupid friends. Sometimes the parties to a trade can dump the costs of their trade onto non-consenting third parties—like when badly managed banks cause a crash or a manufacturer dumps toxins in the air. But, in general, so long as you keep problems like these under control, markets transform selfish behavior into publicly beneficial outcomes.

But governments are not systems of voluntary exchange. Although governments provide various services and do various things, some better than others, you can't "walk away" from government the way you can walk out of a McDonald's. And neither can your neighbors. In general, you get stuck paying for government services regardless of how much you use those services, whether you use them at all, whether they are high or low quality, or whether you'd prefer that the government not provide them. You might well prefer that the government provide, say, national defense or welfare for unemployed parents. But, the government thinks, you wouldn't choose to pay for those things unless they forced you to do so via taxes. And so they force you to pay.

Once you have a system where a service provider can just decide, on its own, to make you buy the service, you stop making that provider compete for your dollar. You remove the main incentive it has to keep you happy.

A-ha!, your sixth grade civics teacher told you, but we do have a check on government! We substitute democratic voting. Democracy allows us to threaten leaders: "Make us happy or we'll vote you out!" As you'll shortly see, though, your sixth grade teacher was wrong. Democratic voting is not much analogous to market trading and a poor check on government behavior. On the contrary, democratic voting is *responsible* for a great deal of the US's dysfunction. Other countries have better criminal justice systems in part because they subject less of their systems to democratic voting.

Another big problem is that because people have to pay for government services regardless of whether they want them or how bad they are, people get a strong incentive to have the government do things they want and pass the cost onto others, even if the benefit to them is lower than the cost to others. To use a cartoon example: Imagine that government passes a new law that any time someone buys a new car, the buyer only has to pay 1/10th of the sale price. The government will make other taxpayers pick up the tab, and, further, it will collect an additional $50,000 for each car sale, which it will promptly burn in a money pit. What would happen under those insane rules? Suddenly everyone would drive luxury cars, the dealers would jack up their prices, and there'd be a big cash bonfire behind the Capitol.

For the rest of this chapter, we'll explain how the key players in criminal justice, from voters to police to politicians to prosecutors, face bad incentives, in which their *self-interest* and the public interest come apart. In the next few chapters, we'll look more in depth about how to realign those incentives, to get those players to act better, as much as possible.

The Voters

We point a lot of fingers in this chapter. When it comes time to assign fault, everyone loves to blame others. We're instead going to start by blaming everyone.

The problem is that American democracy works—and that should scare you. The American criminal justice system is dysfunctional in large part because voters rewarded politicians for creating and maintaining this dysfunction. The question is, why would they do that? The answer, in short, is that democracy encourages voters to act idiotically.

Let's say Pizza Hut is your favorite pizza place. They get your dollar only if they continue to keep you happy. They don't just compete with other pizza places, but with every other possible use of your money. If their food or service starts to stink, you switch to Domino's. If you get sick of pizza, you switch to barbeque or pho.

Your sixth grade civics teacher probably taught you that democracy is supposed to work somewhat like that. Sure, as an individual you can't choose to walk away when your government gives you a bad deal; we all get stuck with the same government. But *we* can vote the bastards out when they do a bad job. So, the hope is that we make a kind of trade with politicians. You give us good government; we give you votes. Mess up, and we'll replace you next election.

The problem with this simple story is that we the voters don't ask for good government. We don't reward politicians for good results, nor—except in extreme cases—do we punish them for bad results.

In the 1950s, political scientists, economists, and psychologists started studying what voters know, how they process information, and what they want. Over the past 70 years, we've acquired a treasure trove of data. The results are depressing. Voters know hardly anything. They reason about politics in silly, irrational ways. Their reasons for supporting particular parties or politicians have little to do with their genuine interests or their sense of justice.[4]

It's hard to overstate how little citizens know about politics. Voters generally know who the president is, but not much else. During election years, most citizens cannot identify any congressional candidates in their district.[5] They don't know which party controls Congress, what Congress has done recently, whether the economy is getting better or worse (or by how much).[6] In the 2000 US presidential election, most voters knew Gore was more liberal than Bush, but significantly less than half knew that Gore was more supportive of abortion rights, more supportive of welfare-state programs, favored a higher degree of aid to black Americans or was more supportive of environmental regulation.[7] Only 37% knew that federal spending on the poor had increased or that crime had decreased in the 1990s.[8] Every two years, the American National Election Studies surveys voters on basic political knowledge; in general, the top 25% are decently well-informed, the middle 50% do little better than chance (they get the same number of questions right you'd get by guessing), and the bottom 25% do *worse than chance* (they are systematically mistaken).[9] Voters are in general myopic; they only remember the past six months of economic change.[10]

Voters engage in what psychologists called "motivated reasoning": they believe what they want to believe is true, rather than what the evidence indicates is true. They tend only to seek out or accept sources of information that reinforce what they want to believe; they ignore or reject sources of information that suggest their current beliefs are false. ("Oh, that study says I'm wrong? Must've been written by a couple of Republican shills!") Their emotional state when they read the news—whether they feel angry, sad, or happy—determines how they'll respond to information. The opinions they offer in response to questions depends on the wording of those questions, and they will switch answers if offered a logically identical question that replaces one word with a synonym.[11] They also tend to presume that anyone who disagrees with them about politics must be evil and stupid.[12]

Voters tend to have intense, long-lasting loyalty to whatever party they support. Most people who claim to be independent are what political scientists call "closet partisans" because they vote for the same party every time. But, oddly, these loyalties don't seem to track voters' interests or their ideologies. In fact, most voters have very few stable political beliefs, and the beliefs they have aren't held deeply. For the more opinionated voters, it's *not* that they first form political beliefs and *then* vote for the party that best matches those beliefs. Rather, we instead find that certain identities—white evangelical, Irish Catholic, Jew, African American—get attached to certain parties for largely accidental and arbitrary reasons, having almost nothing to do with whether those parties support those groups' interests. People with those identities tend to vote for those parties over and over, regardless of what the parties do or how much they help or hurt their partisans. Some of those partisans later learn what their parties actually want to do, and they'll claim they support that platform. It's not that political beliefs determine party affiliation; it's more like party affiliation determines political beliefs.[13]

We could fill entire books explaining all this depressing stuff in fine detail. (Indeed, Jason has already written three.) But the more important question is *why* are voters like that? The answer is *bad incentives*.

To illustrate, let's look again at an example from the first chapter. Imagine a professor has 1000 students. He tells them, "In 12 weeks, you'll take a final exam worth 100% of your grade. But I won't give you each your individual scores. Rather, I'll average your scores together and you'll all get the same grade." You'd guess hardly anyone would study and the average grade would be an F. It's not that the students are lazy, mean, or dumb; it's that the professor's grading scheme incentivizes them to act that way.

Elections have the same logic, but we have millions or, in the case of presidential elections, potentially hundreds of millions of participants instead of 1000. How *we* vote matters a great deal, but how *you* vote does not. Individual votes make no difference and have almost zero chance of changing the outcome of an election. To illustrate, imagine you are a Jewish citizen voting in the last federal election in Germany in 1932—the year the Nazis won power democratically. For you, it's a *disaster* if the Nazis win. But since your individual vote matters so little, the expected effect of you voting against the Nazis equals roughly the expected effect you voting *for* them, both of which are in turn less than the expected benefit of you abstaining and staying home to read your favorite novel. A vote is like a lottery ticket—a winning ticket may be worth millions, but nearly all tickets are worthless. In most major elections, individual voters can afford to remain ignorant, indulge their worse impulses, accept fantasies and fallacies, and use politics as a fun game of us-versus-them and status signaling rather than as a means to achieve their ends.

Let's now discuss how this relates to the criminal justice. From the 1960s to the 1980s, crime rates skyrocketed in the US. Between 1960 and 1980, the murder rate per 100,000 citizens doubled, and the overall violent crime rate nearly quintupled.[14] The US news media knows that A) crime stories and B) "what's wrong with today's teenagers?" stories always grab an audience. In this case, everyone knew there was something wrong. Popular movies depicted American cities as dystopian hellholes ruled by gangs of crack-addicted "super-predators." Citizens in the cities saw the decay firsthand; citizens in the safer suburbs heard about it secondhand. Voters didn't know the exact statistics, nor did they know what was causing the problem.

The news couldn't quite explain *why* crime suddenly rose. Indeed, even today among expert researchers, it's far from clear why crime rose in the 1960s or why it fell dramatically after 1994. While researching this book, we read dozens of books and peer-reviewed social scientific articles trying to explain American crime. To our surprise, researchers are far better at debunking or falsifying possible explanations than they are at offering explanations of their own. There is no consensus scientific view about what caused crime to rise and then fall.

So, by the 1970s, voters are scared, as perhaps they should be. But, like our hypothetical test-takers, they have no incentive to think carefully about what to do. They have no incentive to be careful or cautious when they vote. They have every incentive to accept whatever facile pseudo-solutions politicians offer them, and they have no incentive to track whether the policies their elected officials impose actually worked or backfired. Voters have every incentive to give in to their worst impulses, to dehumanize and destroy criminals. It exacerbates the problem that as crime rose, the criminals were disproportionately black. Even when—for *other* reasons—crime finally started to drop in the 1990s, Americans didn't *know* it was dropping, and kept voting for ever harsher politicians who promised to be ever tougher on crime.[15] Even today, when crime has been dropping for over 20 years, most voters continue to think it's getting *worse*.[16]

Why Politicians are "Tough on Crime"

And this bring us to the politicians. Everyone wants to blame them—and they should! But we need to know why politicians act as they do.

Here's a big lesson from political science: The quality of our politicians depends in large part upon the quality of our electorate, and the quality of the electorate depends on how the background rules incentivize those voters to behave. In American democracy, individual voters are never punished for acting irrationally or out of ignorance, nor are they ever rewarded for casting careful, well-informed, well-researched votes. Our system makes voters simplistic and emotive, so it rewards politicians who cater to a dumbed down electorate.

Politicians are trying to win elections. To win elections, they need to get the most votes. To do that, they need to appeal to as many voters as possible.

In an election, what every *smart* politician is trying to do is behave in ways that he or she hopes will appeal to the typical voter. *Politicians are like this because they respond rationally to the incentives democracy creates.*

If voters were well-informed, dispassionate policy-wonks, then political campaigns would resemble the scientific debates within peer-reviewed economics journals. But, as we discussed, few voters or potential voters are like that. The voters don't know the social science they'd need to know to evaluate policy proposals. They often don't know the basic facts. They don't even know what they don't know—they think they know more than they do.

So, imagine it's 1980. Crime is many times worse than it was a generation ago. Once vibrant cities have become blighted and dangerous. Imagine you're a politician trying to win an election. You can give one of two speeches:

1. My fellow Americans, we have a crime problem. I've read the best academic papers and consulted with the best minds in law enforcement. No one really knows why we have this problem, or what it will take to fix it. But I promise, if elected, we will try carefully experimenting with possible policy fixes in the hopes of finding something that works, at least on a small scale. If what we do works, we'll scale it up. We face a genuine puzzle, but I am committed to figuring this out.
2. Our inner cities are overrun with crime. Crime happens because crime pays. I promise to be tough on crime. It's time we hand out longer sentences. It's time we recognize our police, who keep us safe, should have more rights than the criminals they arrest. Our prisons are practically Hilton luxury resorts—we're giving rapists nice living quarters, three hot meals, and free college tuition, when our law-abiding citizens have to make it on their own. You keep breaking the law, and you lose the right to live among us. Three strikes, you're out!

Which of those speeches do you think would get you elected? Hint: it's the speech you've actually heard a hundred times.

Politicians offered voters simple-sounding solutions, solutions that—if you don't think too carefully and don't look too closely—sound like they had to work. Crime was up and people were using scary drugs. So, the thought was: Let's strip away certain civil liberties, making it easier for police to arrest people and for prosecutors to charge them with crimes. Let's put people in jail for longer and longer. Let's give the cops bigger weapons and train them to be rougher. We'll remove the criminals from the streets and the streets will therefore be safer. Stated so simply, it seems like it's got to work. But, as we'll explain in more detail in a later chapter, it turns out that for the most part, the "tough on crime" approach hurts far more than it helps. While some aspects of it indeed reduce crime, much of it actually increases crime.

We're not saying the politicians were demagogues who lied to voters. They probably were sincere. We're instead saying that politicians had little incentive to think too carefully about the policies they offered, and little incentive to level with voters about how complex the problems are. Their incentive was to enter an "I'm tougher on crime than the next guy" arms race. When being tough on crime didn't work—when crime kept rising even as sentences got tougher and tougher and incarceration rates skyrocketed—they could just say, "We're not tough enough!"

Michael Dukakis was the governor of Massachusetts from 1975–1979 and then again from 1983–1991. For what it's worth, Massachusetts had and continues to have relatively low crime rates and incarceration rates compared to the rest of the USA. In 1988, Dukakis was the Democrat's presidential candidate, running against the Republicans' George H. W. Bush. As governor, Dukakis had overseen a furlough program in Massachusetts, a program that had actually been initiated by a *Republican* governor back in 1972. The point of the furloughs was to allow convicted criminals to remain connected to their communities, rather than completely cut them off and ensure they would only have contact with other criminals. They could leave prison on weekends or select other days to visit family, attend community events, or work real jobs. Overall, statistics show the program was a *massive success*, with low rates of recidivism or crime during release.[17]

Still, one furloughed prisoner, Willie Horton, absconded. A year later, he invaded a home in Maryland, brutally beat one inhabitant and raped the other. Bush ran an attack ad on Dukakis, saying that while Bush supported the death penalty for first-degree murderers, Dukakis instead gives murderers "weekend passes." Willie Horton became a household name, and the ad may have helped defeat Dukakis.

Now, if voters had any incentive to be rational and careful, they wouldn't let one horrible story determine their attitude towards furloughs. They'd demand comparative statistics, including data about rates of recidivism with and without furloughs, and the overall effect of furloughs on crime, and they would want to know whether stories like Horton's were outliers or common occurrences. They'd want to see data about how well furloughs work in the European countries which use them extensively. Had they done their research, they would have realized that most states around the country at the time allowed furloughs and that the furloughs were working. But voters are not social scientists who dispassionately evaluate data. One scary story shuts off their brains and shuts their eyes to the massive piles of evidence for the other side.

So, politicians learned their lesson. For the next few decades, both Democrats and Republicans wanted to be seen as tougher on crime than their competitors across the aisle. Every election, they'd try to one-up each other, ramping up the punishments they would support and bragging about how badly they'd treat prisoners. They wouldn't dare admit the easily verifiable truth—crime was now *falling*, not rising—because that would make them sound soft and unconcerned. And they wouldn't want to admit that their draconian policies all but guaranteed that prisoners, once released, couldn't reintegrate and so would have strong incentives to become career criminals.

Prison Conditions

As we just discussed, politicians have every incentive to be seen as tough on crime. This has a ratcheting effect. If you're not familiar with how a ratchet works, it's a mechanical device that allows for movement only in one direction while preventing movement from going in the other direction. Up until very recently, criminal justice policy in the US has only gone in the direction of more prohibitions, longer sentences, and harsher punishments. Every politician tries to outdo the other in order to win an election, and if a politician dares to claim it's time to reduce sentences, he can be sure his opponent, and perhaps various self-interested prison guard lobbies, will run attack ads alerting voters to this public menace.

Now, consider what this means about prison conditions in particular. You probably already know how bad many prisons are—small, dirty cells, bad food, rampant violence and abuse, sexual assaults, disease, and insufficient medical care. Sheriff Joe Arpaio of Maricopa County, Arizona, openly bragged about only feeding prisoners twice a day, and for housing 2,400 or so inmates in a "tent city" in the sweltering Phoenix sun. When internal temperatures reached 145 degrees, he told the prisoners, "It's 120 degrees in Iraq and the soldiers are living in tents and they didn't commit any crimes, so shut your mouths."[18]

This story illustrates a large incentive problem politicians face. Contrary to what you may have heard, the United States actually has a large "welfare state" in terms of *money spent*; compared to other rich countries, it has the third highest *per capita* government spending on welfare programs.[19] It also has higher overall per person welfare transfers than any other rich country except Norway.[20] The difference between American and European welfare states is not so much size—the US's system is big—but *how* the money is spent. European countries provide more cradle-to-grave welfare and social services; everybody gets something from government. American welfare services are far more targeted; many adults won't consume a dime of welfare spending between the time they graduate until they time they retire and go on Medicare. So, in Europe, welfare is something everyone gets; in the US, working adults sense that welfare is something *other people* get.

Thus, imagine you're a politician worried about prison conditions. Maybe you worry that prisons reinforce criminals' criminality, by forcing them to be hard or to join gangs for self-protection, by cutting them off from their communities and families, by causing their job-related skills to atrophy. Maybe you worry that prisoners are owed more humane conditions as a matter of justice. At any rate, you propose copying, say, the Swedish prison system, which has nicer cells, less violence, more education and training for prisoners, and treats them in respectful ways.

Come next election, your opponent will say:

> My opponent's heart bleeds, sure. Not for our brave soldiers in Afghanistan who face harsher conditions than these thieves, drug dealers, rapists, and murderers. Not for hard-working men and women, who'll be forced to pay out of their own pockets so he can set up Summer Camp for Criminals. I say it's not fair. Our law-abiding citizens are expected to work hard and pay their own way through college or for job-training. Why are we giving *criminals* benefits we don't give good citizens?

Maybe a Democrat would say that less harshly than a Republican. But even the Democrat, who might well wish to offer more European-style social services to middle-class Americans, would probably keep her mouth shut. After all, if she wants to expand or redirect the American welfare state, it's hard to offer services to unsympathetic criminals which regular folks don't enjoy.

Everyone instead has an incentive to produce bad prison conditions, and bad prison conditions are what we get.

The Bad Incentives of Elected Prosecutors and Judges

Crime rose, voters had no incentive to think clearly about how to fix it, and politicians had every incentive to sell voters good-sounding but counterproductive policies. This helps explain why the US has an unusually draconian criminal justice system.

But there's another key piece we haven't yet touched: who the politicians are. The United States is weird in that it's the only major country that *elects* its prosecutors or its judges. In nearly every other country, these positions are appointed by higher politicians or, better yet, run by meritocratic bureaucracies.

Sure, despite voters' bad incentives, it's good to have democratic checks on political power. Democracies generally work better than non-democracies. But that doesn't mean it's a good idea to have any particular *position* elected or subject to direct democratic control. There's extremely strong empirical evidence that certain positions function better when they do not answer directly to voters, or even to politicians.[21]

For instance, unlike the US, most democracies do not elect their chief executives. You might think the Electoral College makes the presidential election imperfectly democratic, but look up how Germany selects its chancellor.

In the US, district attorneys, many prosecutor positions, and many criminal justice judges are elected directly. But, again, voters have no incentive to think like careful social scientists when they cast their votes. So, prosecutors and judges advertise simple, misleading metrics: conviction rates, length of sentences, number of convictions. Never mind that these might be unfair or unjust convictions, disproportionately long sentences that fail to fit the crime, or cases where imprisonment is less effective and less fair than other forms of punishment. Elected prosecutors and judges have every incentive to act like Vlad the Impaler. Voters reward them for *winning*, not for justice.

Here's an example: In 2006, Durham County, NC, District Attorney Michael Nifong charged a number of Duke lacrosse players with raping and assaulting a local stripper. The players were white and the stripper was black. He lived in an area where voters wanted to see themselves as fighting the good fight against racism and white privilege. Nifong used the case to generate publicity for himself, giving at least 50 interviews in the first few weeks. But as the case unfolded, it turned out not only that the stripper was an unreliable witness, but also Nifong himself had withheld DNA evidence which exonerated the accused.[22] Eventually, he was taken off the case and the charges were dropped, as it became clear the students were innocent. Nifong's behavior was so corrupt that he was found guilty of 27 charges, disbarred, and jailed. The disbarment committee chair said it was clear that Nifong's misconduct—including his frequent press statements and interviews—were motivated by his desire to win the upcoming Democratic Primary.[23] He knew he was wrong, but didn't care.

That's just one particularly egregious case, but at least it's one where the misconduct was caught and punished. (This says nothing about how horrifically Duke University, including many of its professors and students, mishandled the internal case.) The real problem is that less extreme versions of Nifong's actions occur every year. Every prosecutor and judge has a strong incentive to ramp up sentences, win at all costs, cut corners, and crush any criminals they convict. America's absurdly punitive criminal justice system emerged from thousands of separate individuals facing bad incentives and taking the bait.

Passing the Buck

Imagine you get a message from your state government:

> Good news! You've been selected to participate in our Fast Food Initiative. From now on, anytime you and your family eat at a fast food or fast casual restaurant, you'll only have to pay 50 cents, no matter what your order. The taxpayers of [Your State] will pay the rest!

Suppose this system turns out, like so many American government programs, to be inefficient and badly administered. Somehow, the new Fast Food Initiative Administration ends up paying $15 per Happy Meal and $20 per Chipotle burrito.[24]

Now, you probably know that fast food, even fast casual food, is less healthy than food you cook at home. It has too many calories and too much sodium. Still, with this program in place, you'd probably start eating out at fast food restaurants more often. You'd start substituting takeout for cooking in. After all, you bear all the costs of buying and preparing your own food, but feeding the whole family Panda Express rice bowl would cost you only 50 cents (though it would cost the state, say, $80.) Perhaps you'd feel bad about taking advantage of taxpayers this way, but if you saw the state made the same offer to thousands of other citizens, you'd probably feel like a sucker if you refused the offer.

In this example, you suffer some of the bad consequences when you switch from eating at home to eating more fast food. But you're tempted because you're able to pass on most of the costs to someone else. It turns out something similar happens in criminal justice.

We sometimes talk about the criminal justice system, but in reality, there are multiple overlapping criminal justice *systems* within the US, with different forms of funding and different priorities. The federal system consists not only of federal and military prisons, but also of a variety of agencies, such as the FBI, DEA, and ATF, which sometimes compete for jurisdiction. Individual states have their own police, regulatory agencies, and prisons. Counties maintain sheriff and/or police departments (sometimes both at the same time) and their own jails. Individual cities, towns, and villages also usually have their own police and local jails.

Each of these systems has a different tax and voting base, though *how* the different systems are funded varies from state to state and town to town. In general, taxpayers pay for state functions through income and sales taxes. They pay for local government functions with property taxes, which are sometimes supplemented with additional sales or income taxes. They pay for federal functions through income taxes.

These overlapping systems create bad incentives. The problem is that everyone has both an incentive and the ability to pass many of their costs onto taxpayers in other counties, or even other states.

Let's say the local town aldermen are trying to decide how to allocate next years' budget. Costs for schools and senior services keep rising, in part because you face unfunded federal and state mandates. You have roads and other infrastructure to repair. And, for reasons you don't understand, you have rising problems in crime, especially in illegal drug use. What can you do? Here are two sets of options:

Strategy 1: Increase police presence. Pay for more officers to patrol the streets, especially in the problem areas in town. Hire drug counselors and offer rehabilitation services. Take proactive steps to prevent crime in the first place.

Strategy 2: Have your local prosecutors push for long sentences. Charge arrestees with felonies or slam them with multiple charges to ensure once convicted they go to a state rather than local prison.

There's good reason to think Strategy 1 works better than Strategy 2; it reduces crime, and it costs less *overall*.[25] Proactive is better than reactive.

But consider the perverse incentives. If the aldermen adopt Strategy 1, the town has to pay the full costs and pass those costs onto local taxpayers. If the aldermen adopt Strategy 2, the town and its taxpayers pay lower costs, as most of the costs of imprisonment are covered by the state through the state tax base.

Of course, every local town faces the same dilemma. But that just increases your reasons to go with 2—you suspect the neighboring towns plan to do Strategy 2. If you try to do the right thing and go with 1, you'll feel like a sucker.

Remember, politicians have an incentive to make voters happy, but voters are—thanks to bad incentives—myopic, ignorant, and irrational. Voters generally want both A) to pay fewer taxes, and B) to expand and improve the quality of government services. (When asked, they'll say they want to cut budgets in general, but they simultaneously oppose cutting any specific item in the budget.) The stakes are also different at the local vs. state or federal levels: in local elections, it's easier to see firsthand what the problems are and how to fix them, and your vote counts for more. As a politician, your incentive is to provide services but pass the costs off to others.

Sometimes this buck-passing is indirect. Most states put prisons in isolated, out of the way places. The majority of prisoners are now housed in rural areas.[26] They give two explicit reasons for doing so: safety and cost. But whether intentionally or not, state prisons have become a workfare jobs program for the relatively poor, generally white people living in rural areas.[27] For a variety of reasons, American cities and suburbs enjoy economic growth while rural areas—which often had economies based on farming, a single factory, or raw materials extraction—suffer decline. These communities' well-being depends on saying yes to building prisons in their backyard. Politicians know that bringing home a new prison development—or increasing the number of prisoners and with it the number of prison *jobs*—keeps rural voters happy. The US has a perverse justice system in which poor black men are overincarcerated in part to create jobs for poor white men.

Unintended Consequences

Imagine you own a piece of property out in the country and you decide you'd get more enjoyment out of that property if you dammed the small stream running through it to create a small lake for swimming and fishing. At first, everything worked out very well. And then the geese came and wanted to enjoy your lake as well. Soon, much of the grass on your property was being chewed up, there was geese poop everywhere, and you could no longer enjoy your property at all (never mind the lake). Even if it wasn't reasonable to know in advance that geese would want to call your lake home, that they did take over was an unintended consequence of your actions and made your situation worse off than it would have been had you done nothing to begin with.

Something similar happened in the US with our approach to criminal justice. Well-intentioned politicians, supported by community leaders and an uninformed but well-meaning electorate, implemented policies that led, not directly but indirectly, to many of the problems we see today. Many examples are fairly straightforward, such as the abuse of civil asset forfeiture laws. Of course we want the police to be able to seize narcotics, vehicles, and cash from drug kingpins, and the law was likely never intended to allow cops to seize Joe Citizen's Camry as he drove across town with a couple grams of weed inside, but here we are.

But other examples are not so obvious or straightforward, such as the increased militarization of our police force and our police becoming increasingly more violent. As of July 12, 2018, police shot and killed at least 543 people in the United States since the beginning of the year.[28] In 2017, they shot and killed 987.[29] Oklahoma and Arizona have a higher rate of police killing citizens than Japan's murder rate, period. To give you a stark contrast, for every *bullet* the German police fired on duty in 2016, American police *killed* ten people.[30] *The Economist* magazine finds that, per capita, Americans are 100 times as likely to be shot by police as their British counterparts, though the UK in recent years has had a worse overall violent crime rate than the US.[31]

There does not seem to be good data on how American police behave compared to their counterparts in other rich democratic countries. Indeed, it's not clear how you could reliably measure certain aspects of police behavior, such as how roughly the police treat suspects. Nevertheless, American police have the reputation of being nastier and more violent than police in other comparable countries. Measured by civilians shot and killed, they certainly are. Further, as video after video goes viral on social media showing police beating and murdering unarmed suspects, American confidence in the police has declined.[32] But we don't know how much of this has to do with social media making us increasingly aware of a problem versus the problem actually getting worse.

Here's one striking number: 100. That's the average number of times *per day* American SWAT teams smash into private homes.[33] The overwhelming majority of these SWAT raids are for victimless crimes, in particular, for rumored possession of small amounts of drugs. As journalist Randy Balko notes, SWAT teams were once used as a last line of defense only against dangerous, armed combatants; now they are being used as "the first option to apprehend people who aren't dangerous at all."[34] Only about 7% of SWAT team deployments are for "hostage, barricade, or active-shooter scenarios"; the overwhelming majority (79%) of SWAT deployments are used to search homes, usually for drugs.[35]

American police violence or abusiveness isn't explained by relatively high crime in the US. As a rough estimate, consider that the American murder rate is about five times Germany's, while its overall violent crime rate is about nine times higher.[36] (Keep in mind that the US classifies more crimes as violent than Germany does, so these aren't exactly apples to apples comparisons.) If this explained why American police killed more people, then, taking Germany as a baseline, we'd expect to see American police kill at most about 250 people per year, not 1000.[37] Still, that's probably a dramatic overestimate. After all, German police somehow get by with firing only about 100 bullets per year during arrests or other confrontations, and about half of these are warning shots.

The United States has pervasive legal gun ownership. Most states allow citizens to openly carry guns, though some require permits. The overwhelming majority of states allow citizens to carry concealed weapons, though most need to acquire a permit first.[38] There are at least 200 million privately owned, operational firearms in the US.[39] So—without saying police brutality is justified or excused—we have to admit that *part* of the problem, frankly, is that American police are rationally more frightened of their suspects than police in other countries. A random American suspect is more likely to have a firearm than a random German or British suspect.

That said, the data shows police officer work is far safer than you might think. Logging, fishing, aircraft piloting, roofing, steel working, garbage collecting, truck driving, and farming each are far more dangerous with far higher death rates on the job than policing.[40] The death rate for cops hit a peak in 1974 and has been declining ever since.[41] The best explanation for the decline seems not to be changes in police behavior, nor the use of SWAT teams, but simply the decline in violent crime in general.[42]

Further, even if American gun ownership could partly explain why American police are more belligerent than, say, German police, it does not explain why American police have become *more* belligerent over the past 40 years. The problem here is that the percentage of Americans who own firearms has been going down—from about 49% in 1973 to about 34% today.[43] Cops today are less likely to be assaulted in the first place, and the public they interact with is far less likely to possess a gun now compared to 40 years ago. But police are more violent.

So how and why did we get here? Like with most of our problems in the criminal justice system, it's a combination of well-meaning policies, public ignorance, and individual actors responding rationally to the incentives that have been placed in front of them. In Chapter 1, we warned that libertarians (and some left-liberals) are too quick to pin dysfunction on the Drug War. But in more specific cases of police aggression, the War on Drugs indeed looks like the main culprit. As journalist Rando Balko documents in

The Rise of the Warrior Cop, over the past 45 years, the government used the Drug War as an excuse to chip away at Fourth Amendment protections. (The fourth amendment supposedly protects citizens from unreasonable search and seizure.) It is now extremely easy for police to search homes, cars, or individual people on "reasonable suspicion"; they rarely need warrants, and warrants are now easy to get anyway.[44] The US Supreme Court has even ruled police can first break into a house to secure it, and then, *later*, obtain a warrant.[45]

In 1981, the Military Cooperation with Law Enforcement Act authorized the US armed forces to cooperate with domestic law enforcement agencies. The military began training police in military tactics—the kinds of home invasion techniques SWAT teams use come from the army's playbook. In 1990, the National Defense Authorization Act (which was further expanded by Bill Clinton and other presidents) authorized the military to donate "excess" military equipment—including armored vehicles, grenade launchers, M16s, helicopters, and weaponized vehicles—to local law enforcement.[46]

Even the conservative political magazine *The National Review* complains that the US has become the "United States of SWAT"; as of 2005, 80% of towns with populations between 25,000 and 50,000 people have a SWAT team.[47] The US police look less like a police and more like a military occupying force precisely because the federal government has trained them and paid them to be just that. The overwhelming majority of SWAT deployments are to serve arrest warrants or search homes in cases where there is no reasonable or probable danger to the police. But using SWAT teams is not only fun for police officers—it also helps justify keeping police budgets high.

Perhaps the scariest part of the SWAT-ification of American police is the growth of the no-knock raid. In a no-knock raid, SWAT teams forcibly break into a house, guns drawn, and immediately subdue any people in the house, including holding young children at gunpoint. Dogs are presumed hostile, so SWAT teams routinely shoot family pets. The supposed rationale behind the no-knock raid is that it prevents suspects from flushing drug paraphernalia down the toilet. In 1981, there were only about 3000 such raids in the US; by 2015, there were over 80,000.[48] These raids leave a bloody path: innocent people get hurt during botched raids on the wrong houses, homeowners get shot when they think they are defending themselves from armed robbers, innocent children get flash bang grenades tossed in their faces—all in the Land of the Free because police got a tip you might have some pot stashed in a closet.

Wrapping Up: The Key Players

When we see bad things happen, it's tempting to blame the bad things on bad intentions. But bad intentions can hardly explain why the American criminal justice system is so unusually cruel, punitive, and violent. Yes, there is racism, and yes, there are bad apples, but we have no reason to believe that in the past 40 years people have gotten meaner.

The simpler explanation is to follow the money—to think of the incentives different actors face. The US had a crime and drug problem, but voters had no incentive to think clearly about it. As a result, politicians had every incentive to sell the simplest sounding pseudo-solutions—to be tough on crime and to wage a War on Drugs. The US is an outlier in that it elects prosecutors and even judges, so the people pressing for and issuing sentences had every incentive to compete by having the highest conviction rates and pushing for the longest sentences. Local jurisdictions had financial incentives to substitute incarceration, which *others* pay for, for police, which they pay for. Small towns lobbied to build more prisons—a source of income and jobs—and politicians build them as pork barrel projects to keep rural voters happy. The federal government militarized local police departments to help fight the War on Drugs, and the result of federal financial incentives is that local police have become increasingly violent "warrior cops," who act less like a constabulary and more like the occupying force they were trained to be.

Many of the peculiarities of the US system—such as elected judges or the how prisons and police are funded—have been in place for a long time. But as we said in Chapter 1, the US did not have an especially dysfunctional or punitive criminal justice system until after the 1950s. What seems to have happened was that beginning in the 1950s, crime in the US got significantly worse. (Just why it did so is poorly understood.) American voters and politicians in many cases overreacted, or reacted badly, because of the bad incentives we discussed above. And when they made these mistakes, they inadvertently created rent seeking opportunities for the other players we mentioned above. So the bad incentives were there are all along, but were somewhat like dry kindle. The spark of suddenly higher crime set the whole system ablaze.

We've given you a basic overview of some the key bad incentives the key players face. In the next few chapters, we'll look at some of these problems in greater detail. We'll pause to ask—and answer—hard philosophical questions about what criminal justice and criminal punishment are for. Finally, we'll offer some practical solutions—solutions which may not be popular right now —but which are feasible in the sense that they will realign individual incentives with the common good and with the demands of justice.

Notes

1 Cowen and Tabarrok 2014.
2 Bhattacharjee, Dana, and Baron 2017.
3 Radford 1945.
4 Achen and Bartels 2016.
5 Hardin 2009, 60.
6 Somin 2013.

7 Somin 2013, 31.
8 Somin 2013, 32.
9 Althaus 2003; Brennan 2016.
10 Achen and Bartels 2016, 93.
11 Kahneman, Slovic, and Tversky 1982; Rasinki 1989; Bartels 2003; Arceneaux and Stein 2006; Westen et al. 2006; Westen 2008; Chong 2013; Lodge and Taber 2013; Taber and Young 2013; Erison, Lodge, and Taber 2014.
12 Tajfel and Turner 1979; Tajfel 1981; Tajfel 1982; Cohen 2003; Mutz 2006; Iyengar, Sood, and Lelkes 2012; Kahan et al. 2013; Somin 2013; Iyengar and Westwood 2015.
13 Achen and Bartels 2016.
14 Latzer 2013.
15 Somin 2013.
16 Gramlich 2016.
17 Pfaff 2017, 170–1.
18 James 2009.
19 Garfinkel, Rainwater, and Smeeding 2010, 45.
20 Garfinkel, Rainwater, and Smeeding 2010, 44.
21 See Jones 2020.
22 Barstow and Wilson 2006.
23 North Carolina State Bar vs. Nifong 2006.
24 That's not unrealistic. Standard microeconomics predicts that when consumption of X is subsidized, sellers of X will raise the price.
25 Pfaff 2017.
26 Beale 1996.
27 Thorpe 2015.
28 Jenkins, Rich, and Tate 2019.
29 Jenkins, Rich, and Tate 2019.
30 Lorei 2018.
31 Moore 2006; D. K. 2014.
32 Jeffery 2015.
33 Balko 2013, xii.
34 Balko 2013, xiii.
35 Burnett 2014.
36 www.nationmaster.com/country-info/compare/Germany/United-States/Crime
37 We get this number by multiplying the number of people German police have tended to kill per year over the past few years by the relative violent crime rate of the US and the relative population size.
38 Most states are "shall issue" jurisdictions; citizens must apply for a permit and will be automatically accepted if they meet certain background requirements demonstrating competence and a clean legal record. They do not need to demonstrate need or cause.
39 Roberts 2014.
40 Fleetwood 2017.
41 Calacal and Petrohilos 2016.
42 Balko 2014.
43 Desilver 2013.
44 Balko 2013, 45.
45 Balko 2013, 151.
46 Andrzejewski 2016.
47 Fund 2014.
48 Jonsson 2006; Hohmann 2015.

3

WHAT SHOULD BE A CRIME?

The Scope of Criminal Law and Government Power

Our goal in this book is to diagnose what's wrong with the criminal justice system and then offer some ideas about to fix the problems. Many of the problems are incentive problems. However, some of the problems aren't just about incentives. Instead, the issue is that the criminal justice system *does too much*. Too many things are subject to criminal penalties and prosecution. We need to first limit the *scope* of criminal justice, then worry about fixing how it works within this reduced scope.

Another reason we may need to reduce the scope is simply because it's the only way to remove the bad incentives. By analogy, if you realize your teenager keeps speeding in his new car, you might try putting in a punishment or reward system to change his behavior. You might try to finagle a limiter to reduce his speed. But in the end you might just have to take away the car. In this chapter, we'll argue there are independent reasons to "take away the car" from US government entities. But part of the reason to do so is that they face all the bad incentives we discussed in the last chapter—plus other bad incentives we'll examine in more depth in later chapters.

In 1650, a man living in Puritan Connecticut interrupted a preacher during his sermon. The Puritans sure took church seriously. He was tried and convicted of a crime. His punishment was to stand in public on a stool for hours on end, wearing a sign proclaiming him an open "CONTEMNER OF GOD'S HOLY ORDINANCES".[1]

The problem here wasn't that his punishment was weird or too severe. The state shouldn't have punished him, period. Fellow parishioners could kick him out of church, sure. Don't invite him to Sunday dinner that week. Maybe unfriend him if he keeps this behavior up. But it's not the state's job to punish people for lack of religious awe.

Fast forward 300 years. Mathematician and computer scientist Alan Turing was a hero. Not only did he help create the modern computer, but also his Enigma code-breaking helped win World War II—he may have reduced the length of the war by two years and saved 14 million lives.[2] For all his heroism, he was nevertheless convicted in 1952 of "gross indecency" for his consensual homosexual relationship with another adult man. Given the choice between imprisonment or chemical treatment, he chose to accept hormone shots, which left him sick and impotent. Two years later, he was found dead in his home, apparently of suicide, though there was some dispute about whether he killed himself.[3]

Again, the fundamental problem wasn't that his punishment was weird or too severe. Instead, the state shouldn't have punished him, period. It's not the state's job or its right to punish adult men for consensual sex.

We've said too many people are in prison for too long. But that statement—"Too many people are in prison for too long"—is ambiguous. It could mean some or all of the following:

1.   Certain things should not be a crime at all and shouldn't be subject to any kind of civil or criminal penalty. Some people shouldn't be in jail because what they did should instead be legal.
2.   Certain actions are wrongful and should face a penalty of sorts, but not a *criminal* penalty per se. For instance, if you negligently rear-end my car, you should pay damages, but generally speaking, your action should be treated as a tort—as a civil wrong rather than a criminal wrong.
3.   Certain behaviors should be subject to some kind of criminal penalty, but imprisonment is not the right way to punish that behavior.
4.   Certain criminal behaviors should result in someone going to jail, but now that person is in jail for too long and under too harsh or bad conditions.

When someone says, "Too many people are in jail for too long," they might mean any combination of 1–4. In our case, we believe all four claims are true of American criminal justice. Too many things are made into crimes that shouldn't be crimes, period, or even a "violation" or "infraction," the way speeding or parking illegally are. In many cases, rather than making offenders serve time, we should make them pay restitution to their victims. In other cases, we should punish them, but not with prison. Finally, even when someone should go to prison, we often put them in for too long.

There's another issue, too: putting people in prison who have merely been accused of crimes. Approximately 462,000 people in the US are in jail right now who are merely awaiting trial.[4] They haven't been convicted of anything, but they are in jail nonetheless. (That they haven't been convicted doesn't mean that they aren't dangerous or a serious flight risk, or that there otherwise isn't a good reason to hold them pending trial, but we believe in most cases of pre-trial detention currently none of these things are true.) In the next chapter, we'll argue that pre-trial detention is usually deeply unjust. Indeed, we'll argue that most people accused of or suspected of a crime should remain free, without even having to pay bail, up until they are convicted. Pre-trial detention or release with bail should be the exceptions, not the rule.

In this chapter, we want to focus on the problem of overcriminalization, which is the idea that too many actions are criminalized. It refers to both 1 and 2 on the list above. Some things that are crimes should simply be permitted. Other things should be handled as a *civil* wrong rather than a criminal wrong.

Arguing for this position requires that we talk about morality and justice. Criminal justice dysfunction in the United States is not just a policy problem, to be investigated and solved with the tools of the social sciences. It's also a *moral* issue. We have to ask some hard philosophical questions, such as when the state should even have the right to punish or criminalize something, or what even counts as an "appropriate" punishment.

There are thousands of philosophy books and articles on what justifies the state, what justifies criminalizing something, and what punishment is for. We don't want to turn this into a 600-page philosophical treatise. So, here, we'll paint with some broad strokes. We want to give you a few ideas and basic arguments which may persuade you that too many things are subject to criminal penalties.

Laws Are Death Threats

We'll start saying something that sounds hyperbolic—the kind of thing only a raving anarchist or libertarian would say—but which is nevertheless true: Laws are death threats. Almost everyone—except those raving anarchists and libertarians, perhaps—likes to ignore this uncomfortable truth. But this is a book on criminal justice, and it's time we experience some discomfort.

Consider what a government is. As the philosopher Gregory Kavka (by no means an anarchist or libertarian) says, the state is a part of society which A) claim a monopoly on the right to create and enforce rules through violence, and B) has effective power to actually maintain that monopoly.[5] Politicians like to say that the state is the name we give the things we choose to do together. If we the authors were running for office and trying to win power over other people, we'd say high-falutin' bullshit like that too. But philosophers know better. The state is the name we give the part of society that has the power to create rules by fiat and which has enough guns to make others comply with those rules.

This isn't meant to be an attack on the state per se. Kavka and most other political philosophers accept this definition of the state but also think a state is necessary to solve various problems. The difference between an anarchist and a statist isn't whether they think the state is a form of monopolistic, institutionalized violent control. It's whether they think such a monopolistic, institutionalized violent control is necessary, good, or better than the alternatives. Anarchists say it's not; statists say it is.

Governments enforce their rules, regulations, codes, and laws with violence or threats of violence. It's easy to miss that because many of us never see the threats or the violence, except on TV. Your taxes get deducted from your paycheck and you pay sales tax at the point of sale. You follow the rules you know about, though you speed a bit and hope you don't get caught. When you get pulled over, the officer usually doesn't draw his firearm; he instead hands you a ticket. The violence isn't visible the majority of the time for the majority of people.

But the threat is still there. As philosopher Michael Huemer says, imagine you get a $100 ticket for running a red light. When the government issues you a ticket, it thereby commands you to pay it $100. So far, that's just words. But what happens if you do not pay? At first, the state will issue *more* commands. It will increase the fine, which means it commands you to pay it more. If you don't pay, it will eventually revoke your license. If you think about it, when the state revokes your license, what that really means is that the state thereby commands you not to drive.

But suppose you ignore all of these commands. Eventually, the government will arrest and imprison you. It will command you to submit to the police. If you do not heed its command to submit, it will use violence to make you submit. If you continue to resist, it will beat you, tase you, or shoot you. Heck, if the cops are American, they might beat you, tase you, or shoot you even if you do exactly what they say. Once you are arrested, the government will continue to use violence and threats of violence to contain, control, and punish you.[6]

Yale law professor Stephen Carter—neither an anarchist nor a libertarian—concurs:

> Law professors and lawyers instinctively shy away from considering the problem of law's violence. Every law is violent. We try not to think about this, but we should. On the first day of law school, I tell my Contracts students never to argue for invoking the power of law except in a cause for which they are willing to kill. They are suitably astonished, and often annoyed. But I point out that even a breach of contract requires a judicial remedy; and if the breacher will not pay damages, the sheriff will sequester his house and goods; and if he resists the forced sale of his property, the sheriff might have to shoot him.[7]

He continues:

> It is an argument for a degree of humility as we choose which of the many things we may not like to make illegal. Behind every exercise of law stands the sheriff—or the SWAT team—or if necessary the National Guard. Is this an exaggeration? Ask the family of Eric Garner, who died as a result of a decision to crack down on the sale of untaxed cigarettes. That's the crime for which he was being arrested. Yes, yes, the police were the proximate cause of his death, but the crackdown was a political decree.[8]

This bring us to what we hope is the most fundamental and basic idea behind criminal law—or really any law:

> Nothing should be made illegal unless it's at some point permissible to kill people, or at the very least severely incapacitate them, to stop that kind of thing from happening.

To say, "There ought to be a law against X!" is the same thing as saying, "The government ought to threaten people with violence to stop X!" So, a general heuristic is that when you say there ought to be a law forbidding this or requiring that, you need to ask: Do I think it's right, if necessary, to eventually kill or severely incapacitate people to make them comply with that rule? If you answer no, then you shouldn't want that rule to be a law.

What makes laws distinctive is the *way* we enforce them. Laws come with threats of violence. Non-compliance begets greater violence, even if the police and other enforcers act as professionally as possible.

Of course, this is more a heuristic than a solid moral rule. We the authors are not willing to threaten people with violence to ensure compact discs have warning labels about dirty language. But Tipper Gore is perhaps happy to kill a few people to stop children from buying gangster rap. Maybe philosopher Sarah Conly is willing to kill a few people to stop most others from smoking deadly cigarettes.[9] We won't take their willingness to use violence as proof it's okay. The heuristic is "make it illegal *only if* you're willing to kill," not "if and only if."

We won't try to offer a full answer to the question "When is violence justified?" here. Nevertheless, we remind you that every law is a death threat. So nothing should be law unless it's in principle permissible to kill people to enforce that law. Now ask, how many things are criminalized that—by that reasoning, in your own opinion—ought not to be?

A few years ago, a comic called "Marijuana ruins lives" went viral on Facebook. It showed a kid taking a joint from another kid. A police officer arrests the first kid and says, "Sorry, it's for your own good. This drug will ruin your life." Next panel: The kid gets six months in jail. Next panel: A fellow inmate threatens to rape him. Next panel: The newly released drug criminal gets turned down for a job. The interviewer says, "I'm sorry, but we don't hire ex-convicts." The last panel shows the kid homeless, sitting on the street, holding up a "HELP" sign. The arresting police officer walks by and says, "Called it."[10] Think about that. Some people think pot is bad for you, so they threaten to ruin your life if you possess it. On net, is this helping people?

Glenn Greenwald says the government

> destroys the lives of individuals that proponents of the drug war are trying to help. What is it we do to those we are trying to help? We take them and charge them with crimes. We turn them into felons which ... renders them unemployable. We put them into cages for many years, and keep them away from their children and families.[11]

About one in five American prisoners is in jail solely for drug crimes. We admit that number is partly misleading: just as Mafia Don Al Capone was convicted for tax evasion, *some* of these drug convictions were proxies for more serious but harder to prove crimes. But regarding the people who really are in jail just for drug crimes, ask yourself: Should we threaten to kill people—or ruin their lives—for smoking pot? Eating mushrooms? Snorting cocaine? Doing meth? For selling or exchanging these drugs?

Morality ≠ Law

Our readers disagree about what the state should and should not enforce through law. However, pretty much everyone understands that it's not the state's job or right to enforce all of morality. Some rules may be morally important or even required by morality, but nevertheless, the state should not enforce those rules. Morality and the law often overlap, but some things are part of morality but not law, while other things are part of law but not morality.

For instance, killing your neighbor for fun is both morally wrong and illegal, rightly so. So rules against murder are both part of morality and the law. But some laws are not connected to morality. The law requires you to turn in your tax return by April 15, but morality doesn't set a date on when you pay taxes. Some legal rules are unjust and violate moral rules. As Martin Luther King, Jr. reminds us in his letter from Birmingham jail: "We should never forget that everything Adolf Hitler did in Germany was 'legal' and everything the Hungarian freedom fighters did in Hungary was 'illegal.'"[12]

Many people are too quick to think that if something is morally wrong, or at least deeply morally wrong, then there ought to be a law against it. But hold on. Upon reflection, you'll notice that most of our moral obligations to one another are not legally enforceable, and rightly so. To illustrate, consider a hypothetical jerk named Mark. Suppose Mark does each of the following:[13]

A. Mark promises Allison he'll drive her to the airport. When the time comes, he reneges, saying he'd rather play video games.

B. Mark promises to marry Allison. On the day of their ceremony, he reneges, saying he'd rather play video games. He offers to elope the next day instead, after he kills the Ender Dragon.

C. Mark does not celebrate his first anniversary with Allison. He does not buy her a present or do anything special for the day.

D. Allison is a devout Catholic and so will not divorce Mark for any reason. Mark decides to sleep around, knowing Allison will not leave him, even though his infidelity devastates her.

E. When Mark and Allison have children, Mark does the minimum he can as a father, showing the children little affection or love. He provides them with the material goods they need and never abuses them. But he never says "I love you," never cheers for them, and never smiles at them.

F. Mark wins millions of dollars in a lottery, more than he could ever use. He pays his taxes in full, but never gives any money to charity. He does not help his sick mother with her medical bills.

G. At work, Mark does the bare minimum not to get fired. He frequently promises his boss to get things done at certain times, but doesn't do so.

H. Mark frequently promises co-workers that he will help them with projects, but he never does so.

I. Suppose God exists. Mark is aware that God exists, but never worships Him. In fact, he openly mocks God. He worships Satan instead, just for the hell of it.

J. Mark is aware of his character flaws, but actively chooses not to improve his character in any way.

K. Mark decides to smoke, overeat, and overdrink, not because these things bring him joy, but just to spite health fanatics and upset Allison.

L. Whenever Mark does something wrong, he refuses to say he is sorry or to make amends.

M. Mark never shows gratitude to anyone for anything.

N. Mark has a managerial job. He decides to promote workers who share his taste in music, rather than promoting the best or most deserving workers.

O. Mark joins the Communist Party. He starts writing communist literature, advocating that workers rise up and murder all the property owners— except Mark, of course.

Mark is a bad person and bad at each of the roles he plays. He's violated a wide range of moral duties.

Yet most readers in modern liberal democracies would agree that the state should not compel Mark to act better in these cases. It should not prosecute him, stigmatize him, or even force him to pay a small fine for his behavior. In each case, A–O, both criminal and civil intervention goes beyond the scope of the state's rightful authority over Mark. (At most, the state might be involved if Allison chooses to divorce Mark or if Mark's employers fire him and he tries to sue.) Mark acts wrongly, but it's also wrong for the state to intervene.

Our point here is that the state may intervene only in special cases. From "This behavior is morally wrong" we cannot infer "The behavior should be proscribed by law." Some moral obligations—such as a duty not to commit murder or the duty to feed our children—should be legally enforced, but most of our moral obligations should not. The state is not a vehicle for creating a righteous society or for expressing our contempt for immoral behavior.

Criminalization Has to "Work"

Imagine an evil demon appears and decides to cast a bizarre spell on the world. The demon cackles his evil laugh, then explains:

> You have laws making murder illegal. But I have cast a magic spell which ensures your attempts to punish murder will backfire. Every time you penalize someone for murder, my spell causes even more murders to take place! The more your laws criminalize or punish murders, the more murders you'll see!

Now, ask yourself, if a demon did that, what should we do?

The demon's magic spell doesn't change the *moral* status of murder. But it does change what the law should do about murder. In this case, the demon's spell makes it so that criminalizing murder begets more and more murder. So, in the face of this terrible spell, we ought to completely decriminalize murder. And the reason we ought to decriminalize murder is precisely because murder is so terrible and bad.

This thought experiment may seem silly, but it has a not-so-silly upshot. Politicians and voters tend to judge laws by their *intentions*. They think a law is good if and only it *aims* at doing something good. As we discussed in Chapter 2, they have no incentive to think more clearly about the laws. They don't bother to trace cause and effect and instead settle on symbolism.

That's a stupid way to design laws. Economists and social scientists know better: We should never judge laws by their intentions, but instead we should judge them by their outcomes. A good law needs to make things better, all things considered. And note that this is a necessary but not sufficient condition for something being a good law. A bad law makes things worse, all things considered. That is a sufficient condition for something being a bad law.

Many laws backfire, making things worse than before. For instance, there is very strong evidence that the War on Drugs is counterproductive in a number of ways.

One problem is that demand for drugs is—to use a technical term from economics—relatively *inelastic*.[14] This means that when drug prices go up, people do not reduce their consumption of the drug by a corresponding amount. Criminalizing inelastic goods usually backfires. People still want to buy the good. Criminalizing it means that the effective market price of delivering the good goes up, not down. Since demand is fairly inelastic, when the law makes the price higher, suppliers can then acquire higher-than-normal profits—they *benefit* from the law criminalizing the sale. Criminalizing the drug and preventing its legal sale doesn't stop the sale, but instead increases the potential profit margins while simultaneously relegating the sale to the black market. Instead of being sold in nice retail shops, the drug gets manufactured and sold by violent criminals. (Consider how alcohol prohibition in the 1920s led to the rise of organized crime.)

On this point, the Nobel Laureate economist Milton Friedman once joked, "If you look at the drug war from a purely economic point of view, the role of the government is to protect the drug cartel."[15] He might have added that the purpose of the Drug War is to increase the profitability of selling hard drugs.

Another problem is that criminalizing drugs changes the way drugs are shipped and consumed. If you are trying to smuggle drugs into the US, or hide them on your person when selling on the streets, you'll want to hold the drug in the most compact, highest potency form. You'll prefer carrying small crack rocks to bulky cocaine powder, and prefer carrying powder to chewable coca leaves. Similarly, underage kids in college dorms tend to hide bottles of Everclear and 151, not large and bulky cases of less potent beer.

The Drug War predictably if unintentionally makes selling drugs more profitable. It creates criminal cartels, which violently compete to manufacture and sell drugs in territories they control. It allows drug suppliers to acquire monopoly profits. It induces suppliers to produce stronger and more dangerous forms of the drug. The Drug War is tremendously expensive to wage.

Yet for all this, the Drug War doesn't even appear to reduce drug addiction. Countries like Portugal, which have decriminalized drug use, generally see rates of drug use, drug addiction rates, and the problems associated with drug use go *down*, not up.[16] In contrast, despite all the efforts in the US, drugs remain extremely easy to acquire. A 1996 National Institute on Drug Abuse survey revealed that 85% of high school seniors believe that marijuana is very or fairly easy to acquire.[17] Jason often asks his students—the posh, well-behaved, bound-for-success students at Georgetown University—how many of them could, if they wanted, acquire cocaine, heroin, narcotic pills, meth, and other hard drugs in 24 hours. They almost unanimously answer yes, they could do so easily.

The evil demon thought experiment is not so silly after all. There are indeed cases where criminalizing certain behaviors backfires, as if the evil demon had cast a spell on us. In those cases, we're better off legalizing that behavior precisely *because* the behavior is bad. (Similar remarks might apply to prostitution or other "sins" we tend to criminalize.)

Is Criminalization Worth the Price We Pay?

Imagine a different evil demon appears. This one casts a different evil spell. He cackles and declares,

> I will cast a magic spell that makes prosecuting murder exceptionally expensive. Henceforth, it will cost you a minimum of $1 trillion to investigate and prosecute a single murder.

If a demon did that, what should we do?

If something is a matter of justice, then it feels callous or monstrous to ask whether we can afford it. How can you put a price on justice?

The economist and philosopher David Schmidtz responds, "Some things are priceless. So what?"[18] We might decide that dolphins are the world's priceless heritage. But if it costs $2 billion to save one priceless dolphin, that's still $2 billion we're not spending saving all the other priceless things out there.

The world doesn't care what you regard as priceless. It doesn't give you the luxury of treating things as priceless, not even justice. You still have to choose, and every time you choose, you are forced to put a price on everything.[19]

If trying a single murder cost us a bare minimum of $1 trillion, then criminalizing murder wouldn't be worth the price. Again, it wouldn't mean murder is right—it doesn't change the ethics of murder. But it does change what we should do in response. In this case, trying a single murder case is about as expensive as the total spending on kindergarten through college education in the USA. We might leave the law prohibiting murder on the books, but we'd better off having the state turn a blind eye to murder. We'd have to use social sanctions instead.

This new evil demon case may again seem silly. But, again, there are real life examples quite like this.

Take the Drug War again. The United Nations estimates that three quarters of imported drugs would need to be seized before the profitability of the illicit drug trade is significantly compromised. At current levels of police power, only 13% of heroin and on average 25% of other drugs are confiscated.[20] This means that effectively enforcing the law—enforcing it to a level that would actually significantly reduce drug use—is prohibitively expensive.

Are there other examples? Perhaps. While some government regulations are critical, some regulations have little real benefit. They just waste money and distort the economy. Other regulations produce benefits, but their costs far exceed their gains. For instance, in a famous study, Harvard researcher Tammy Tengs and her colleagues measured the cost-effectiveness of 587 regulations. They found great variation. While the Federal Aviation Administration's regulations cost, on average, $23,000 to extend one person's life one year, the Environmental Protection Agency's regulations averaged $7.6 million per life-year extended.[21] That was back in the mid 90s. Maybe the EPA's rules get us more bang for the buck today. But as of 1995, the EPA's rules generally weren't worth the price we paid. Note: that's not to say we shouldn't protect the environment, or that all EPA regulations were bad. It's just to say that as of 1995, the EPA's regulations *on average* weren't worth the price we paid for them.

Now consider all the money we spend on criminal justice in general. Remember, as of 2010, governments in the US spent at least $80 billion on all forms of law enforcement, including prisons.[22] California spends about $75,000/year housing and feeding each of its 130,000 prisoners.[23] All of this money could be spent on other valuable causes.

So, this brings us to another heuristic: Before criminalizing something, you need to ask, how much will it cost and is it worth that cost? That also means asking, of all the ways to enforce and punish that behavior, which way gets us the most bang for the buck?

Government spending always involves trade-offs. When we point this out, many people get angry and deny any such trade-offs exist. But refusing to acknowledge such trade-offs shows a lack of moral seriousness.

The Right to Competence and Good Faith

Imagine a third evil demon. This one comes armed with a third horrible spell. He declares:

> Whenever you investigate a murder, I will possess your police officers, DAs, judges, and associated bureaucracy. I will ensure they use the power you give them for their own selfish ends at the public expense! I will make them act in abusive, violent, and nasty ways!

This third demon also increases the costs of enforcement. It does so by corrupting the enforcers.

Once again, there is a real lesson to learn from this thought experiment: *What you should enforce depends on who the enforcers are and how well they will enforce the rules*. The more corrupt they are, and the more incompetent they are, the less power we should give them.

The deeper lesson, though, is that how "corrupt" people are is itself a function of the rules we create. As you saw in Chapter 2, some rules *make people act worse*. The problem isn't that we have bad apples; it's that some rules turn the apples bad.

The historian Lord Acton says, power tends to corrupt, and absolute power tends to corrupt absolutely. The government's power to serve justice is also the power to do evil or to serve oneself. When we create regulatory or enforcement bodies, we may have noble goals. However, the people who seek to possess the power we created will not always have noble intentions. The power we create to save our children may be used against them instead.

Remember everything we discussed in Chapters 1 and 2. Our current criminal justice system incentivizes nearly everyone involved—including voters—to act badly. One response to that problem is to fix the incentives. But sometimes that's not possible. Sometimes a better response is to reduce the scope of their power and jurisdiction. If we can't trust people, even ourselves as voters, to use power wisely and competently, then they shouldn't have much of that power.

Imagine you are a criminal defendant accused of capital murder. During the trial, though, imagine your jury has any of the following pathologies:

1. *They are ignorant*: They pay no attention to the facts of the case. They decide to find you guilty on the basis of coin flip.
2. *They are dumb*: They pay attention to the facts, but don't understand them, because the case is "too hard." They've been given a calculus problem but barely understand arithmetic. Still, they decide to find you guilty, even though they don't understand the facts.
3. *They are irrational*: They pay attention to the facts, but they process these facts using unscientific, fallacious, and unreliable forms of reasoning. Thus, while the facts point to you being not guilty, they find you guilty, thanks to their incompetent reasoning skills.
4. *They are partial and act in bad faith*: They pay attention to the facts, which suggest you are not guilty. But they don't like people like you. One of the jurors is a business competitor, so he convinces the others to find you guilty because doing so would benefit him.

In each of these situations, if we knew the jury acted like that, we would not consider their decision binding or authoritative. We would conclude that the jury acted wrongly. In many states, if we knew the jury did that, you'd be entitled to a new trial. After all, you are entitled by law to a fair trial, and a fair trial requires jurors to be competent to decide the case, to act competently, and to act in good faith.

Consider what makes the jury trail important: The jury is charged with and given the power to carry out justice. They agree to serve society, not themselves. Their decision is high stakes—they have the power to greatly affect a possibly innocent person's life prospects, and to deprive that person of property, liberty, and even *life*. Their decision will be imposed using violence and threats of violence. In a high-stakes decision like this, it seems that they owe it to the defendant, and really to all of us, to make their decision competently and in good faith. If they fail to do so—if they act incompetently or in bad faith—they shouldn't have that power.

We think this idea generalizes—it applies to *all* major government decisions, not just to jurors in a trail. Many other government entities, including regulators, district attorneys, the police, forensic lab operators, and so on, have the same features as the jury. They too are charged with and given the power to carry out justice. They too agree to serve society, not themselves. Their decisions are also high-stakes, with the power to greatly affect a possibly innocent person's life prospects, and to deprive that person of property, liberty, and even *life*. Their decisions will also be imposed upon potentially innocent people using violence and threats of violence—indeed, unlike the jury, they are often the ones directly making the threats and acting violently to enforce their choices.

In a high-stakes decision like these, it seems that they owe it to the defendant, and really to all of us, to make their decision competently and in good faith. If they fail to do so—if they act incompetently or in bad faith—they shouldn't have that power.

We thus think that governments are subject to a constraint we call *The Competence Principle*:[24]

> People have a right not to be governed by incompetent people or people who act in bad faith, or to be subject to high-stakes political decisions made incompetently or in bad faith. Government agents and entities should be granted power only insofar as they use that power competently and in good faith.

The Competence Principle isn't a left-wing or right-wing principle, liberal or conservative. It's an ideologically neutral test of what power governments ought to have. The idea here is that government bodies (such as the legislature as a whole) or particular agents (such as the local beat cop) should have power over some issue only if they will use that power the right way. If they are too incompetent, corrupt, or selfish to use that power correctly, they shouldn't have it. Power: use it well or lose it.

When we decide how much power to give people, we shouldn't imagine them to be omniscient angels who always and only do the right thing. Instead, what government is allowed to do depends on how well they'll actually do it.

There are things we might want a government of angels to accomplish but which we shouldn't dare let a government of real people even attempt.

Harms vs. Crimes

Given how badly things have gone, what is the viable path forward? Let's start from the beginning. Philosophers and political theorists frequently like to start discussions by thinking about what theoretical principles would be best and then crafting practical policy suggestions from these theoretical principles. More often than not, this approach produces results that are both philosophically implausible and politically impractical.

At the root of our problem of overcriminalization is that the government polices too many day-to-day decisions of private individuals. It acts in this way because other private individuals profit from this behavior, either financially or because they enjoy seeing arbitrary power exercised over other people who value different things or who otherwise want to live their lives in different ways.

Even in our current, overcriminalized system, there's lots of bad behavior that the state does not punish and we would think it wrong for the state to punish. The state does not imprison or fine people who cheat on their romantic partners, have excessive body odor while riding public transportation, fail to show the appropriate amount of gratitude to others who have helped them, or who intentionally spoil the plot of a movie or the conclusion of a football game that you've recorded. All of these behaviors are bad, make society worse, and cause harm to others. But we think it's outside the appropriate domain of the state to intervene.

There's nothing obvious that ties all of these examples together beyond that most reasonable people don't seem to think any are the kind of thing that warrants punishment from the state. That is, we don't believe that these behaviors are or should be considered *crimes*. It's not that these examples are unserious, or that the matters are all private and not public, or that they don't involve real victims, or that we don't think someone has been harmed. Look back to the list of bad things our hypothetical agent Mark did above—many of these are very harmful and terribly wrong. Still, most people recognize it's not appropriate for the state to get involved, either by passing laws that would prevent the actions that lead to people being harmed in these ways, or by punishing people who have harmed others in these ways after the fact.

This situation gets more complicated when we look at examples of other behaviors that are criminalized currently or were criminalized in the relatively recent past such as smoking marijuana in the privacy of one's home, participating in an interracial or homosexual romantic relationship, or listening to certain types of music. Why would any of these actions be illegal? While you may not believe they should be, many people in the US still do.[25]

Beyond obviously bad acts like murder, rape, and assault—and even with these we go to great lengths to parse out different severities based on the circumstances—there seems to be no obvious standard for determining when certain bad behaviors should be considered crimes, or even when certain behaviors should be considered bad. Consider the wide range of actions that can cause harm to someone else. Not all of those actions are bad or unjust.

For example, a child's parents tell her that she can only invite one other child over to play. That child's decision to invite her friend Emma over instead of her friend Kristen negatively affects Kristen because she wasn't picked, especially if Kristen finds out. But that Kristen is negatively affected does not mean that she has been wronged or that a crime has taken place, and no one who is reasonable thinks that the state should intervene by, for example, requiring the child to invite Kristen over next time or face some type of punishment.

While this example is private, there are similar examples in the public sphere. Even in 2019, some people seem to have a certain set of personal preferences that leads them to become physically ill every time they see a same-sex couple express affection for each other in public. But similar to the previous example with Emma and Kristen, no reasonable person believes that legislation should aim at restricting exchanges just because they produce yucky feelings within a handful of people. Rather, if the free actions of someone else (or multiple someone elses) are going to be restricted via legislation, the only reasonable justification for such restrictions is when they aim to protect third parties from real harms.

Both of these examples connect to what economists call *externalities*. An externality is a consequence—usually of an economic transaction or commercial activity—that affects individuals who were not involved directly in that transaction or activity. Externalities can be negative or positive. No one complains if they benefit from a positive externality, but negative externalities are different. In the examples above, Kristen's hurt feelings or the "yucky feeling" experienced by the person who is made uncomfortable by seeing same-sex relationships are both negative externalities.

While it seems reasonable to think that the state shouldn't get involved in trying to prevent or alleviate negative externalities like those just mentioned, there are many negative externalities where we may think it is necessary for the state to get involved if the people affected can't resolve things for themselves. For example, if you contract with someone to build a house on your vacant land, that may negatively affect the person living next to you. In some cases, we may say "tough luck" if that negative effect is that his view of the nearby river is now obstructed or that he now has to contend with additional traffic going down the street. But if in building your house you channel additional water onto his property, causing damage to his property or diminishing his property value by making certain parts of his land unusable, then this seems to be the type of thing where we're not inclined to say "tough luck."

While certain harms require the actor to repair the damage he has caused or otherwise make things right, that does not mean that those actions are *criminal* or that the state should get involved beyond its role as a neutral arbiter to settle the dispute and then ensure that the resolution is carried out appropriately. *Criminal* behavior requires a higher standard. When an act is *criminal*, we also believe that the person who has been harmed should be restored to the position he was in before being harmed and possibly compensated for this bad experience (as with non-criminal harms). But, beyond this, we believe that the person who perpetrated the harmful act should receive some punishment administered by the state beyond simply what was necessary to make things right with the person who was harmed. In other words, while criminal acts harm individuals, they also seem to harm society in a way that warrants additional punishment or proactive legislation to prevent them (or both).

Overcriminalization in the US

If you watch enough NFL football, sooner or later you'll find a situation that takes the coaches or players by surprise—not so much because of the circumstances, but because they were unfamiliar with the rules of the game. One of the most memorable examples came in 2008, when Donovan McNabb, a ten-year veteran and six-time Pro Bowl quarterback for the Philadelphia Eagles, was surprised when the game he was competing in ended in a tie after the first overtime period. "I've never been part of a tie. I never knew that was in the rulebook. But it's part of the rules and we have to go with it."[26] Perhaps McNabb could be forgiven. The NFL rulebook is quite long—now 89 pages[27] —and it isn't surprising to think that many players haven't committed the entire thing to memory, even if they are paid to play the game governed by those rules.

But if you think an 89-page rulebook is bad, try the US code of criminal law. In 1982, Ronald Gainer was an official at the Department of Justice and was tasked with counting the number of federal criminal offenses contained within the over 23,000 pages of the federal criminal code. According to Gainer, Justice Department lawyers took on this project "for the express purpose of exposing the idiocy [of the system]."[28] The project took over two years and produced only an estimate: nearly 3000 federal, criminal offenses were on the books. Even today, no one is quite sure how many offenses are on the books, never mind the hundreds of thousands of existing federal regulations that can be just as forceful as federal criminal law.

And that's just *federal* criminal law. Each state has their own code of criminal law. Louisiana, for example, has confined their criminal code to one, volume that is usually around 400 pages in length—good luck trying to keep all of these laws straight, never mind attempting to comply with them all.

The consequences are alarming. Retired Louisiana State University law professor John Baker claimed that it is not an exaggeration that "there is no one in the United States over the age of 18 who cannot be indicted for some federal crime."[29] This sentiment was echoed by Boston attorney Harvey Silverglate, author of *Three Felonies a Day* and co-founder and Chairman of the Foundation of Individual Rights in Education. Silvergate argued not only that Barker was correct, but also that in the normal course of the day nearly everyone in the United States commits at least three felonies, and that if motivated to do so, prosecutors can pin federal crimes on any of us and likely get them to stick. His concern is not that this kind of behavior is happening on some grand scale at this point, but rather that the machinery is in place for this type of abuse to happen and no one should feel safe from becoming the target of a vindictive federal or state prosecutor.

The problem isn't just that there are too many criminal laws, but rather that many go far beyond the scope of addressing what reasonable people think crimes should be. Below is a brief list of ten somewhat ridiculous federal crimes in the US, all brought to our attention by "A Crime a Day" (@CrimeADay) on Twitter (yes, Twitter is good for some things). While this list is amusing, it also goes to show just how far the federal criminal code has extended:

1. 21 USC §333, §352(c) & 21 CFR §332.30(a) make it a federal crime to sell over-the-counter antiflatulent drugs if the label doesn't identify them as "antiflatulent," "antigas," or "antiflatulent (antigas)."
2. 15 USC §7704(d)(1)(A) & 16 CFR §316.4(a)(1) make it a federal crime to send a promotional email that includes unsolicited pornography unless the first 19 characters of the subject line are "SEXUALLY–EXPLICIT:" in all caps.
3. 16 USC §730 & 50 CFR §27.33(c) make it a federal crime to pull a water-skier in a clockwise circle in the Upper Mississippi River National Wildlife and Fish Refuge.
4. 40 USC §1315 & 7 CFR §501.6 make it a federal crime to gamble at the US Meat Animal Research Center.
5. 21 USC §§331, 333, 352 & 21 CFR §344.50(c)(4) make it a federal crime to sell earwax removal aids without telling people to avoid getting it in their eyes.
6. 7 USC §8313 & 9 CFR §93.301(f)(5)(vii) make it a federal crime to temporarily import a horse older than 731 days into the United States for entertainment purposes and let it have sex with other horses while it's here.
7. 21 USC §§331, 333, 379e & 21 CFR §73.275(b)(1) make it a federal crime to put dried algae meal into chicken feed unless it's being used to make the chickens and their eggs look yellower.

8. 21 USC §§331, 333, 348 & 21 CFR §184.1973(d) make it a federal crime to sell chewing gum that's more than 0.065% beeswax.
9. 16 USC §668dd & 50 CFR §32.28 make it a federal crime to drink liquor while fishing in Florida's Lower Suwannee National Wildlife Refuge.
10. 21 USC §331, 343(g) & 21 CFR §139.125(c) make it a federal crime to sell vegetable spaghetti bigger than .11" in diameter.

The issue isn't if criminal law has been extended too far, but rather what can be done to reel it back in. For starters, we need to refocus on associating criminal law with actual crimes. A crime not only requires a victim—who cannot be a person who consented to and desired the interaction—but also requires that in doing harm to the victim the perpetrator also harmed society to such an extent that significant punishment is warranted. Under these guidelines, gambling, consuming recreational drugs, prostitution, braiding hair without a license, and all ten of the federal crimes listed above would no longer be considered crimes.

Consider #8 above, selling chewing gum that's more than 0.065% beeswax. If a company was found to be selling chewing gum or some other product that wasn't as described on the label, then this issue could be addressed as a civil matter by anyone who was harmed as a result of the false advertising. Again, the aim is not to minimize harms or prevent people who have been unjustly harmed from receiving appropriate restitution. Rather, the aim is to reduce the scope of *criminal law* and the number of offenses that are considered to be *crimes* by the state.

Expanded Use of Tort Law

US law differentiates between *crimes* and *torts*. *Crimes* are actions that the state has identified as wrong and subject to some type of penalty. *Torts* are acts that wrongfully cause harm to someone else. Not all crimes are torts, not all torts are crimes, and some bad acts are both torts and crimes. Tax evasion is a crime but not a tort; breaking a contract is a tort but not a crime; and murder, rape, assault, and theft are both torts and crimes.

Procedurally, there are important differences between torts and crimes. The most obvious is that proceeding against someone who has committed a crime is a *criminal* case, while proceeding against someone who committed a tort is a *civil* case. Only the state can prosecute someone who has committed a crime, which is why criminal proceedings are always *The State vs.* so-and-so. But anyone can bring a civil suit—individuals, corporations, or state entities. In civil cases, there is a plaintiff and a defendant, and the remedy the plaintiff seeks against the defendant is almost always financial compensation.

Another important difference is the burden of proof. In criminal trials, the state must prove "beyond a reasonable doubt" that the person being accused of the crime did, in fact, commit the crime. But in a civil case, a plaintiff must only prove that the defendant is responsible by a "preponderance of the evidence" or with "clear and convincing evidence," both of which are much lower than the burden in a criminal case. As a result, often there are cases where the state fails to convict someone for a crime like murder, rape, or assault, but where the victim, as a plaintiff in a civil case, can receive a judgment against the person who harmed him, the defendant in the civil case.

For example, in 1995 the US was captivated by the high-profile murder trial involving NFL Hall of Fame running back O. J. Simpson. The jury *in the criminal trial* found Simpson "not guilty" for the murders of Nicole Brown Simpson and Ronald Goldman, mostly due to the higher burden of proof and the general ignorance regarding DNA evidence.[30] But in 1997, a second jury, this time *in the civil trial*, found Simpson "legally liable" for their deaths and ordered him to pay $25 million in damages to the families of the two victims.[31]

This chapter has argued that one solution to the problem of overcriminalization is to reduce the number of crimes. For criminal actions where there are no victims, such as the private use of recreational drugs, simply striking these laws from the books is the best path forward. But there are still lots of other actions—actions that harm other people—where we want to hold people responsible for that bad behavior and compensate the victims for the harm they experienced. The default right now is to turn first to criminal law to punish bad actors, pursuing a civil trial only in cases where a miscarriage of justice has occurred in the criminal trial or when the perpetrator is wealthy (and more often than not only when both of these conditions are met).

We believe that the first move in almost all cases should be to pursue the action as a civil matter and not a criminal matter, reducing the number of criminal prosecutions. But the primary reason for a victim to proceed with a criminal prosecution first is financial. Prosecuting someone costs a lot, both in time and money. In a criminal prosecution, the state bears all of the financial costs of the investigation and prosecution, including collecting and processing evidence, finding and interviewing witnesses, and attorney costs during the trial. Most individuals could not afford to front these costs on their own. Even if a victim could recoup these costs as part of a judgment, the vast majority of defendants don't have the money to cover these costs themselves, never mind any financial award to compensate for the bad act or punitive damages associated with it.

So how could it work? One possible step is to address the obvious financial hurdles. For most tort claims, the state would need to bear the responsibility and financial cost of collecting and processing evidence, as well as finding and interviewing witnesses. This information would then be available to both the would-be plaintiff and defendant. That takes care of costs that aren't connected to litigating the case.

Litigation costs could be incorporated into the trial process. Currently, plaintiffs and defendants in the US have to pay their own attorney's fees, a policy known as the "American Rule." But the US is unique here. Most other countries have adopted a policy known as the "English Rule," which requires the loser to pay the reasonable attorney's fees of both parties. Instead of adopting the "American Rule," we would adopt the "English Rule" or a modified fee-shifting system (like Alaska, the only state in the US operating in this way) that requires the loser to bear the financial costs for both parties. Not only would this reduce the number of litigated cases, likely replace them with formal arbitration, but it would also provide an incentive for plaintiffs' attorneys to take up cases where the damages are likely to be low.

The other financial challenge is with the defendants. Most defendants will be "judgment-proof," which is a fancy legal term to mean that they are too poor to pay any financial judgment against them. If they can't pay the judgment, then they certainly can't pay any legal fees for the attorneys on the other side. One way to address this problem is through an expanded use of victim restitution funds, which can be financed by all of the fines and fees collected by state agencies. This fund could pay for judgments against judgment-proof defendants, including attorney's fees. Further, by directing the revenue from fines and fees to this fund, we eliminate the added incentive for law enforcement agencies and other state entities to act as a secondary, revenue-generating arm of the state.

Other details would need to be worked out, but this at least provides a blueprint for how we can move in the direction of expanding the use of civil trials to reduce the number of criminal proceedings, compensate victims, and punish offenders. While this change could work for many torts such as theft, minor assaults, defamation, and contract violations, it's hard to see this route being politically viable for dealing with violent crimes. While it may not be unreasonable for the rape victim to see financial compensation from his attacker, most of us also believe that the perpetrator should be punished beyond simply paying some amount of monetary restitution. So, although appealing to criminal law and the power of the state may not be a *last* resort, it also should not be the *first* resort, which is often what it is right now.

Overcriminalization in the US is one of the most significant problems in need of serious reform. The first step is to decriminalize any and all acts that do not cause harm to someone else or do not bring significant instability to the community or state. But after that, we need to look at other alternatives to ratchet down the scope and volume of criminal law. Here, we've suggested expanding the scope of civil law, as well as some practical changes that will make this expansion possible. The primary barrier to this solution is public perception. People see criminal law as the mechanism by which we punish people for their bad behavior. But it is this view that has led to its overexpansion and many of the problems you see today. Reducing its scope as much as possible puts us on the right path towards meaningful reform.

Notes

1 New England Historical Society 2018.
2 Copeland 2012.
3 Pease 2012.
4 Prison Policy Initiative 2019b.
5 Kavka 1995.
6 Huemer 2013.
7 Friedersdorf 2016. Hasnas 2017 disputes whether contracts must be enforced through violence.
8 Hasnas 2017.
9 Conly 2012.
10 TheismComics 2016.
11 Siriram 2011.
12 King 1963.
13 We take this list from Brennan and Hill 2014, 63–4.
14 Manski, Pepper, and Thomas 1999.
15 Perry 2015.
16 Ferreira 2017.
17 Brennan 2004.
18 Schmidtz 2001.
19 On this point, see Brennan and Jaworski 2016, 55–9.
20 Brennan 2004.
21 Tengs et al. 1995.
22 Kearney and Harris 2014
23 Associated Press 2017.
24 Jason first defended this principle in Brennan 2011.
25 Pew Research Center 2017; Hartig and Geiger 2018; Marcin 2018.
26 Nabone 2008.
27 https://operations.nfl.com/the-rules/2018-nfl-rulebook/
28 Emshwiller and Fields 2011.
29 Emshwiller and Fields 2011.
30 Littlefield 2016.
31 Drummond-Ayres 1997.

4

INCARCERATION ON TRIAL

In March 2018, Charles and Cynthia Jones were doing what many married couples with children do every once and a while—they were fighting. They weren't fighting physically, but they were going at it loud enough in front of their home that one of their neighbors decided to call the police. New Orleans police officers arrived and found Charles and Cynthia arguing in front of the house. The police declared that because they had come out to the house, a report would need to be filed and at least one of them would need to be charged with something and held in the parish jail until things got sorted out. (In fact, that's false and there's no such rule, but such is life for a black American couple when the police are called).

This sent Charles and Cynthia into a panic. Both Charles and Cynthia were employed by the local Waffle House, but they worked different shifts so that they could take care of their children. So, when Charles was at work, Cynthia watched their children; and when Cynthia was at work, Charles watched their children. Charles and Cynthia lived paycheck to paycheck and had no savings, and so if either went to jail, coming up with the money to bail the other out—even a couple hundred dollars to pay the bail bondsman fee—would be difficult. So not only would that person have lost his or her job, but also the other would likely lose their job as well, since they had no one else to watch their children. No jobs mean no money, and no money means missed mortgage payments, missed car payments, and no way to provide for their family. All because the police were called on two people arguing outside of their house.

Fortunately, this specific story has a happy ending, thanks to the New Orleans Safety and Freedom Fund. The people who operate the Safety and Freedom Fund collect donations from private individuals and corporations to do what the name suggests—bail people out of jail when they have been arrested for minor offenses, pose no danger to the community, and don't have resources to bail themselves out. Although Charles was arrested and was being held in the local jail, thanks to this organization—which the Orleans Parish District Attorney has been highly critical of (no surprise, right)[1]—he was out before the end of the day. Once he was bailed out, his case was dropped by the district attorney, just like nearly 80% of the cases in which the Fund has bailed people out. That's right—nearly 80% of the time in Safety and Freedom Fund action cases, the district attorney simply drops the charges once the person has been bailed out. It makes you wonder why they were arrested and held to begin with.

This story of Charles and Cynthia Jones is not unique. Every day in the United States, hundreds of poor people are arrested and held for trivial offenses, spending days, weeks, or even months in jail because they lack a couple hundred dollars to bail themselves out. Once in jail, they are subjected to all sorts of horrific treatment and conditions—conditions that often make them suicidal. Consider this statistic: In 2017, approximately 70 people in California *already in police custody* were killed by police officers (and this number is likely higher because nearly 200 in-custody deaths from 2017 are still pending investigation).[2] 70 deaths is more than the total number of people killed by police in Europe period, including all people in custody, not in custody, whatever. And California is only one state and these 70 people *were already in police custody*. 162 other people were killed by California police officers in 2017 before being apprehended.[3] Fortunately, this number dropped to 115 in 2018,[4] but it is still ridiculously high by global standards. And, again, California is just one state.

Beyond the problem of being killed by police while in custody, the experience is so horrific that suicide is one of the leading causes of deaths in custody and suicides have been rising since 2013.[5] In many cases suicides occur within the first 72 hours and the people who kill themselves have shown no signs of psychological problems. One of the highest profile cases of in-custody suicide was of Sandra Bland, a seemingly healthy, 28-year-old woman who hung herself in a Texas jail cell less than 72 hours after being arrested during a traffic stop. Bland's death attracted national attention—HBO even made a movie about her case in 2018—highlighting the problems of policing and punishment in the US, and raising important questions about the appropriate aims of punishment.

We already described the basic problem in previous chapters. For largely unknown reasons, the US had a spike in crime beginning sometime after World War II, which (again, for largely known reasons) peaked and began falling dramatically in 1994. Voters had little incentive to be informed about what the best policy solutions were to crime, and indeed, little incentive even to know that crime started falling in 1994. Voters formed mistaken beliefs about policies, and politicians had perverse incentives to be seen as "tough on crime" even when such policies were counterproductive. Once the criminal justice system expanded, a whole range of different special interests—from poor rural communities who wanted the state funding that came with hosting prisons, to localities that wanted to take advantage of federal revenues attached to the Drug War, to other localities that wanted the revenue streams that come with enforcing petty offenses—acquired a stake in the system continuing to expand.

Fixing the problem means fixing the bad incentives. In this case, though, we think the best response is to use incarceration as a punishment only in special cases. One reason to do so is it will fix the bad incentives. We can't trust certain actors to use their power appropriately, and we can't easily craft rules to make them behave better, so we should take the power away. But, in addition, there are independent reasons to oppose incarceration.

Why Punish?

In the last chapter, we asked whether the *scope* of criminal justice is too expansive. Too many things are subject to criminal law. Some of those things should simply be allowed, period. Some of those things should be considered *civil wrongs*, where the wrongdoer should *compensate* the victim for the harms he's perpetrated, but that's it. Not everything that's bad should be a crime.

Ken promises to drive Barbie to the airport. He decides to get drunk and sleep in. Barbie misses her flight. That makes Ken a jerk, and Barbie is rightly angry. The rest of us might think twice before befriending Ken. But that's it. We wouldn't normally think in a case like this that the state should force Ken to pay Barbie damages. We wouldn't normally think more strongly that the state should charge Ken with a crime and punish him.

New story: Ken drives too close behind Barbie in stop and go traffic. Barbie hits her brakes. Andy hits his too late. He rear-ends her car and causes $1500 in damages. In this case, Ken should pay Barbie damages. If he refuses, we may well think the state should force him to do so, and at some point his refusal to pay should be a crime. (Maybe not: there are ways of enforcing torts without criminalizing refusal to pay.[6]) But in the first instance, the state shouldn't charge Ken with a crime.

New story: Ken and Barbie have broken up. In a fit of rage and jealousy, Ken stalks Barbie and tries to hit her with his car as she exits hers. She jumps out of the way, but he smashes her car, causing $1500 in damages. In this case, sure, he should pay her damages. But here it also seems appropriate to charge Ken with a crime. This case is different from the first two.

Most people think in this third case, the state should *punish* Ken. But, no surprise, just *why* the state should punish is a big, seemingly never-ending philosophical controversy. Philosophers and legal theorists have spent thousands of years trying to produce good theories of both A) what actions should be punished, B) why the *state* in particular should punish people, and finally C) what the *purpose* of punishment is. You won't be surprised to learn they've produced many competing theories, but no one has produced a compelling theory that wins general agreement. People have strong intuitions that we should punish, but rather weak explanations for why and how. There is no consensus.[7]

It would take us 100 pages to outline the main arguments for and against each of these major theories. Our goal in this book, though, is to talk about problems caused by bad incentives and possible reforms. We doubt we need to settle the 2000+ year debate to do that. We also doubt we can settle that debate. We don't find any of the extant major theories of punishment particularly compelling. If you were to take a class on philosophical theories of punishment, you'd learn that each major theory, despite its initial plausibility, has serious flaws.

With that caveat, then, here are the basic "theories" of the purpose of punishment on offer:

1. *Retribution*: Wrongdoers ought to suffer in proportion to the harm they have caused others. It's not right that a murderer goes free when his victim lies in the ground. In slogan form: "An eye for an eye."
2. *Deterrence*: Criminal justice should disincentivize potential offenders. If criminals know there is a high enough chance they'll be caught and punished, and if the punishments are bad enough, they'll commit less crime. Slogan: "Crime shouldn't pay."
3. *Communication*: Criminal justice should communicate society's anger or moral judgment of the wrongdoer. We punish to express our moral values. Slogan: "The criminal law is how society expresses its abhorrence of the criminal's behavior and motives."
4. *Removal/incapacitation*: Criminal justice should remove dangerous wrongdoers from society in order to protect the innocent. Slogan: "Keep the criminals off the streets."
5. *Rehabilitation*: Criminal justice should reform wrongdoers and turn them into productive, peaceful, functioning citizens. Slogan: "Turn criminals into honest, productive citizens."
6. *Restitution*: Criminal justice should require the wrongdoer to make his victims whole, to compensate them for the harms he has caused. Slogan: "Make your victims whole."

Some philosophers think we shouldn't use the word "punishment" for the last two kinds of reasons. If we make Ken pay back Barbie for damages, it's not clear we're *punishing* him per se. If we put deviant Ken in a facility which educates him, teaches him anger management, gives him marketable skills, and then releases him when he's good to go, it's also not clear we're punishing him per se. (It's also not clear it matters whether these qualify as "punishment" or not.)

The boundary between criminal and civil wrongdoing is fuzzy. The boundary between criminal punishment and other reactions to wrongdoing is also fuzzy. We don't plan to settle on a sharp distinction here.

You might find any of 1–6 compelling. Fair enough. We won't try to dissuade you. But now the question is, what does any of this have to do with throwing people in *jail*?

From "Why Punish?" to "Why Incarcerate?"

We grew up and live in a world where incarceration is the most common way that states punish criminals. As a result, punishment via incarceration just seems natural and normal to us. But throughout history, around the world, throwing people for prolonged periods in a jail, dungeon, or prison was rather uncommon. Indeed, many societies in the past would have seen incarceration as perverse. If one person wrongs another, you make the first person pay restitution to the second. Jailing the wrongdoer doesn't help the victim, and simply makes the wrongdoer an even greater burden on society, which now must pay for wrongdoer's upkeep while he does nothing useful.[8]

Instead, in the past, societies around the world often used other punishments, including:

1. Expulsion/exile: Criminals were forced to leave, either to live outside society or to move to a new society.
2. Confiscation: Criminals lost some or all of their property.
3. Restrictions: Criminals lost some of their legal rights.
4. Slavery: Criminals were made into slaves and sold off.
5. Execution: Criminals were killed.
6. Pain: Criminals were given some form of painful corporal punishment.
7. Humiliation: Criminals were subject to social sanctions. Their crimes were advertised or they were made to stand in public advertising their crimes.
8. Mutilation: Criminals were branded or had body parts cut off.
9. Partial confinement: Criminals were forced to stay at home or forbidden from going to certain places.
10. Labor: Criminals were forced to do work for the public benefit.
11. Conscription: Criminals were made to join the military.

It wasn't until relatively recently, in the past 150 years or so, that most countries started substituting imprisonment/incarceration for these other forms of punishment.

It's not so obvious to us the change was for the better. Of course, the idea of cutting off a thief's finger sounds horrible to us. Part of that horror comes from mutilation being genuinely horrible. Part of it, though, stems from it seeming *weird*—we're just not used to that sort of thing happening anymore.

We're not going to advocate we resume chopping off hands. But we do think prison is in general a bad way to punish criminals. In the last chapter, we argued that in many cases, the best thing is simply to make criminals pay restitution to their victims, and then move on. Here, we want to argue that in cases where someone genuinely ought to be punished through criminal sanctions, incarceration is usually a bad way to punish them. It's bad because it's often *an unjustifiably harsh* penalty. But it's also bad because—with the exception perhaps of a few highly functional systems in other countries—it's a counterproductive form of punishment, which tends to reinforce and increase criminality.

To make our case here, we're going to start by arguing that for a large number of criminal actions, we should use *corporal punishment*—specifically caning—instead of incarceration. That's not because we're sure it's the best punishment. (Indeed, at the end of the chapter, we'll discuss why forced labor and other forms of punishment will often be better.) Instead, we pick it because caning sounds awful and barbaric. However, upon reflection, we hope you'll see it's probably *less barbaric* and also *more effective* than incarceration. If so, that tells us something about how awful our system is, since even caning would be a serious improvement.

Does Incarceration Work?

One thing is clear: If you want to prevent someone from committing another crime against other people in the free community, the most effective ways of accomplishing this goal are either to kill that person or place him permanently in a cage by himself. If someone is dead or locked up alone, they're not committing any more crimes. But we wouldn't think the death penalty is an appropriate response to all bad behavior, and that incarceration is effective in the same way doesn't mean that it's an appropriate method for punishment. Whether incarceration as a punishment works shouldn't just take into account its ability to keep threats out of the community, but (1) if it's an appropriately proportional or fair response to the bad action, (2) if it helps to correct the bad behavior of the person who is punished, (3) if it deters both the individual and others in society from performing similarly bad acts in the future, (4) and if it does all of these things at a lower cost than other options that achieve similar results. In most cases, prison as a response to bad behavior fails to achieve (1), (2), (3), or (4).

(1) Proportionality and Fairness. Is incarceration proportional or otherwise fair? We're not sure what the appropriately proportional punishment should be for rape, violent assault, murder, or other crimes that could scar a person for the rest of her life or otherwise end her life. In such cases, incarceration may not severe enough. Does throwing a serial killer in jail for 90 years mean he suffers in proportion to his victims?

But for other crimes like drug possession, theft, and public disorder, is jail too harsh? Set aside concerns about holding someone in jail while they await their trial, which can often be months and during this time they lose their job, house, and sometimes their children. Assume someone has been convicted of theft or some type of public order crime—prostitution, drug use, public intoxication, drunk driving, etc. Is the appropriately just punishment something that causes the person to lose their job, house, kids, etc.? Being convicted of a crime in itself can sometimes cause people to lose their jobs, families, and so on, but being incarcerated at great length makes some such losses inevitable.

Even if you think the answer to this question is yes, the use of incarceration as a punishment causes collateral damage, punishing other individuals connected to the bad actor who have done nothing wrong. One of the hallmarks of just punishment is that people who we know haven't done anything wrong shouldn't be punished. The wives, girlfriends, and children of men who are incarcerated are often negatively affected, putting additional strain on the schools, community organizations, and governmental entities who then must step in to provide additional support.[9] In addition to studies showing that children with incarcerated parents do worse in school and suffer from a variety of social problems,[10] families with at least one close relative incarcerated suffer from economic hardships at a greater rate than families from the same community without an incarcerated member.[11]

Now, it's true that even restitution can have such negative effects. If Bob has to pay Tom $100,000 as restitution for harms, Bob's family may suffer hardships. But, again, the hardships incarceration imposes are more severe. If Bob goes to jail, he can't support his family or parent his children. Further, at least with restitution, people could in principle buy insurance policies which would cover some such claims. (Perhaps no one would sell a liability policy that pays out restitution on intentional murder, but you can buy umbrella policies which cover the civil liability associated with negligent homicide.)

(2) Rehabilitation. Prisons in the US fail to rehabilitate offenders and, in most cases, make people worse. According to government's Bureau of Justice Statistics, 83% of all released prisoners returned to prison within nine years of their release,[12] and included in this number are the prisoners who have aged out of crime. "Property criminals, like burglars and car thieves, tend to stop in their 20s, while violent criminals are more likely to continue into their early 30s. Drug-crime careers can be lengthier, stretching into the mid-30s."[13] If one aim of US prisons is to rehabilitate, "teaching people a lesson" and making it less likely that they commit crimes once they come out, it is failing at this goal—and failing miserably.

One reason why is because of what is happening in our prisons currently. When journalist Eileen Rivers went to investigate US prisons, she "expected to find stories of inmate violence and of former felons who encountered discrimination as they struggled to find work." But what she actually found was far worse:

> [P]ervasive corruption and systems too overwhelmed to offer desperately needed services that give ex-convicts a fighting chance to succeed in the outside world. We learned of inmates who worked with prison guards to deal drugs. We heard about others who used drugs for the first time while incarcerated. Instead of getting rehab, those who came in addicted often got worse. We found inmates who used their time not to gain a trade but to learn how to more craftily commit crimes upon release.[14]

Not good. Even worse, research by psychologist Marieke Liema and criminologist Maarten Kunst showed that people who had been in prison for any significant period of time developed "institutionalized personal traits," which included "distrusting others, difficulty engaging in relationships [and] hampered decision-making."[15] No wonder people who leave prison are so likely to reoffend and end up back there soon after their release.

(3) Deterrence. Perhaps you think that long prison sentences deter crime? You'd be wrong. Mark Kleiman,[16] David Kennedy,[17] and Steven Durlauf and Daniel Nagin[18] have all published significant and comprehensive studies on the effects of punishment and criminal activity. They've all found that ratcheting up the length or harshness of the punishment has almost no effect on the rate at which people commit certain crimes. In other words, longer or harsher punishments don't deter criminal activity. What they found deters criminal activity is an unpleasant punishment *coupled with* certainty and immediacy. That is, knowing that you'll be caught if you commit the crime and knowing that the punishment you receive will be immediate or otherwise happen very soon after the bad act.

So why don't longer and harsher sentences fail to deter criminal activity? The answer is not surprising: The vast majority of criminals don't think they're going to get caught. And they have good reason to think this. When a crime is committed and the police arrest someone for the crime, a crime is considered to be "cleared," even if the charges are dismissed later or the person is found not guilty in a trial. In 2017, the clearance rate for violent crimes—murder, rape, and aggravated assault—in the US was only 45.6%; the clearance rate for property crimes was a pathetic 17.6%.[19] In many inner-city neighborhoods throughout the country, the clearance rate for murder is 0%,[20] never mind property crimes and other less violent offenses. When people are not worried about getting caught, the punishments for bad behaviors are irrelevant.

(4) Cost. Not only do prison sentences fail to achieve the aims of justice when it comes to proportionality and fairness, fail to rehabilitate, and fail to deter, they fail to accomplish these things at a higher cost than nearly every

other option. According to the Federal Bureau of Prisons, in 2017 the average cost to incarcerate a federal prisoner was $36,299.25 per year, up from $34,714.12 in 2016.[21] For state prisons, costs in 2015 per inmate per year ranged from $14,780 (Alabama) at the low end to $69,355 (New York) at the high end.[22] It is hard to imagine a system of punishment that could be more expensive and accomplish so little.

The good news is that making people aware of the costs of incarceration seems to motivate them to advocate punishment reform. Research by Eyal Aharoni has shown:

> a curious bias in people's punishment attitudes. Under normal conditions, they neglect to consider the quite large costs of incarceration and punish as if the punishment is cost-free. But when you gently remind them that there are substantial taxpayer costs associated with that sentence—money that could otherwise be spent on other social services—people recommend smaller punishments, indicating that they do care about cost saving to some degree.[23]

Perhaps it's time to consider some alternatives.

Does Caning Beat Incarceration?

On March 3, 1994, Singapore sentenced American student Michael Fay to four months in jail, a small monetary fine, and six strokes of the cane, after Fay pled guilty for vandalism.[24] The American reaction was revealing. Hardly anyone complained that Fay would be locked away and deprived of freedom for months on end, but many Americans regarded Singapore's practice of caning offenders as alien, barbaric, and backward.

We think Americans have their values backward. What they should have complained about was Fay's incarceration, not the caning. Incarceration is a far more barbaric and inhumane practice. Indeed, if given the choice, Americans should replace incarceration with caning.

Caning is a form of corporal punishment in which an officer lashes a criminal offender's buttocks or feet with rattan cane. Highly trained professionals administer the lashes, making sure not to strike the offender in places that leave visible scars. Afterward, the punished person receives medical care for his wounds, and is set free.

To contemporary Westerners, caning—still practiced in Singapore, Malaysia, and elsewhere—seems horrific. Many of their complaints are legitimate. Nevertheless, we think that practice of imprisonment, especially as practiced in the US, is even worse. Depriving someone of freedom, subjecting them to extended risk of physical and sexual abuse, forcing them to remain locked in a small space, and in some cases, keeping them isolated and without entertainment for extended period, is more barbaric than simply lashing an offender and letting him go. Again, we aren't claiming that caning is the best possible response to the problem of criminal justice. However, we will argue that it is *superior* to incarceration in most cases.

Three Intuition Pumps

We in the West are accustomed to incarceration, while caning seems alien. If we were to watch a video of a flogging (yes, you can find them online), we would likely react with horror and disgust. It seems only natural to conclude that caning is unjustifiable. But we hope the next three sections will help alienate you from those intuitions. Because we are accustomed to incarceration, we fail to see that incarceration is the more horrifying practice.

Making Contact

Imagine a twin Earth, like ours, in which corporal punishment had never been invented. Instead, suppose every country punishes its criminals the way the United States does. Now, suppose in the near future, this twin Earth makes contact with the Vulcans, the highly rational humanoid race from *Star Trek*. Suppose that shortly after making contact, we send ambassadors to planet Vulcan to learn about differences in cultural practices, institutions, and norms.

We are surprised to learn that the Vulcans use corporal punishment in response to crime. In particular, when a criminal is convicted, he is immediately brought to a caning station. There, a trained medical doctor evaluates the criminal to ensure he is healthy enough to withstand the caning. If the criminal passes, he is placed on a special structure that holds him intact, which exposes his buttocks, and which ensures that his genitals or vital organs will not be struck. Then, a highly trained guard administers a set number of lashes, with more severe crimes leading to a higher number of lashes. For severe crimes, the criminal is struck with a cane that may break open his skin. For less severe crimes, the criminal either pays a monetary fee, or is subject to a far less severe form of flogging which does not break the skin. Lashes come at set rate of one minute apart. After the convict is flogged, a medical doctor treats and dresses his wounds. He is kept in a hospital as he convalesces, and then is set free. The wounds are painful, but superficial, and impose no long-term ill-effects other than scarring in areas that are always covered by clothing.

However horrified we Earthlings are when we discover that the Vulcans use corporal punishment, they are even more horrified to discover what Earthlings do. We explain that when a prisoner is convicted (and often even simply suspected of a crime), the prisoner is sent to live, for a long time, in a tiny, grey concrete cell with other criminals. In some cases, e.g., in Maricopa

County, Arizona, the convict is made to live in cramped tents baking underneath the hot desert sun. The prisoner is deprived of all privacy and required to shower, piss, and shit in front of others. We require the prisoner to wear bright orange clothing and remove as many vestiges of individuality as we can. We deprive prisoners of sexual satisfaction, even forbidding them (though unsuccessfully) to masturbate, and forbidding them from having access to materials (such as pornography) to aid in achieving private sexual satisfaction. However, we also fail to protect prisoners from one another, and as a result, many prisoners are raped and sexually and physically abused by the others, and even those who escape rape live with constant fear of rape and assault.

Prisoners are surrounded by metal bars. They face a set daily routine, and are told what to do, where to be, when to eat and when to sleep by poorly educated, poorly paid guards who regard them as subhuman. Their conditions are so unsanitary that no blood bank will accept their blood for at least a year after their release. Most receive only a modicum of leisure time. If they misbehave, they are forced to spend weeks in even tinier isolated cells, with no form of entertainment. Further, the prisons are filled with violence, drugs, and alcohol, and many prisoners find they need to join violent gangs for some protection against violence.[25]

Prisoners spend years of their lives behind bars; some even spend the rest of their lives there. Most receive only a few visits from loved ones. Over time, their loved ones tend to abandon them and move on, as they have to, since the prisoners are shut off from society.

When (and if) prisoners finally are released, most are not fully free. Instead, they are subject to a wide range of restrictive rules about how and where they live, work, and play. They must check in regularly with a police officer, who has the power to send the prisoner back to prison for even minor transgressions, such as having a glass of wine.

Most released prisoners find it difficult to integrate back into normal, outside life, in part because they are stigmatized, in part because they have spent months or years living and making friends with other criminals, and in part because their lost time and lost skills make them unemployable. A large percentage become desperate and commit further crimes.

Now imagine how the Vulcans might react:

> Sure, we beat our convicts, but we let them go. You Earthlings enslave your convicts, place them under constant surveillance, remove their privacy, dehumanize them, bore them, psychologically torture them, and subject them to near constant threats of capricious physical and sexual abuse. You *ruin* their lives, and you make it so that these people provide nothing of value to society, either. And you do this all at tremendous monetary expense. We punish criminality with a moment's brutality; you punish criminality with prolonged dehumanization punctuated by capricious, unexpected brutality.

What American Sentencing Guidelines Reveal

Our own criminal justice system reflects the judgment that caning someone is far less bad than imprisoning them. Though it varies from state to state, the criminal penalty we assign to battery is generally far less severe than the penalty we assign for prolonged false imprisonment or kidnapping.

According to criminaldefenselawyer.com and similar websites, if you beat a person unlawfully with a wicker cane, you might receive a prison sentence of six months; if you unlawfully imprison someone in your basement for six months, you would go to jail for many years. The difference in the penalties attached to these crimes is meant to reflect the difference in the harshness or wrongness of treatment the criminal inflicted on the victim. By parity of reasoning, caning is less harsh than imprisonment.[26]

The Choice

Peter Moskos asks readers to consider, if they were convicted of a crime, which would they choose, incarceration or flogging?

> Before you're led out of the courtroom, the judge calls for order and offers you the flogging option. "Five years or ten lashes," he says. If you choose flogging, an appointed state flogger will cane you immediately. Ten lashes, a little rubbing alcohol, a few bandages, and you'd be free to go home and sleep on your own bed. No holding cell. No lock-up. A quick and painful caning, and you'll be on your way. Would you choose years in the joint over a brief punishment, however cruel?[27]

Keep in mind the description of American prisons from the previous section. Moskos expects most of his readers would choose flogging over incarceration. If he's right—admittedly, he did not take a survey—then that tells us something about how to compare incarceration to flogging. If someone would choose flogging over incarceration, then incarceration must be, all things considered, *worse*.

Moskos suggests that instead of having US criminal courts *mandate* flogging, they should simply offer it as an option. We could follow his suggestion here. On Moskos's scheme, convicts can choose incarceration (or perhaps some other punishment) if they so desire. Adding a new option simply expands the range of punishments, while letting the prisoner decide on the punishment means that the prisoner will likely receive the least bad punishment.

If a person is free to choose from a range of options, the fact that a person chooses one option over the other is strong evidence that that is his best option. For instance, suppose Ivan is about to executed. Suppose the executioner offers him a choice of execution methods: guillotine, burning at the stake, or boiling. If the prisoner chooses the guillotine over the others, that is strong presumptive evidence that this is the least bad/best option from the prisoners' point of view. This point holds even though the prisoner is not fully free or autonomous, and even though all the options are bad.

Further, we do not generally harm the prisoner by simply *adding* a few other options to choose from (e.g., lethal injection, being eaten by lions, etc.) If an option is better, the prisoner will take it; if it's worse, he will not.

In Moskos's scheme, prisoners are offered the choice between incarceration or flogging. He suspects most would choose flogging. We certainly would. What this means, then, is that to defend incarceration over flogging, we must in general take one of three stances. One stance is vindictive: it holds that in some way flogging *goes too easy* on prisoners, i.e., that the reasons they should be imprisoned is that flogging is not painful enough. A second stance is *paternalistic*: It holds that when prisoners choose flogging over incarceration, it must be because they are uninformed or irrational, and so we should choose incarceration on their behalf. A third stance holds that flogging will not work on some prisoners, as they are too dangerous to be set free. This point may be true but holds for only a minority of prisoners. We will discuss this further below.

Caning and the Purpose of Punishment

Recall that philosophers and legal theorists haven't reached a consensus on what criminal punishment is even for. However, these are the six major reasons they tend to defend:

1. Retribution
2. Deterrence
3. Communication
4. Removal/incapacitation
5. Rehabilitation
6. Restitution

Let's consider these putative purposes, and ask how caning fares compared to incarceration.

Regarding retribution: The main idea behind retribution is that wrongdoers deserve to suffer the harm they have caused others. Of course, there are problems in interpreting just what that means and how one could implement it. A mass murderer has only one life to give—so there's no "eye for an eye" there. Few people seriously advocate having the courts punish rapists with rape, though many look sideways or laugh when such rapists are raped in prison.

Putting people in jail and depriving them of freedom may seem like just retribution for kidnappers, or perhaps for murderers (who deprive their victims of freedom by killing them). But for most others, it seems out of sorts. If a person steals my car, it does not seem as though he "suffers the harm he caused me" by having to spend a few years in jail.

Moskos argues that flogging serves the desire for retribution far better than incarceration.[28] He asks us to imagine that someone has developed a machine —call it the "reformatron"—which instantly rehabilitates any criminal placed inside it, curing that person of vice, and instilling in that person perfectly good character and desires. Moskos says that even if such a device were created and widely used, many people would feel something is missing. If you had been beaten by an attacker and that attacker were placed in the reformatron, you would feel that justice had not been done. You might be glad the attacker was reformed, but you would feel he got away with wrongdoing.

Flogging, Moskos says, seems to satisfy the desire for retribution, while prison does not. "[B]ecause prisons do not punish in a comprehensible manner, incarceration will never satisfy the public's legitimate desire for punishment ... Without satisfactory punishment, the public brays for more punishment."[29] And so, he claims, the public demands ever longer sentences, but remains unsatisfied.

Regarding Deterrence and Rehabilitation: According to the rehabilitation theory, the purpose of criminal justice is to reform criminals. They should be taught useful skills, taught to correct their impulsive behaviors, and somehow induced to have more pro-social attitudes. The goal is to take people whom society is better off without and turn them into people society is better off with.

In contrast, deterrence theory claims that the point of punishment is to scare criminals off from committing crime in the first place. The deterrence theory relies largely upon a "rational criminal" theory of crime, according to which criminals commit crime because the expected benefits of crime outweigh the expected costs. Punishment is supposed to change the calculus of the expected costs. For instance, suppose all crimes were punished by placing the criminal in a pain amplifier for eternity. In that case, it would never be rational to commit crime if there was even the slightest chance of being caught.

In a pair-wise comparison, which does better from a rehabilitative or deterrence standpoint, incarceration or flogging? Since flogging is not widely practiced, it is not widely studied. No one thinks that receiving a lash somehow induces virtue. It's also not clear that most criminals actively weigh the costs and benefits of crime before committing crime; on the contrary, they appear to be "impatient, myopic, or both," and to act impulsively.[30] The extant research indicates clearly that having a high probability of being caught and punished deters crime, but it does not appear that incarceration per se does much to deter criminals, and there is little evidence that adding extra length to sentences does much to deter criminals.[31] In fact, some of the empirical work finds that increased sentences promote recidivism, as the longer a prisoner is in jail, the more he becomes institutionalized and the weaker his ties to his community become.[32]

Overall, rates of recidivism remain very high in the US and places with heavy incarceration. It makes sense: putting a criminal in a camp with other criminals, where he therefore makes friends with criminals or must adopt a tough, alpha male mindset to survive, all while breaking him off from civil society and the family and community ties that give him a stake in behaving well, is not an obvious strategy for rehabilitation.

In short: Incarceration per se does not seem to work as an effective means of rehabilitating or deterring criminals. It even seems to backfire, by making it more likely a convicted criminal will commit future crimes. What matters is not how severe the punishment is, but that criminals believe there is a high probability of being caught and punished. A priori, there is little reason to think that caning would fare even worse. However, if we give people lashes, let them suffer through healing for a few weeks, then let them go about their lives, we at least avoid some of the problems incarceration causes. We return people to their communities. We let them get back to work. We do not break off their ties to law-abiding citizens and friends. We give them a stake in and a chance to contribute to society.

Further, since incarceration is very expensive but flogging is cheap, if the state replaces incarceration with flogging, it could use some of the leftover funds to A) increase policing in high crime areas, B) fund community policing efforts, C) invest in community development or D) create job training programs, welfare programs, and the like.

Regarding Communication: Some theories of criminal justice hold that the point of criminal justice "is to communicate to offenders the censure or condemnation that they deserve for their crimes."[33] While this theory of criminal justice is popular among philosophers, it faces a serious problem: which *particular form* of communication is best?

If we want to communicate to a criminal that he deserves censure, instead of incarcerating him or requiring him to do hard labor, we might make him wear a scarlet letter, put him in the pillory, post a billboard condemning him, write a scathing poem about him, build a mocking statue, or have an insult comic dress him down in public each day for six months. There is no obvious connection between communicating censure and incarceration. On its face, flogging a criminal seems just as good a means to communicate disapproval as incarceration.

Our culture has adopted a symbolic code of meaning by which we use incarceration to signal society's disapproval. But this is at most a contingent, recently developed social construct that incarceration has that meaning. It is not written into the fabric of the universe.

In general, we can judge such social constructs by their utility. For instance, consider that when I utter the sounds, "I love you," this signals concern and care. It really is a fact of the matter that the words express such. But this is only because of meaning English speakers have attached to those sounds. In most languages, the sounds "I love you" mean *nothing*. In an alternate universe, "I love you," could be used by speakers to signal hatred or contempt.

Now, suppose we discovered that uttering the sounds "I love you" had certain negative consequences. It turns out, thanks to bizarre laws of physics, that saying "I love you" to another person increases that person's chance of developing cancer by half a percent. If we discovered that this form of communication had such negative consequences, we would not shrug our shoulders and continue talking that way. Instead, we would change the meaning of the English language, stop saying "I love you," and find some *other* way to express concern and love. It would be monstrous of us to continue using such a dysfunctional and damaging method of communication.

Similar remarks apply to incarceration. Incarceration is replete with problems. It is dysfunctional. It does not "work". It causes more problems than it solves. Thus, even if American culture has fixated on using incarceration as a method for expressing disapproval, this just seems to show that Americans should find some other way to communicate censure.

Regarding Removal: Removal and incapacitation theories hold that the purpose of criminal justice is simply to remove dangerous criminals from society and prevent them from committing further crimes. Pure versions of these theories face a problem in that is unclear why we should wait until after a person commits a crime to remove him from society—after all, certain people (e.g., black American men who drop out of high school) who have not yet committed crimes are statistically very likely to commit crimes, while certain people who have committed crimes (e.g., upper class white collar criminals, or men who murder their cheating spouses in crimes of passion) are statistically unlikely to do so again.

These problems aside, this may be the one theory of criminal justice against which incarceration fares better than flogging. When we incarcerate a person for a long time, we deprive him of freedom and remove him from the outside world. He may continue to commit crimes, but at least his criminal activities will be directed against other criminals. When we flog a person, we let him go. If the criminal is dangerous, he is free to hurt more innocent people.

Still, there are things to balance here. Incarceration for lengthy periods has a high recidivism rate in part because it disrupts a prisoner's life, removes his contacts in civil society, ruins his résumé, institutionalizes him, and socializes him with other criminals. Incarceration prevents the criminal from hurting outsiders during his term, but it may lead to more crime once he is removed.

That said, there may be some people so dangerous that they should not be allowed back in civil society at all. Flogging may not stop serial killers, unrepentant child rapists, and others. So, perhaps incarceration (or exile or even execution) is a better response to extremely dangerous criminals. But this applies only to a minority of criminals. Even for those criminals, we needn't jump immediately to prison. We might instead require in-house arrest or otherwise limit their mobility while requiring them to wear ankle monitors.

Regarding Restitution: The restorative or restitution theory of criminal law holds that wrongdoers should compensate their victims or make their victims whole. Proponents of this theory, sometimes reject the idea of criminal justice altogether and instead hold that all "crimes" should instead be treated as torts. In the last chapter, we argued that many crimes should indeed be turned into torts.

Incarceration does not make compensate victims or make them whole. On the contrary, it is tremendously expensive and must be paid for via taxes. When we throw a criminal in jail, we not only fail to compensate the victim, but also in many cases make the victim partially pay (through taxes) for the criminals' incarceration. You spend, say, $4 a year in property and sales taxes to keep your assailant in jail.

On its face, flogging does not compensate the victim either. However, since flogging is far less expensive for the state than incarceration, Moskos proposes an in-between solution: If the criminal agrees to a flogging, some portion (say half) of the money the state would have spent on incarcerating the prisoner will go to the victim.[34] In this case, while the criminal himself does not compensate the victim, at least the victim receives some degree of compensation from the state. Of course, this gets funded by taxpayers, not the perpetrator. But while this arrangement is imperfect, it still seems better than incarceration. We spend fewer tax dollars, the victim is partially compensated, and the perpetrator gets punished without reinforcing his criminality.

To summarize, we took no stance here on what the purpose of criminal justice ought to be. However, it appears that on most of the theories of criminal justice, including retribution, deterrence, rehabilitation, communication, and restitution theories, caning either beats or ties incarceration. It only fares worse on removal theories, and even then, only when applied to the most dangerous criminals.

Is Caning Torture? Degrading? Dehumanizing?

One possible objection to caning goes roughly as follows:

1. Caning is a form of torture.
2. Torture is either always wrong, or wrong except in bizarre and unique circumstances (such as ticking time bomb cases).
3. Therefore, caning is always wrong, or wrong except in bizarre and unique circumstances.

The idea here is that we just need to show caning falls into the conceptual category of torture, and that is sufficient to show it is wrong.

Matthew Kramer offers what is perhaps the most thorough and rigorous definition of torture.[35] He claims it consists of six components:

1. Torture involves the infliction of severe pain and suffering.
2. Torture is conducted for a purpose, such as punishment, the enjoyment of the torturer, or some other purposes.
3. Torture generally continues until the purpose is achieved.
4. Torture shows indifference to the well-being of the victim.
5. Victims do not consent to the torture.
6. Victims lack control over the length of the torture.

Now, one may certainly dispute whether this is the best characterization of torture.[36] Maybe it's too hard to a give a real definition for the concept.

However, if we accept Kramer's definition, caning arguably escapes it. Judicial caning does meet criteria 1–3 and 6. However, we need not suppose that caning shows indifference to the well-being of the criminal. On the contrary, we might practice caning precisely because it is a form of punishment that shows *greater* concern for the victim's well-being than incarceration.

After all, as we discussed above, incarceration is generally worse than caning. If we could wave a magic wand and replace American-style prisons with caning, that would make things *more humane.* If 1–6 constitute torture, then American-style jails are more like torture than caning is.

It is not just that caning could show more concern for a person's well-being than incarceration. Rather, the kind of caning we are discussing here involves carefully monitoring a person's health, carefully ensuring that he is not grievously or permanently injured, and then providing him with medical care afterward. These are not behaviors that indicate a lack of concern for the victim's well-being.

Further, as Koskos recommends, the most defensible form of caning does not to require criminals to be caned. Instead, criminals are offered the choice between caning or incarceration (or other penalties). Since this is a forced choice between two unpleasant options, the criminal cannot be said to fully consent to the caning, in the way that perhaps a masochist might consent when he enters a torture dungeon. Nevertheless, when we offer a person a choice between two bad options, he can still freely choose between those two options. If a person chooses caning over incarceration, or would choose caning if given the option, we certainly do not show respect for his capacity to consent by imposing incarceration anyway.

At any rate, the torture objection is too simple. Moral philosophers tend to think the way to argue against a policy is simply to list its faults and or to fit it into some objectionable category. This is one way in which philosophers tend to exhibit less intellectual seriousness about moral matters than supposedly amoral social scientists such as economists. An economist would not ask whether torture is absolutely right and wrong. Instead, she might ask, what are the available options in light of the technical and motivational constraints we face, and then try to determine which of these is best. We don't know what an ideal criminal justice system would look like. However, we are pessimistic about American federal or state governments' competence to implement anything like well-functioning, productive rehabilitation centers. We are competent to cane prisoners, and we would do it better than we do incarceration.

A closely related objection to caning holds that caning is shameful and degrading. To cane someone lowers that person's status and standing. It treats them in an inhumane way. The entire spectacle is embarrassing. It violates their bodily integrity. Since at the very least the criminal's buttocks will be exposed, it also violates their privacy.

David Benatar has a powerful response to this objection:

> Here it is noteworthy that there are other forms of punishment that lower people's standing even more than corporal punishment, and yet are not subject to similar condemnation. Consider, for example, various indignities attendant upon imprisonment, including severe invasions of privacy (such as strip-searches and ablution facilities that require relieving oneself in full view of others) as well as imposed subservience to prison wardens, guards, and even to more powerful fellow inmates. My intuitions suggest that this lowering of people's standing surpasses that implicit in corporal punishment per se ... If corporal punishment is wrong because it involves violating the intimate zone of a person's body, then surely the extreme invasions of prison inmates' privacy, which seem worse, would also be wrong.[37]

When we cane someone, we intentionally inflict severe pain on that person for a short period of time. That is of course distinct from incarceration. But incarceration generally involves long-term severe restrictions on a person's liberty, long-term constant surveillance, long-term exposure to risk of capricious abuse and physical harm, forced boredom, forced labor, deprivation of privacy, deprivation of sexual satisfaction, and separation from loved ones, friends, and civil society, and so on. As Benatar concludes, incarceration is even more degrading. So the objection that caning is degrading does not rule out caning unless it also rules out incarceration.

Do We Just Need Nicer Prisons?

One major objection to our argument is that we're contrasting caning to American-style prisons. Sure, American-style prisons are horrific, and so caning is plausibly preferable to imprisonment. However, perhaps an alternative prison system would be better. Consider this description of the Scandinavian and Finnish model:

> Suomenlinna Island has hosted an "open" prison since 1971. The 95 male prisoners leave the prison grounds each day to do the township's general maintenance or commute to the mainland for work or study. Serving time for theft, drug trafficking, assault, or murder, all the men here are on the verge of release. Cellblocks look like dorms at a state university. Though worse for wear, rooms feature flat-screen TVs, sound systems, and mini-refrigerators for the prisoners who can afford to rent them for prison-labor wages of 4.10 to 7.3 Euros per hour ($5.30 to $9.50). With electronic monitoring, prisoners are allowed to spend time with their families in Helsinki. Men here enjoy a screened barbecue pit, a gym, and a dining hall where prisoners and staff eat together. Prisoners throughout Scandinavia wear their own clothes. Officers wear navy slacks, powder-blue shirts, nametags and shoulder bars; but they carry no batons, handcuffs, Tasers or pepper-spray.[38]

In these prison systems, prisoners are only partially removed from society. They are made to live together, but in humane conditions. They are put to work or allowed to keep their jobs, and paid real wages. They retain their outside relationships. Their main "punishment" is a loss of freedom, but it is a loss of freedom closer to that of having strict parents than the kind of loss American prisoners face.

Note that the Scandinavian countries and Finland also have closed, high security prisons in the American style. Conditions there may be somewhat better and more humane, but prisoners are still kept under more constant surveillance and are in greater danger from one another.

In some sense, we are willing to concede this kind of argument. However, there a number of difficult questions we would have to answer in order to reach a judgment either way. First, it is not clear that just because something works in Sweden it can work in the United States. (We admit, this applies to caning as well.) The Scandinavian countries have remarkably low crime, have small, relatively homogenous populations, are very conscientious and have high mutual trust, and so on. It may turn out, empirically, that such forms of incarceration only "work" in that kind of context.

Second, there are cost trade-offs that need to be considered. The Scandinavian model, with its focus on humane treatment and rehabilitation, may be more expensive up front, though perhaps less expensive in the long run. That said, compared to caning and setting someone free, it will certainly be more expensive.

However, even if we concede that these points come in favor of the Scandinavian model, there are still reasons to prefer caning. First, we might ask, if you were convicted of, say, grand theft auto, would you prefer A) to spend four years in a Scandinavian open prison, or B) be lashed eight times and then set free? Many people (including me) would find B preferable to A. Perhaps some would find A preferable to B. But that indicates that the Scandinavian model is arguably harsher than caning, though perhaps it should be preferred all things considered if it turns out to have a better rehabilitation rate. Second, consider that if I convicted for A) kidnapping you and keeping you imprisoned in a Scandinavian-style open prison for a few years, I would receive a harsher sentence in most countries than I would if I simply B) lashed you eight times with a cane. So, while the Scandinavian prison model is better than the American, even it is not clearly better than caning.

Other Punishments

As far as we can tell, caning is in most cases better than incarceration. That doesn't mean we'd recommend immediately dispensing with prisons and using caning instead. Maybe we should instead experiment with caning on a small scale in certain districts, measure the effects, and if it works—where "it works" just means "all things considered, it's better than incarceration"—we should scale it up.

Perhaps *other* punishments are superior to both caning and incarceration. Let's consider some options, and discuss some of the potential pros and cons. Remember, whatever proposal we consider, we have to ask how it would realistically work with the kinds of people working in the criminal justice system. We shouldn't ask how angels would run the punishment. We need to imagine imperfect, selfish, sometimes corrupt and often corruptible players running the show.

Partial Restrictions on Liberty: Incarceration usually involves a mix of A) very severe restrictions on a convict's liberty, B) separation and confinement from society. But perhaps we should experiment with doing A without B. A person might be deprived of the right to go certain places, participate in certain activities, enjoy certain hobbies, and so on. The problem, though, is that enforcing such restrictions in the absence of state confinement is terribly difficult and costly.

Forced Labor: Already, criminals are sometimes made to do "community service" in addition to or in lieu of prison time. We could expand that, perhaps requiring convicts to do significant and more severe forms of labor, all while letting them keep living at home and working their regular jobs. In this case, we can have convicts serve society by doing something useful, and it may be that forcing some of them to work on a schedule has significant rehabilitative value.

But we have to keep in mind that the same incentive and cost problems we discussed in Chapter 2 will reappear here. One problem is that forced labor is expensive to monitor. Laborers may be subjected to abuse from supervisors and co-workers, who know that the workers must work to avoid more severe penalties. Just as right now, certain groups and people—prison guard unions, public prison administrators, private prison companies, rural workers—have a strong financial incentive to increase the number of hours people spend in jail, so people will have a bizarre incentive to game the system to get "free" laborers. Just as cash-strapped towns in the US often issue too many punitive tickets or abuse civil forfeiture laws, so they might start handing out sentences in order to create a "free" workforce for their local needs. So, forced labor might be better, but it will almost certainly be abused, and we'd have to be very careful about it.

Another possibility is to substitute *partial* confinement to full incarceration. This could mean making heavier use of house arrest, but with the stipulation that prisoners are free to continue working at their jobs. In this case, they are allowed to leave the home during their work hours, and even allowed to, say, get lunch or gas while out, but must return and remain at home during non-work hours. We can use electronic monitors to ensure compliance.

Alternatively, we might follow certain Swedish or Norwegian models, in which convicts are required to sleep at state-funded confinement centers at night, but may leave during the day to see family, work, do community service, and so on. However, this model may in the American context reintroduce many of the dangers and dysfunctions of prisons, just from the hours of 8pm to 7 am.

Public Humiliation: Maybe the *Scarlet Letter* had the right idea—their problem was just that they punished a behavior that should not have been a crime. One cheap way to punish criminals might be to force them to stand on the pillory or in the stocks. After a person is convicted, her or she is led outside to a public place, where they are required to stand, perhaps with a sign declaring their names and crime. Maybe they have to dress in a silly costume. Perhaps states should publicize who has been convicted of what. Fear of public disgrace is a powerful motivator for many people. Already, thanks to social media, we have a tendency to form mobs who spew their anger at wrongdoers. Perhaps that's a good idea, but we first add the *due process of law* to ensure the accused get a fair hearing.

Of course, this also has its limitations. Some people might not feel humiliated or might even revel in the notoriety. Perhaps there would be too many criminals and we'd end up polluting or ruining our public spaces with such punishments. Perhaps the social ostracism that would result would go too far; convicts would lose their jobs, become desperate, and commit more crimes.

Exile: In some cases—e.g., when a person acts violently because he has joined a gang—requiring him to leave, live, and work elsewhere could at first glance be an effective solution. A convict is told he gets two weeks to month to get his affairs in order, after which time he will be not be allowed to re-enter the city, county, or even US state for some period of time.

But there are a few obvious problems with this idea. For one, it may incentivize jurisdictions to get into an arms race where they use their criminal justice systems to dump their most problematic citizens onto neighboring towns, counties, or states. You could easily imagine, say, Baltimore using exile to unload its gang members elsewhere. Further, monitoring and enforcing exile rules might be extremely expensive or impossible.

Conscription: Throughout history, many countries required convicts to serve in the military, or instead gave them the option of military service in lieu of other punishments.[39] Should we give that another shot?

The pros are speculative. The military imposes harsh discipline. Perhaps it can both A) teach certain unconscientious criminals to get their act together and B) simultaneously teach them useful, valuable skills while also (after years of service) credentialing that they have become trustworthy people.

However, to demonstrate that, our best proxy would be to examine whether, say, citizens drafted into Vietnam who had various criminal records or similar problems at home were made better off from their conscription (assuming they weren't killed or injured). Turns out there are studies on how conscription affects criminality (as well as lifetime earnings potential and other measures of success), but the results are rather mixed.[40] Some papers argue that conscription reduces criminality, some that it has little effect, and others that it increases criminality.

But there is another issue. Part of the reason why, e.g., the Vietnam War draft led to a low quality army was that our most successful young men, including college students, generally got furloughs and deferments. War is a serious business, requiring high levels of discipline and smarts. Weapons must be maintained. Orders must be followed. Goofing off is dangerous. Smart soldiers fight well and live; lazy, undisciplined, and dumb soldiers fight badly and die. Convicted criminals tend to have low levels of conscientiousness and low IQs. We don't want to flood the military with low IQ, undisciplined soldiers, and hope they somehow make it work.

Mutilation: This is a far more severe form of corporal punishment than flogging/caning. Nevertheless, if there are cases where flogging is not "good enough," it's not obvious to us a priori that all forms of mutilation are worse than incarceration. If we were convicted of, say, grand theft auto, we'd choose having the state chop off a pinky over spending a year in jail.

We often hear people say that repeat sexual offenders should be castrated or emasculated. But rather than literally chopping off bits, we might require offenders to undergo chemical castration and hormone therapy.

When to Use Prison

Incarceration is a horrific punishment with a terrible track record. On its own, it has little to no deterrent effect. It's expensive and in many cases counterproductive, as it tends to criminalize convicts ever more.

In some cases, it reduces crime (or relocates it), because it gets criminals off the streets. A violent criminal might remain violent in prison; his victims there will be other inmates. But incarceration at least successfully removes dangerous criminals from society. At the same time, though, when young men and to a lesser extent women grow up in neighborhoods where half the men are missing because they are incarcerated, they also become more likely themselves to become criminals.

In this chapter, we haven't settled on which alternative to incarceration is best. We defended caning at some length, but we admit certain other alternatives might be even better.

In our view, incarceration is something close to a last resort punishment. It might not literally be the last resort, but it's not a first or second choice either.

We see prison as a good *punishment* only if the following conditions are met:

1   The person must have been convicted of a violent crime.
2.   There must be very strong evidence that the person represents a persistent and ongoing physical threat to other people.
3.   There is strong evidence that there is no other more effective (including cost-effective) way of removing that threat.

Prison isn't obviously the best punishment. It doesn't sate our desire for retribution. It's expensive and ineffective. The special case where prison works best is when we know letting a convict go free puts us in serious physical danger. Even then, very few dangerous criminals remain dangerous for long periods of time. In saying prisons are a last resort, we aren't thereby endorsing the extremely long prison sentences the US imposes.

Notes

1 Perlstein 2018; Sledge 2018.
2 Open Justice 2017.
3 *Washington Post* 2018a.
4 *Washington Post* 2019.
5 Grinberg 2017.
6 See Hasnas 2017.
7 See Bedau and Kelly 2015.
8 Hasnas 2017.
9 Reckdahl 2014.
10 Wildeman 2010; Galea et al. 2015.

11 Schnittker, Turney, and Wildeman 2012.
12 Alper, Durose, and Markman 2018.
13 Goldstein 2015.
14 Rivers 2017.
15 Jarrett 2018.
16 Kleiman 2010.
17 Kennedy 2008.
18 Durlauf and Nagin 2011.
19 Statista 2019.
20 *Washington Post* 2018b.
21 www.federalregister.gov/documents/2018/04/30/2018-09062/annual-determin
   ation-of-average-cost-of-incarceration
22 Vera Institute 2016.
23 Aharoni et al. 2019.
24 Shenon 1994.
25 Skarbek 2014.
26 Thanks to Alexei Marcoux for this wording.
27 Moskos 2011, 9.
28 Moskos 2011, 22–3.
29 Moskos 2011, 95–6.
30 Lee and McCrary 2005.
31 Farrington, Langan, and Wikström 1994; Gendreau, Little, and Goggin 1996; Levitt
   1998; Langan and David 2002; Doob and Webster 2003; Levitt 2004; Nagin 2013.
32 Gendreau, Goggin, and Cullen 1999
33 Duff 2013.
34 Moskos 2011, 143.
35 Kramer 2014.
36 e.g., Lenta 2015.
37 Benatar 1998, 243–4.
38 Larson 2013.
39 Betaud 1988.
40 Hjalmarsson and Lindquist 2016.

5

CRIME DOESN'T PAY, UNLESS YOU'RE THE STATE

One of the earliest recorded accounts of a system of laws that aims at just punishment dates back to 18th century BC Mesopotamia and the Babylonian King Hammurabi. For Hammurabi, the role of the state and function of juridical law was "to bring about the rule of righteousness in the land, to destroy the wicked and the evil-doers; so that the strong should not harm the weak."[1] Hammurabi's Code contained 282 "laws of justice" for addressing topics as wide ranging as adoption, inheritance, the appropriate amount of payment for certain services, and penalties for harming other citizens or causing damage to their property.

Punishments dictated by the Code varied widely, with many being relatively severe by today's standards. For example, 28 laws prescribe death as the appropriate punishment for behavior ranging from murder, kidnapping, and negligent homicide to theft, making false accusations, adultery, and withholding compensation from mercenary soldiers. Perhaps more surprising is that for some crimes, such as when a man strikes a free-born woman and causes her to die, death is prescribed as the appropriate punishment, not for the perpetrator, but for one of his children. Beyond these 28 laws that prescribe death as the appropriately just punishment, other laws prescribe punishments that may strike us as even more barbaric: amputation of ears and hands, bone breaking, eye gouging, blows from an ox-whip, indentured servitude, and fines to be paid directly to the people who were harmed.

Noticeably absent from Hammurabi's Code are the types of punishment that we see most frequently in our own society—fines paid to the state and imprisonment by the state. Although the Code makes reference to prisons, these prisons appear to have been private and were used for holding individuals who owed debts and were working those debts off through forced labor. The

Code provided certain protections for these prisoners and outlined penalties for any individuals who mistreated them or caused their death while in custody. Although it is not clear why the early Babylonians did not utilize fines paid to the state or state imprisonment as methods of just punishment, one reasonable explanation is that they believed these two types of punishment failed to contribute to the goal of restoring the appropriate balance to the community that was upset by the unlawful behavior.

So why do we rely on these two types of punishment almost exclusively, especially when other options may be more successful at realizing the differing aims of just punishment? Follow the money. Policing and punishment is big business in the United States. Just how big? All included, it is at least a $300-billion-a-year industry. This number includes $100+ billion in yearly expenditures nationwide on police[2] and the $182+ billion in direct costs of the criminal justice system.[3] It does not include the $136+ billion in fine and forfeiture revenue reported by the states that goes back into supporting the criminal justice system. To put this number in context, it is about half of what the US spends on primary and secondary education nationwide, and about four and a half times what the US spends on the Supplemental Nutrition Assistance Program (food stamps).[4]

While public attention usually focuses on the profits of private individuals and corporations, focusing solely on private contractors distracts us from the reality that vast majority of state-sanctioned policing and punishment in the US today, whether carried out by a government or private entity, is motivated by financial gain. This statement is true up and down the line, from prisons to parking tickets. But most of us are unaware of just how bad this problem is, as well as how the use of our criminal justice system as a revenue-collecting arm of the state has exacerbated existing social and economic problems.

The Prison-Industrial Complex

Incarceration is big business in the US. As a nation, the US incarcerates more people than any other nation in the world: 2.3 million or just under 1% of its total population. Of this total, just over 20% are in prison for the possession of illegal drugs,[5] and it is estimated that over 50% are in prison for drug-related activities (consumption, distribution, violence associated with the drug trade, or committing crimes due to drug influence or addiction).[6] On a per capita basis, the US incarcerates more people than any other nation in the world with the exception of the tiny island nation of the Seychelles, which comes in first only because it volunteered its prison system to house all of the Somali pirates captured in the Indian Ocean. While we often think of incarceration as a national problem, of the 2.3 million people incarcerated in the US at the start of 2017, 2 million are held in state prisons and local jails, not federal prison.[7] If US states were nations, the District of Columbia and eight states—Louisiana, Georgia, Oklahoma, Alabama, South Dakota, Arizona, and Texas, and Florida, in that order—would have a higher per capita incarceration rate than the circumstantially inflated rate of the Seychelles.[8] After the Seychelles, 25 other US states have a greater per capita incarceration rate than the next highest nation on the list, Turkmenistan.[9]

When thinking about the ethical issues related to the business of policing and punishment, as well as possible paths for reform, it is important to keep in mind not only how many people are incarcerated in the US, but also that there is no one, uniform set of rules governing their incarceration or the laws that put them there. There are at least 52 different sets of rules—50 states, the District of Columbia, and the federal government—and 52 different arenas for private parties to try to advance their interests. What is also important is just how big a business incarceration in the US has become. While the focus is often on the business of private prisons, put in terms of dollars, private prisons represent only $4.2 billion of the $80.7 billion a year spent on the corrections industry.[10] This number includes the cost for corrections employees, health care, building upkeep, food, and utilities, but it does not include the cost of policing, the court system, or expenses charged to the inmates or their families, such as bail fees, items from the commissary, or telephone calls. The complete incarceration pie, from arrest to release, represents a $182-billion-a-year industry.

Police departments and municipalities are not the only ones who profit from the US criminal justice system. Private companies and individuals do as well. Thus far the 21st century has been kind to most investors in US financial markets. From January 2001 through May 2017, the S&P 500 index has nearly doubled, and investments in blue chip companies such as Microsoft, Exxon Mobil, Proctor & Gamble, and Nike all would have returned 300% to 800% during this same period. While there have been a handful of really big winners during this time period—Amazon and Apple come to mind—two less well-known companies, CoreCivic and the GEO Group, have each returned a whopping 5000% to their investors. CoreCivic, formerly known as the Corrections Corporation of America, and the GEO Group own and manage prisons, detention centers, and correctional mental health facilities throughout the United States and abroad under US government contracts. Together, as of the end of 2018, they own and manage over 200 US facilities, have a combined yearly revenue of $4 billion, and a combined market capitalization of nearly $6 billion. In short, CoreCivic and the GEO Group are not small companies, and business has been very, very good over the last 16 years.

Few areas of our criminal justice system elicit stronger reactions from the general public than the use of private prisons. Motivated by negative public attention directed at the use of these facilities, in 2016 the US Department of Justice (DOJ) Office of the Inspector General (OIG) initiated a systematic investigation into private prisons to compare them to their state-run counterparts. The OIG released this report in August 2016. It concluded that private prisons not only offered no significant cost savings over prisons run by the Federal Bureau of Prisons (BOP), but also performed worse than BOP facilities in most of the important metrics, including contraband, inmate incidents, and lockdowns.[11]

As a result of these findings, the DOJ announced that same month that it would begin the process of winding down its use of private prisons, leading ultimately to their discontinuation in the federal prison system.[12] But no contracts were terminated and reductions in use were nominal at best. In November 2016, just three months after this supposedly landmark directive was issued, CoreCivic announced that the Federal Bureau of Prisons had renewed their contract on a facility in McRae, Georgia for an additional two years, with a bed reduction of less than 10%.[13] Other renewals of private prison contracts followed, either with no reductions or similarly nominal reductions. Then, in February 2017, the DOJ formalized what everyone already knew, rescinding the directive to reduce its reliance on private prisons.[14]

Why the change of heart? Although no formal explanation was provided, it is not unreasonable to follow the money. The GEO Group was one of only a handful of publicly traded companies to make significant contributions to super PACs during the 2016 election, all to support Republican candidates, including more than $225,000 to pro-Trump super PAC Rebuilding America Now. While federal law prohibits federal contractors from making political contributions, in an effort to get around the law, contributions from the GEO Group were made through "GEO Corrections Holdings Inc.," a separate but wholly owned subsidiary of the company.

While a complaint regarding these contributions was filed with the Federal Election Commission (FEC), the FEC declined to pursue it based on prosecutorial discretion. When the party that filed the complaint sued to compel the FEC to pursue it,[15] the Court sided with the FEC and granted summary judgment on the suit, dismissing it. Even if the FEC would have pursued this case and found that the GEO Group knowing and willfully violated federal law, it would have been up to the DOJ to enforce any criminal penalties. Such enforcement seems unlikely in part because in October 2016 the GEO Group hired three former aides of Jefferson Sessions, Attorney General and head of the DOJ at the time of their hiring, to serve as lobbyists for the company.[16]

Their lobbying efforts seemed to have paid off. CoreCivic and the GEO Group have become the primary beneficiaries of President's Trump zero-tolerance immigration policy, which involved, among other things, detaining entire families who had come to the US to seek asylum or otherwise migrate. CoreCivic and the GEO Group run many of these detention facilities, including the two largest: the Karnes County Residential Center in Karnes City, TX, and the South Texas Family Residential Center in Dilley, TX. Before

Trump's policy change in spring 2018, Homeland Security had requested funding for 2500 "family beds" in these migrant detention facilities.[17] After President Trump's executive order, this number jumped to 15,000. According to a report by the Center for American Progress, "At a cost of $318.79 per bed per day, this sixfold expansion of current capacity would mean the government would pay $5.6 million per day to jail families seeking asylum—an annual cost of more than $2 billion."[18]

While it is reasonably clear how companies such as CoreCivic and the GEO Group profit directly from government policies laws that put more people in prison and keep them there for longer periods of time, only around 7% of persons incarcerated in the US are held in private prisons. The rest are held in government facilities, at either the federal, state, or local level. So, who makes money off of them? In short, almost everyone. The easiest group to identify are employees of the correctional institutions themselves. In 2016, we spent 38.4 billion dollars on the salaries and benefits for these employees, and they're very much interested in protecting their jobs and growing their ranks. Police and prison guard unions and lobbying groups are some of the strongest and most vocal in the country. They have been at the center of efforts to implement mandatory minimum sentences and three strikes laws,[19] as well as some of the most vocal opponents of efforts to decriminalize the use of recreational drugs.[20] Given the financial incentives at play, it should not be surprising that they have been opposed to almost any program or law that would reduce the number of people sentenced to prison, reduce the length of time inmates spend there, or otherwise disrupt the flow of resources to prisons.[21]

There are also less obvious financial beneficiaries of mass incarceration. Prison health care is a $12.3-billion industry.

> In a bid to cut costs, more state prisons and county jails are adding healthcare to the growing list of services that are outsourced to for-profit companies, … [and] more than half of all state and local prisons have outsourced their healthcare.[22]

The largest provider of prison health care nationwide is Corizon, which has contracts with over 300 correctional facilities in 22 states, covering 220,000 prisoners or just under 10% of the US prison population.[23] But Corizon's ability to secure additional contracts and keep its existing ones seems to depend not so much on its ability to provide quality health care for the lowest cost, as on its effectiveness at lobbying the relevant decision-makers at the state and local level.

In 2013, Corizon's $42 million per year contract with the city of Philadelphia to provide health care at city correctional facilities came up for review. Many observers thought that Corizon would likely lose the contract to one of its competitors—such as Correction Medical Care, which offered to provide the same services for $3.5 million less per year, saving the city $35 million over the life of the ten-year contract. Not only did competitors offer to provide the same services at a lower price, but also Corizon had just settled with the city for $1.85 million after it came to light that Corizon had passed money through a dummy subcontractor to satisfy the city's minority-participation requirements.

How was Corizon able to secure the contract? As with many of its contracts around the country, and as with many businesses that depend almost entirely on government contracts, it successfully lobbied the relevant government decision-makers. Corizon has actively lobbied officials in Alabama,[24] California,[25] Florida,[26] Washington DC,[27] and so forth. Find a state where Corizon has government contracts, and you'll find that they have lobbied significantly to get those contracts. But Corizon is not unique and operates like any other company dependent on government contracts. As Ice-T says, "Don't hate the player, hate the game."

Philadelphia is a great example of lobbying in action. In addition to donating to the campaigns of several local politicians in Philadelphia, including $26,600 to Mayor Michael Nutter's campaign committee, Corizon also hired S. R. Wojdak & Associates, a Pennsylvania lobbying firm with strong ties to Philadelphia's City Hall and Mayor Michael Nutter's administration. When the City of Philadelphia's Inspector General recommended that Corizon be banned from competing for city contracts for a period of two years after participating in the dummy subcontractor scam, "not only was [Corizon] allowed to keep doing business with the city, the [Nutter] administration went out of its way to make sure it could bid on the next prison contract," including extending

> the [contract submission] deadline by six months to give Corizon time to implement reforms it was required to adopt as part of its settlement [with the city]. And in the meantime, the city simply extended Corizon's existing contract for those six months for a cool $21 million.[28]

If you're uncomfortable with private companies profiting from housing and caring for inmates, then you likely will be even more uncomfortable with private companies and state entities profiting from prison labor. There are two kinds of prison labor: "First, there are [jobs] ... where inmates work for the prison, and the employer—the government—doesn't make a profit per se off prisoners' backs, though it holds down expenses by paying little or nothing to get essential tasks done."[29] These jobs include working in the prison laundry facility, painting prison walls, and doing other jobs that connect to the proper functioning or upkeep of the prison facilities. The second "are jobs under the Prison Industry Enhancement (PIE) program, in which inmates are employed by a private business that has contracted with local correctional authorities for low-cost labor,"[30] or by Federal Prison Industries (abbreviated as FPI or UNICOR), a wholly owned US government corporation.

UNICOR partners with government entities and corporations to produce a wide range of products, including body armor, office furniture, clothing, and food (milk, beef, fish, etc.), and services, such as word processing, call center operations, and data encoding.[31] As of September 2016, UNICOR "has agricultural, industrial and service operations at 63 factories and 3 farms located at 52 prison facilities" and employs over 12,000 inmate workers.[32] And business at these factories and farms is quite good. During 2016, UNICOR had a yearly revenue of nearly $500 million and a net income or profit of just over $44 million.[33]

You have almost certainly bought UNICOR products or used UNICOR services without even knowing about it. In the past few years, they have provided Whole Foods with tilapia and goat cheese;[34] McDonald's with plastic utensils, packaging, and uniforms;[35] Victoria's Secret with casualwear and lingerie;[36] AT&T with call center operations;[37] and BP with oil cleanup crews after the Deepwater Horizon explosion.[38] But many of these companies have kept their use of prison labor hidden, and for good reason. Not only do corporations receive lucrative tax write-offs for hiring work-release inmates—up to $2,400 per year per inmate through the Work Opportunity Tax Credit Program—inmates working in UNICOR factories or on UNICOR farms make between $0.23 and $1.15 per hour,[39] a fraction of the federally mandated minimum wage of $7.25 per hour. (The salary for prisoners working non-industry jobs, the first type listed above, is not much better—they earn between $0.00 and $2.00 per hour.[40]) And UNICOR passes these savings on to its business partners. The $12-a-pound tilapia at Whole Foods, for example, was raised by prisoners who were paid as little as $0.74 per day.[41] As UNICOR says on its website, "Imagine … All the benefits of domestic outsourcing at offshore prices. It's the best kept secret in outsourcing!"[42] (Seriously, they actually say this directly on their website.)

How are prisons, as well as UNICOR and its partners, able to get around federal wage requirements and pay prison laborers so little, operating in a way that many opponents have called modern day slavery? While the 13th Amendment to the US Constitution outlaws slavery and indentured servitude, an exception is made for prison labor. It reads: "Neither slavery nor involuntary servitude, *except as a punishment for crime whereof the party shall have been duly convicted*, shall exist within the United States, or any place subject to their jurisdiction" (our emphasis). Prisons have taken advantage of this exemption, as well as being able to deduct up to 80% of earned wages to account for costs of room and board. For UNICOR and its partners, although they should be required by law to pay "prevailing wages … for similar work performed in the locality, and comparative benefits (overtime, worker's compensation, etc.),"[43] a requirement outlined clearly on their own website, they have found ways to get around it. One loophole is that all prison laborers working as part of UNICOR are considered to be volunteers,[44] and, as volunteers, generally are exempt from prevailing wage requirements. They're considered to be volunteers because they volunteer to participate in UNICOR instead of working a regular prison job.

Fines and Fees

While the so-called prison-industrial complex has a large financial impact on both public and private entities, other programs and punishment mechanisms —although smaller in total dollars—are actually more important to fiscal health of county and municipal budgets. If you've driven US Route 301 in Florida between Gainesville and Jacksonville, you've gone through the small town of Waldo, population 1000. With the exception of having a name that might lead your kids to say, "There's Waldo!" from the back seat, the town is otherwise indistinguishable from the other small towns along 301 or across Florida generally. Driving through Waldo would take only a few minutes, unless you are pulled over by one of Waldo's finest. And if you drove through in 2013, this outcome was not unlikely. In 2013, Waldo's seven police officers wrote 11,603 traffic citations, an average of just over 1658 citations per officer for the year.[45] For comparison, that same year the 300 police officers in the nearby town of Gainesville, a town with 128,000 residents and an additional 50,000 students at the University of Florida, wrote 25,461 citations, or just under 85 per officer per year. On average, each police officer in Waldo wrote 1850% more tickets than each police officer in Gainesville, the town where the University is Florida is located.

Why were police officers in Waldo writing so many citations? Similar to almost every other problem we've identified thus far, we can follow the money. In 2013, the 11,603 citations generated nearly $500,000 for the town, half of its total yearly revenue. Things got so bad in Waldo that the Automobile Association of America (AAA) not only identified the town as having one of the nation's worst speed traps, but also the group bought multiple billboards on US Route 301 to warn drivers to be especially cautious when driving through.[46] In 2014, as a result of numerous citizen complaints and the negative attention generated by the AAA, Florida's Department of Law Enforcement opened an investigation into Waldo's police department and the town suspended Police Chief Mike Szabo. When the investigation revealed that police offers had been given orders to write at least 12 tickets during each 12-hour shift or face repercussions, violating Florida state law that prohibited ticket quotas, Waldo's city council voted to disband the police department.

How dramatic was this move on the finances of Waldo? Consider the difference between the city's 2015 and 2016 General Fund Budgets.[47] For 2015, the city projected police revenue to be $434,000. This number was then revised down to $98,153.30 after the investigation and vote to disband the department. The 2016 budget indicated that Waldo actually generated $177,216.24 in "police revenue" in 2015. After the disbanding of the department, Waldo projected that they would generate only $5000 in "police revenue" in 2016.

While this story has a somewhat happy ending, many municipalities around the country have turned to their police to act as an additional source of revenue. A 2016 study by the Sunlight Foundation found that "thousands of American cities and towns [depend] on judicial fines and forfeiture to fund public services," with municipalities in Louisiana, Arkansas, Georgia, Illinois, and Mississippi topping the list of "states where city governments rely heavily on fines and forfeits for funding."[48] The most egregious abusers, calculated in terms of the percentage of revenue derived from fines, were smaller towns with populations under 1500, towns similar to Waldo. That these tiny towns are the worst offenders "suggests that most of those fines were probably paid by people who did not live in those towns, but who nonetheless had to drive through them."[49] For example, the town Olla, LA, population 1400 and located on the highly traveled US Route 165 between Alexandria, LA, and Monroe, LA, collected $250,699 from fines in 2017, over 25% of the town's total yearly revenue and almost five times what the town collects in tax revenue from its citizens.

Although tiny towns seem to be the worst offenders on a percentage basis, larger municipalities, often assisted by private companies such as American Traffic Solutions, get in on the action as well. American Traffic Solutions (ATS), and a handful of similar companies in the US, have contracts with municipalities to install traffic cameras and process violations. While the specifics of each contract vary depending on the municipality, generally ATS will pay to install the equipment, send video of each violation to local law enforcement for review, and then take on some of the payment processing (mailing the violation notice, collecting the fine, etc.). For their work, ATS receives a percentage of fine revenue collected, often with certain guaranteed minimums. Given that many municipalities are trying to increase revenue at no cost and without taking steps that are seen by the public generally as tax increases, it is not surprising that they have turned to these arrangements with companies such as ATS.

For 2017, the cities of Atlanta, New Orleans, and Chicago *projected* that they will collect $28 million, $46 million, and $359 million in revenue from fines and forfeitures, which comes to 4.6%,[50] 7.5%,[51] and 9.7%[52] of their total yearly revenues, respectively. These numbers represent significant percentages of the projected yearly revenue for each of these cities. Not all cities have budgets that rely so heavily on revenue from fines and forfeitures. Mobile, Detroit, and Houston, for example, project that they will collect $3 million, $24.8 million, and $40 million from fines and forfeitures, which comes to 1.2%,[53] 1.3%,[54] and 0.9%[55] of their total projected revenue.

The projected numbers are important because this is what each city counts on coming into its pocket and a shortfall in fine and violation revenue could cause significant budget problems for each city. By contrast, consider a different budgeting model that projected $0 yearly from fines and forfeitures. In that model a city wouldn't be dependent on its citizens breaking the law to have enough revenue to operate. You can see the dangers with a budget model that depends on a certain amount of citizen law-breaking to function. It's not unreasonable for people who live in or around these cities to be especially concerned about the likelihood of receiving questionable parking tickets, running into speed traps, or otherwise being negatively affected by the city's dependence on these funds.

Comparing budget projections to the actual amount of revenue collected is also interesting. For 2017, those same three cities of Atlanta, New Orleans, and Chicago *collected* $23 million,[56] $41 million,[57] and $327 million.[58] Although each represented year-over-year increases from the previous year, the collected amounts were less than the projections in each of the three cities. Fine and fee revenue coming up short had led to some interesting political situations. For example, in New Orleans, newly elected mayor LaToya Cantrell learned that it's not always easy keeping campaign promises. Cantrell ran on a number of reform issues including ending the city's controversial traffic camera program.[59] What she didn't realize was how difficult it would be to wean the city off of this revenue stream. She tried to back out of this commitment,[60] faced significant public backlash, and then moved forward with a partial shutdown while launching a campaign to generate more revenue for the city from other sources.[61]

The pattern connecting cities that rely disproportionately on revenue from fines and forfeitures is not what might be expected. One might expect that these cities would have features such as having a contract with companies like American Traffic Solutions to handle traffic enforcement or having many non-residents passing through or visiting for one reason or another. But neither of these features predict higher than average reliance on revenue from fines and forfeitures. What does predict it, according to recent empirical research, is the racial composition of the city and its elected leaders—the higher the black population, the more likely the municipality will rely on fines to generate needed revenue.[62] Further, cities with at least one black member of the city council reduced the connection between race and fines by about half. Perhaps most worrisome, these same researchers found that "police departments in cities that collect a greater share of their revenue from fees solve violent and property crimes at significantly lower rates."[63]

But even for cities in which a relatively low percentage of revenue comes from fines and forfeitures, actions that disrupt this flow can cause significant problems. New York City generates less than 1% of its total revenue from fines and forfeitures, $702 million in 2017.[64] In 2014, New York City made international news when two NYPD officers killed Eric Garner, an unarmed African-American man who was selling "loose" cigarettes on the street near the Staten Island Ferry Terminal.[65] In December of that year, the relationship between the office of Mayor Bill de Blasio and the New York Police Department began to deteriorate following statements made by de Blasio after a grand jury's decision not to indict the two officers. The situation reached a tipping point on December 20 when two NYPD officers, Rafael Ramos and Wenjian Liu, were shot and killed in their squad car by an attacker who wanted to avenge Eric Garner's death.[66]

The major police unions in the city, citing concerns about the safety of their officers and perceived lack of support from Mayor de Blasio, issued orders to their members to make arrests "only when they have to"—let that sink in for a second.[67] The result of this virtual work stoppage, which had the secondary effect of hitting City Hall in the pocket by cutting off the flow of violation revenue until the police unions' demands were met, was a 92% reduction in parking violations, a 94% reduction in traffic violations, a 94% reduction in criminal court summonses, and a general reduction of 66% in overall arrests. While the police unions ultimately got what they were asking for, their actions sparked a national conversation about the necessity of much of the policing done in the United States, "shin[ing] a light on the use of police officers to make up for tax shortfalls using ticket and citation revenue."[68]

Civil Asset Forfeiture

Ticket revenue is not the only place where municipalities are using police officers to help fill the coffers. Lumped together in the city revenue numbers cited above are both fines (i.e., ticket and citation revenue) and forfeitures. Forfeitures are assets—cash or property—seized by the state under the justification that they were acquired illegally or are otherwise associated with the commission of a crime. Seized cash can be used by law enforcement to support their crime-fighting activities, while seized property can be sold to generate cash that can be used in the same way.

While the use of forfeiture has risen dramatically over the last 20 years, it has always been on the books in the US as a possible punishment for participating in criminal activity. The first mention of asset forfeiture in US law is in the Act of July 31, 1789, which allowed the equivalent of customs officers to seize and retain goods unloaded from merchant ships if the merchant had not paid the appropriate taxes to receive the required permits. Its use expanded significantly after 1978, when Congress authorized its use to allow for the seizure of money connected to the buying, selling, and trafficking of illegal drugs, and then again in 1984 when Congress revised the statue to allow for the seizure of property connected to those activities. Since then, the amount of assets seized by the federal government has increased constantly and consistently.

Forfeiture programs exist at both state and federal level, and on both the criminal and civil sides of the law. There is an important distinction between criminal and civil forfeiture, one relevant to understanding how forfeiture programs have been abused to help generate revenue for states and municipalities. Criminal forfeiture is a penalty resulting from legal action brought against *a person* who is acknowledged to have broken the law, because he was convicted of or pled guilty to a crime. The property is forfeited because it was used in or otherwise derived from the crime. Perhaps the best-known case of criminal forfeiture in recent memory is that of Bernard Madoff, who in 2009 was arrested and pled guilty to running the largest Ponzi scheme in US history, swindling over $50 billion from his investors. In an effort to provide restitution to these investors, the federal government seized Madoff's assets and auctioned them off, including his houses, vehicles, collection of fine wines, and even his wife's fur coat. Even though these assets were held jointly between Madoff and his wife and it seems she had no knowledge of her husband's fraudulent activity, they were seized because they were purchased with money acquired through Madoff's criminal activity.[69]

Civil forfeiture, by comparison, does not require a conviction or guilty plea for the government to seize an individual's assets because civil forfeiture is an action brought against *the property itself* and not the person who owns that property. The property is seized under the suspicion that it is somehow connected to a crime, which is a much lower burden than proving that it was used in or derived from a crime. The burden is then on the individual to demonstrate that the seized property was not connected to a crime before it is returned.

How does civil forfeiture work? Here's a story out of Nebraska, but similar stories happen around the country on an almost-daily basis. In 2008, Mark Brewer, decorated veteran of the United States Air Force, was medically discharged after becoming disabled while serving in Afghanistan. He set aside money from his Air Force and disability income for a down payment on a house. Brewer was moving to Los Angeles to be near family, and like many people who make cross-country moves, he packed everything he owned into his car and planned a route across the country that allowed him to hit various rest stops along the way.

Everything went smoothly until Brewer hit Interstate 80 in Nebraska—a Douglas County sheriff's deputy pulled him over, allegedly for changing lanes without signaling. After the deputy's roadside background check of Brewer came back empty, the deputy asked Brewer if he could walk around the car with his drug-sniffing dog. Brewer consented. (Never consent to a search of your vehicle!) As the deputy and the dog walked around Brewer's car, the dog signaled at the trunk, creating probable cause for a search. During the search, the deputy found two backpacks containing $63,530 in cash which he claimed smelled strongly of marijuana. The deputy seized Brewer's cash and had the car towed.

No charges were filed against Brewer—not even for the supposed traffic violation. He was able to produce disability documents, paystubs, and tax returns showing that all of the money had been acquired legally. Still, the Sheriff refused to return the $63,530, claiming—correctly—that federal asset forfeiture laws allowed the government to seize and keep any assets, including US currency, that they believed were tied to criminal activity. To get those assets back, Brewer would have to provide an affirmative defense, proving that the currency was not in any way connected to drug trafficking and was not going to be used to purchase drugs. Amazingly, his documents and stubs weren't good enough. He would have to prove something impossible to prove. In the United States, you may be innocent until proven guilty, but your money is guilty until proven innocent.

The district court sided with the government finding that the "quantity of currency" and "manner in which it was bundled and concealed" (i.e., in a bag in the trunk) "provided sufficient evidence to prove a substantial connection between the currency and drug activity".[70] Brewer appealed the district court's decision to the US Court of Appeals for the Eighth Circuit, one step below the US Supreme Court, where the district court's ruling was affirmed. It is worth your time to read the ruling. Aside from the substance of the decision, there are at least two interesting things to note from the structuring of the original action:

First, the case is "the United States of America" (as plaintiff) versus "$63,500 in United States Currency" (as defendant), with "Mark A. Brewer" as the claimant and appellant. This structure makes sense given that civil forfeiture is an action against the property itself and not against the person, but it is still odd to think about actions being brought against real property or currency in this way.

Second, the plaintiff is the United States of America, not the State of Nebraska as one might expect given that Brewer was pulled over by a Nebraska county sheriff's deputy. Instead of trying the case under state law, which in many states (including Nebraska) requires a more substantial burden to be met, the sheriff's office asked the federal government to adopt the seizure so that the case could proceed under federal law.

Why would Douglas County do that? Individual states have benefitted from the federal government's involvement in asset forfeiture, via adoptions, joint task forces, and other arrangements, to take advantage of the DOJ's "Equitable Sharing Program," which "distributes an equitable share of forfeited property and proceeds to participating state and local law enforcement agencies that directly participate in an investigation or prosecution that result in a federal forfeiture".[71] This program gives state law enforcement agencies the option of prosecuting some cases involving asset forfeiture under federal law (which has more permissive forfeiture rules), instead of state law. Taking this route, state agencies receive up to 80% of the assets seized under federal law.[72] Assisted by state law enforcement agencies motivated by this program, the federal government seized over $5 billion in assets (yes billion, with a "b") in 2014, a 550% increase over the amount seized in 2004 and 50% more than what was stolen by burglars in the US during the same year.[73]

States benefit from their participation in the DOJ's Equitable Sharing Program, as well as from their own state-level forfeiture laws, laws that vary greatly by state in terms of what assets can be seized under what conditions, the procedure for reclaiming seized assets, and how forfeited cash or funds generated by the sale of forfeited property is distributed among various state agencies.[74] Hawaii, for example, has one of the most lucrative and aggressive asset forfeiture programs in the country, generating nearly $2.5 million during 2014, 1.4M from assets seized by state and county agencies directly[75] and an additional 1.1M from its participation in the Equitable Sharing Program.[76] States like Hawaii have gone to great and sometimes ridiculous lengths to defend these programs. Hawaii's Attorney General even has a website dedicated to this purpose. It not only provides a brief history of asset forfeiture as a penalty—complete with biblical references—but also provides a justification based on its benefits, which includes generating revenue to support law enforcement activities.[77]

That asset forfeiture programs generate revenue to support police activities is not a problem in and of itself, but when states and municipalities want to raise revenue and turn to forfeiture programs as a means to that end, we should not be surprised when those programs are abused. As in the case of Mark Brewer, one troubling feature of civil asset forfeiture is that individuals do not have to be convicted of a crime, or even charged with a crime, to have their assets seized. Then, once assets have been seized, the burden is on the individual to prove that those assets are *not* connected with criminal activity, an almost impossible burden in many cases. Another troubling feature of how incentives are aligned relative to asset forfeiture programs is that it has changed how municipalities police. For example, when disrupting drug trade activities, any illegal drugs seized by law enforcement agents must be destroyed, but they can retain seized cash believed to be connected to drug activity and use it to fund their own operations. That cash can be kept but drugs must be destroyed has led many police departments to establish checkpoints and otherwise run operations to target individuals after sales have been made, rather than preventing those sales from being made in the first place.

One of the more egregious examples of this policy in practice comes from central Tennessee. In 2011, reporter Phil Williams of Nashville's NewsChannel 5 investigated drug traffic stops along Interstate 40 west of Nashville, a well-known route for drug trafficking to northeastern states.[78] Although increased traffic stops to prevent drug smuggling would be expected, Williams uncovered that nearly all of the stops took place on the westbound lanes of I-40, lanes used by cars returning from the northeast, not the eastbound lanes, which would have been used by cars transporting drugs to the northeast. Instead of trying to seize illegal drugs to prevent them from being distributed, law enforcement officers seemed more interested in seizing the cash connected to their sale to help fund their own operations. As a result of this selective policing, I-40 became a cash cow for a handful of county police departments taking advantage of state asset forfeiture programs. It was such a cash cow that the two multi-county agencies patrolling this stretch of I-40 engaged in a turf war with each other that ended only when they reached a formal agreement outlining who would patrol the westbound lanes on which days.

Although some of these examples seem especially egregious, there is reason to be hopeful when it comes to the reform of civil asset forfeiture laws in the United States. In the past two years New Mexico, Nebraska, North Carolina, and Connecticut have passed sweeping asset forfeiture reform bills that have effectively eliminated civil forfeiture. Eleven other states—California, Iowa, Minnesota, Missouri, Montana, Nevada, New Hampshire, Ohio, Oregon, Utah, and Vermont—now require a criminal conviction for all or nearly all forfeiture cases, which abolishes one of the more objectionable components of the asset forfeiture program. Seven states—Arizona, California, Colorado, Maryland, Nebraska, New Mexico, and Ohio—and the District of Columbia have passed legislation that aims to close the equitable-sharing loophole that has allowed transferring of state cases over to federal jurisdiction. Progress on this issue has been made and likely will continue being made until the use of forfeiture programs to generate revenue is greatly reduced or eliminated. But even if these steps are taken with asset forfeiture programs, the history of policing in the US suggests that police departments and municipalities will turn to other law enforcement programs to generate revenue, programs operated under the banner of promoting public safety.

A Path Forward

There are at least three important takeaways from this discussion: (1) Government agencies are not immune from responding to financial incentives and operating as if they were for-profit corporations. (2) Private actors, either individuals or corporations, will spend significant sums of money to lobby government agents or agencies when doing so will benefit their bottom line, and they will usually get what they want, even if it's at the expense of sound public policy. (3) People are not perfectly virtuous, and it is not reasonable to expect them to act against their own interests when those interests conflict with doing what is best for the community as a whole. Programs created with good intentions can cause more harm than good when they are implemented without considering how real-world actors—who are not motivated by the goals that the program was enacted to realize—respond when operating inside of the rules of that program. Any strategy for reforming the current approach to policing and punishment must take into account (1), (2), and (3).

Incentives matter, especially financial incentives. Resolving many of the problems connected to policing and punishment in the US requires greatly reducing or eliminating the financial incentives that lead to abuse, or aligning those incentives in such a way that we are able to achieve desirable social outcomes when individuals, corporations, or government entities act from self-interest. Accomplishing this goal in practice is much easier said than done.

Perhaps the most obvious challenge is identifying what the appropriate aims of justice are and how they manifest themselves in policy decisions. Consider UNICOR, the prison work program discussed in the last section, a program that many people believe (perhaps wrongly) is morally problematic. No reasonable person would object to requiring prisoners to perform basic upkeep functions in the prison (mopping floors, painting walls, doing laundry, etc.), as long as they are capable of doing so, are not being overworked, and are otherwise treated humanely. Since it's not unreasonable to require them to perform these tasks for no compensation, no injustice is done if they are given a nominal amount of money as a reward for this work, money that they're then able spend in the commissary on small luxury items like nicer personal hygiene products, snacks, and coffee.

The relevant ethical issue is as follows: Suppose someone is required to do something. After he does it, is it just to (1) pay him nothing, (2) pay him a regular wage, or (3) pay him a token amount? Considerations of justice would not make any of these responses impermissible, although the relevant circumstances may dictate when we would choose one response over another. While the common objection to prison labor is that the prisoners are being treated like slaves because they are not provided with at least the federally mandated minimum wage for their labor, this position misunderstands the nature of prison labor and the relationship between the prison and the prisoners. Prisoners are not employees of the prison. No amount of pay would justify compelling prisoners to perform tasks that were dangerous or otherwise inappropriate for them to perform for free. Any financial rewards they receive for doing work that is required of them, or that they volunteer for beyond what is required of them, is not compensation, but a reward. In this way, any pay received by prisoners for their labor is more appropriately thought of like a child's allowance rather than a worker's wage. If my wife and I give our daughter a dollar a week for making her bed every morning, no reasonable person would accuse me of violating labor laws, even though her wage would be around a dollar an hour. That we choose to give her a small amount of money for completing this task, perhaps as a way of teaching money management or to minimally incentivize her to make her bed without a fuss, has no bearing on whether it is reasonable for us to require this behavior of her.

For prisoners participating in programs like UNICOR, there are additional factors in play: prison labor provides a direct or indirect financial benefit to third-party organizations, and prisoners are not required to participate in UNICOR; they do so voluntarily. So, the relevant ethical questions are: (1) Is it just, or even obligatory, to pay a volunteer nothing, a regular wage, or a token amount for performing the task he volunteered to do? (2) Are prisoners who volunteer for UNICOR actual volunteers? And (3) Is it objectionable to realize financial gain from someone else's volunteer work?

Someone who volunteers for a task does so freely and without the expectation of receiving monetary compensation. While volunteers may expect to receive something for volunteering—feeling good about themselves, future considerations, etc.—none of those things are owed to the volunteer and are not guaranteed. As for the prison workers being volunteers, although many are under an obligation to do some kind of work, they are under no obligation to work in UNICOR. They choose to work in UNICOR because they would rather spend their time manufacturing furniture, raising goats for milk, or working in a call center, than cleaning the floors in the prison, either because they find these activities to be a better way to pass the time or because they believe doing so will put them in a better position get a job when they are released. Given that prisoners who participate in programs like UNICOR are "24% less likely to recidivate and 14% more likely to be gainfully employed,"[79] holding this belief is not unreasonable.

As for companies receiving financial gain from prisoner labor, in general it does not seem objectionable for one party to gain financially from someone else's willingness to volunteer, as long as no deception is involved. There are many examples of this practice in the world around us, none of which seem controversial or exploitative. People who work for non-profit organizations gain financially, through their employment with that organization, from the volunteer work of the organization's board members. Companies frequently have unpaid student interns help to produce things of value.[80]

What is consistent about all of these unproblematic cases is that no deception is involved. The volunteer knows that someone is gaining financially from his work, either directly or indirectly, and chooses to volunteer anyway. Applying this reasoning to UNICOR and similar prison-work programs that operate in the same way and benefit third-party corporations or government agencies, while the public may be unaware of UNICOR, public ignorance is not the same as deceiving program participants. Prison workers know the tasks they will be performing, whether they will be paid for that task, and, if so, how much.

The real concern relevant to prison work programs is rent-seeking (manipulating public policy to increase private profits) and abuse, which is the same concern we should have about all aspects of policing and punishment capable of generating revenue or otherwise allowing for financial gain. Just as asset for-feiture programs have been abused by police departments and municipalities to serve as a secondary revenue stream, if it were the case that more people were being sent to prison or that prison sentences were increased for the purpose of having more laborers in the prison work program, then public outrage would be appropriate. While prison guard unions and police unions have pushed for public policies that send more people to jail or keep them there longer as a way of protecting their own interests, there is no evidence to suggest that the prison work program is being taken advantage of in this way. That doesn't mean that such rent-seeking and abuse couldn't happen with this program in the future, as some sheriffs right now see their prisoners as sources of free labor,[81] and so it's not unreasonable to be on the lookout for policies or pro-grams that can be abused, putting a stop to them before that happens.

No matter what problem we identify, it is likely that we can find a solution —at least in theory—that could align financial incentives with what is in the interest of justice. We suggest a number of solutions in Chapter 7. But no matter if a solution can be found, implementing it will require significant pol-itical maneuvering for some fairly obvious reasons: First, many individuals and corporations have their financial interests aligned with maintaining the status quo. Second, it is incredibly difficult to cut off revenue streams from govern-ment agencies or municipalities that are now dependent on them for regular operations. Third, and perhaps the greatest barrier to widespread outrage that would bring about significant change more quickly, is that current social cul-ture in the US is to regard criminals, especially those convicted of felonies or in prison, as second-class citizens or worse. People in the US seem to care more about the welfare of animals in shelters than they do are about the wel-fare of prisoners or how people are treated once they enter the criminal justice system. A sound approach to reform should consider operating within this social constraint, not imagining that it will somehow change overnight—because it won't.

Notes

1 Hammurabi 1910.
2 Justice Policy Institute 2012.
3 Wagner and Rabuy 2017a.
4 USDA 2017.
5 Wagner and Rabuy 2017b.
6 Bureau of Justice Statistics 2017.
7 Bureau of Justice Statistics 2017.
8 Wagner and Walsh 2016.
9 Wagner and Walsh 2016.
10 Wagner and Rabuy 2017a.
11 US Department of Justice 2016.
12 US Department of Justice 2016.

13 CoreCivic 2016.
14 Zapotosky 2017.
15 Campaign Legal Center, et al. v. Federal Election Commission 2018.
16 Arnsdorf 2016.
17 Department of Homeland Security 2018, 114.
18 Gruberg 2018.
19 Reilly and Knafo 2014.
20 Fang 2014.
21 Jethani 2013.
22 Neate 2016.
23 Corizon 2017.
24 Toner 2014.
25 Swan 2016.
26 Bottari and Persson 2014.
27 Hauslohner 2015.
28 Walsh 2013.
29 Bozelko 2017.
30 Bozelko 2017.
31 UNICOR 2017a.
32 UNICOR 2017a.
33 UNICOR 2016a.
34 Aubrey 2015.
35 Flounders 2011.
36 Winter 2008.
37 Prison Legal News 1995.
38 Young 2010.
39 UNICOR 2017b.
40 Sawyer 2017.
41 Curry 2015.
42 UNICOR 2017c.
43 UNICOR 2017d.
44 UNICOR 2016b, 17.
45 Dearen 2014.
46 O'Neill 2014.
47 City of Waldo, Florida 2015, 2016.
48 Shaw 2016.
49 Shaw 2016.
50 City of Atlanta, Georgia 2017b.
51 City of New Orleans, Louisiana 2016.
52 City of Chicago, Illinois 2016.
53 City of Mobile, Alabama 2017.
54 City of Detroit, Michigan 2016.
55 City of Houston, Texas 2016.
56 City of Atlanta 2018, 61.
57 City of New Orleans 2018, 11.
58 City of Chicago 2018, 17.
59 Adelson 2017.
60 Williams 2018.
61 Bridges 2019.
62 Sances and You 2017.
63 Goldstein, Sances, and You 2018.
64 The Council of the City of New York, Department of Finance 2016.
65 Baker et al. 2015.

66 Celona et al. 2014a.

67 Celona et al. 2014a.

68 Taibbi 2014.

69 CBS News 2009.

70 Sibilla 2015; United States of America v. $63,530.00 in United States Currency 2015.

71 US Department of Justice 2017a.

72 Ingraham 2016.

73 Ingraham 2015.

74 Hall and Mercier 2017, 216–20.

75 State of Hawaii, Department of Attorney General 2016.

76 US Department of Justice 2015.

77 That justification via benefits is contained within one paragraph, which reads: "As a result [of asset forfeiture], criminals are deprived of their working capital and their profits, thereby preventing them from operating. A secondary benefit of forfeiture laws is that forfeited property, or the proceeds of its sale, has been turned over to law enforcement and is used to fight against crime. While the purpose of forfeiture and the evaluation of a forfeiture law or program should never be based solely on the generation of revenue, it is only fitting that forfeited property be used to combat those who seek to profit from crime." The entire discussion can be found on the Attorney General's website, http://ag.hawaii.gov/cjd/asset-forfeiture-unit/history-of-asset-forfeiture/.

78 Williams 2016.

79 UNICOR 2017e.

80 The US Department of Labor has set requirements outlining the conditions under which unpaid internships are legal or illegal. They include: "1. The internship, even though it includes actual operation of the facilities of the employer, is similar to training which would be given in an educational environment; 2. The internship experience is for the benefit of the intern; 3. The intern does not displace regular employees, but works under close supervision of existing staff; 4. The employer that provides the training derives no immediate advantage from the activities of the intern; and on occasion its operations may actually be impeded; 5. The intern is not necessarily entitled to a job at the conclusion of the internship; and 6. The employer and the intern understand that the intern is not entitled to wages for the time spent in the internship" (US Department of Labor 2010). The easiest way to get around these requirements is to hire interns who are receiving academic credit from a college or university. So not only are these students not being paid by the company to work, they are also paying the university for the opportunity to work for the company for free.

81 O'Donoghue 2017.

6

POVERTY, RISK, AND CRIME

In 2015, President Obama commuted the sentences of 163 inmates in federal prison, most of whom were serving lengthy sentences for non-violent drug offenses.[1] One of those sentences belonged to Sharanda Jones.[2] In 1999, Jones was found guilty of one count of conspiracy to distribute cocaine. Even though Jones had no prior criminal record—not even a traffic violation—the guilty conviction plus the various sentencing enhancements gave the federal judge no choice but to sentence her to life in prison. *Life in prison*, for a non-violent drug conviction.

While Jones's story is one of the horrors of mandatory minimums and illustrates how unjustly punitive many of our sentencing laws had become, it is not one of obvious police misconduct or arresting the wrong person. Jones admits to trafficking illegal drugs, but the reasons why can help us understand the connections between poverty and crime, as well as why many people in Jones's situation feel like there's nowhere else to turn.

Jones grew up poor and was raised by her grandmother after her mother broke her neck in a car accident and became a quadriplegic. From an early age, Jones had to help take care of her family. At age 14 she was working, and soon after that she opened her own businesses: first a hair salon, then a hamburger restaurant, and then another restaurant that served Southern-style food. But with a young daughter to take care of, she couldn't make ends meet. Driving shipments of drugs from Houston to Dallas seemed like the best available solution.

Sharanda Jones isn't alone. Imagine you're a teenage boy growing up in a poverty-stricken neighborhood.[3] Around you are dilapidated buildings, closed businesses, and graffiti. You have little and infrequent contact with your biological father, who has provided you and your single mother with little financial or emotional support. Your mother perhaps did her best, but she faces burnout, as she struggles with providing full-time care for you while also making ends meet. Perhaps, as a result, she was more emotionally distant from you than mothers in better conditions, and perhaps, as a result, you formed a weaker sense of attachment and self-worth, and in turn have less empathy for others.

We could be describing an inner city populated by blacks and Latinos. We could also be describing a decaying rural town populated by whites.

Let's say it's a bad part of a city. Perhaps, then, young men in your neighborhood gain status and power by joining various criminal gangs.[4] Your school has armed cops and metal detectors at the door. Conditions are poor, learning outcomes are poor, and dropout rates are high. Few people in your neighborhood learn a skilled trade or go to college. Your neighborhood has little economic development, and when neighborhoods like yours do develop, it usually means outsiders coming in rather than growth from the inside. Your mom doesn't let you play outside at night, and often not even during the day. You can hear gunshots a few times per week when you're supposed to be sleeping.

Let's say it's a white-dominated rural town—places where violent crime now exceeds the national average.[5] Old economic opportunities have vanished. The factory or mill has closed down or the coal mine is shut. Learning outcomes in your schools are poor, and dropout rates are high. Most students don't go to college, and the ones that do don't come back. Many of your fellow students, and the adults you depend on, drink, smoke, and abuse prescription narcotics. Some of your friends get pregnant in schools. The girls end up raising the children with their parents help but the dads disappear. There may not be organized gangs per se, but there are plenty of bands of young men up to no good, regularly engaging in criminal activities for fun and status.

In either case, it wouldn't be surprising if you tried experimenting with petty crimes. You probably won't invest heavily in schooling and won't think too much about the future. You don't have much parental support, and your family lacks the human capital to help you move forward. You might not know how to escape your situation. Starting at a young age, when you lack good impulse control, you make some mistakes or some bad choices, and find yourself caught up in legal troubles. The spiral begins, and you become a criminal. Once you commit a serious crime, it becomes difficult for you to return to society, get a job, get government help, and succeed.

We're not making any excuses for "you" here in this hypothetical story, nor are we making excuses for the countless real people who actually fit these stories. We're not saying people who grow up poor in poor neighborhoods had no choice or are without blame. Plenty of people living in such places make the right choices, better their lot, and escape poverty. Indeed, if one simply doesn't commit petty crimes, graduates from high school, waits until marriage to have children, and both parents work as janitors or maids, that's about enough to guarantee the family will live far above the poverty line. Further, American "poverty" is relatively rich by world standards. As of 2015, a person living at what the American "poverty line" is—adjusting for the cost of living—among the top 15–20% of income earners alive today.[6] Yet plenty of far poorer people in far poorer countries commit crimes at far lower rates.

Further, not every historically poor group in the United States had high rates of crime—for instance, poor Jewish and German immigrants had low rates of crime, while poor Italian and Irish immigrants had high rates of violent crime.[7] Rural Scots-Irish in West Virginia commit crimes at high rates, but even poorer Jewish communities in 1920s Brooklyn committed crimes at far lower rates. So, poverty does not ensure high crime.

Nevertheless, from a policy perspective, wishing for greater virtue gets us nowhere. Further, though poverty is not destiny, we can still see that poverty, lack of opportunity, and social malaise are not conducive to producing productive, cooperative, highly successful citizens. It's no surprise that people living and growing up in poor conditions are far more likely to become and remain criminals than people growing up in well-to-do, high social capital neighborhoods, with high human-capital parents, with excellent schools, and with plenty of opportunity. Poverty is not the sole cause of crime, nor is at a guarantee of crime, but it is a strong predictor and influence.

In general, with a few exceptions, poorer people commit more crimes than richer people. Part of the reason may be that the kinds of dispositions—such as poor impulse control, a lack of conscientiousness, or a low IQ—that make you more likely to commit crime also make you less likely to be rich. But, as we'll discuss below, part of the reason is probably that people who grow up in wealthier environments filled with opportunity have less incentive to commit crime.

Violent Crime in the United States

The United States has an incarceration problem, but we also have a crime problem. And not just petty crime—violent crime. Murder, rape, and aggravated assault. Of the 2.3 million or so people incarcerated in the US, nearly 1 million or 40% are there for violent crime. This is double the number of people in prison for either drug-related activity or property crimes like theft or vandalism.

Just how bad is violent crime in the US? For 2017, the FBI estimated that over 1,247,00 violent crimes occurred in the US, which is roughly 383 violent crimes per 100,000 people.[8] But national statistics here are almost irrelevant because crime is local, not national; different departments classify the same actions in different ways; and many departments (and even some entire states) don't report their crime statistics to the federal government.[9]

While comparisons of "violent crime" generally are difficult, comparisons when it comes to a specific violent crime—murder—are not. You can always count bodies. In 2017, there were 17,284 reported cases of murder and non-negligent manslaughter in the US,[10] which is roughly five murders per every 100,000 people. That's a lot, at least when compared to the nations we like to compare ourselves to. In Canada, for example, there were roughly 1.8 murders per every 100,000 people in 2017, so about a third as many as the US.[11] Japan (0.28), Norway (0.51), and Italy (0.67) provide even starker comparisons.[12] The US is far from the worst here: El Salvador's rate was 50.3 murders per 100,000 people in 2018,[13] Jamaica's was 44.4 in 2018,[14] and Mexico's was 25.8 in 2018.[15]

But while national averages tell a story about crime in a country, they often don't tell the whole story because violent crime—homicides especially—are concentrated in urban areas. While the US as a country had five murders per 100,000 people last year, city statistics tell a different story. New Orleans, where Chris lives, had only 146 murders in 2018, and we say "only" because it was the fewest number of murders in New Orleans in a year for over 50 years.[16] Even still, with the population of New Orleans proper being only 400,000 people, the homicide rate in 2018 was 36.5 murders per 100,000 people. Many other US cities fare just as bad or worse than New Orleans. In 2018, Detroit had 261 homicides, for a rate of 37.3 per 100,000 people;[17] Baltimore had 309 homicides, for a rate of 50.7 per 100,000 people;[18] and St. Louis had 186 homicides, for a rate of 60 per 100,000 people.[19]

But like national statistics, city statistics are deceptive as well. When you fly into New Orleans and drive from the airport to downtown, you may think you're in New Orleans the entire time. But you're not. You land in Kenner, drive through Metairie, and then enter New Orleans, and the crime statistics for New Orleans do not take crime in Kenner, Metairie, or any of the towns in Jefferson Parish (i.e., the Louisiana equivalent of a county) that surround New Orleans and make up the general metropolitan area of the city. In 2018, there were 24 murders in Jefferson Parish, which had a population of just over 400,000 people. That's right—the suburban area around New Orleans which is mostly indistinguishable from New Orleans had a murder rate of six per 100,000 residents as compared to 36.5.

Even if you set aside the suburban areas of the city, crime statistics within the city itself have a great deal of variation when you move neighborhood to neighborhood. New Orleans has eight police districts that cover the entirety of the city. The plurality of murders occurred in police districts five and seven, which are the poorest districts in the city and where the residents are predominately non-white.[20]

Not only is the murder rate in these parts of the city high, but also the murder clearance rate is abysmally low, close to 0%. The "clearance rate" is the rate at which the police *arrest* people for crimes. Over the past eight years, there have been 54,868 homicides in 55 of the largest cities in the US.[21] In just over 50% of these cases, no one was arrested. We see more violent crimes in poor, minority communities, and we also see a much lower crime clearance rate in these communities. Want to kill someone without being arrested? Target a non-white person in a poor neighborhood. New Orleans is no exception. Over the past eight years, New Orleans police failed to arrest someone for 65% of the murders in the city. When the *Washington Post* plotted these uncleared murders on a map, nearly all of them took place in poor, minority communities.

Poverty and Crime

Criminologists can't identify what exactly causes crime. It's complicated. Poverty doesn't cause crime and crime doesn't cause poverty, but they're linked. We know that certain kinds of crime, especially violent crime, are generally concentrated in poor areas. We also know that it is far less likely for the police to arrest someone for a crime in a poor area than when it occurs somewhere else. Part of it is the willingness (or lack thereof) of the people in those areas to engage with the police (and understandably so), part of it is that most cities devote less resources to people in those areas, and part of it is simply the volume of criminal activity.

But we do know that people who grow up in Metairie, Louisiana (and other communities like it) live very different lives than people who grow up in New Orleans's 5th or 7th District. And these areas are about ten minutes from each other. Perhaps the most obvious example—in addition to the amount of criminal activity and the different in crime clearance rate—is the access to basic things like grocery stores. If you live in a neighborhood without a grocery store—a real grocery store, not some corner market with limited goods at much higher prices— your life is much more difficult than if you live with a grocery store close by.

In most cities throughout the US, neighborhoods that have high criminal activity and low crime clearance rates also lack grocery stores and other businesses that make it easier to live our lives, take care of our families, and do the types of relatively mundane day-to-day activities that most of us take for granted.[22] The result is that although the cost to buy or rent a house in these areas is low, the actual cost of living in these areas is higher than in wealthier parts of the city. Not only do people living in these neighborhoods have to worry about an extreme amount of crime and violence—levels similar to what we see in the most violent countries in the world—but they also have to spend more time and money to accomplish basic tasks like going to the grocery store. Either that or they have to make do with the limited resources in their neighborhood, resources that often may cause them long-term harms.

Sometimes these long-term harms are negative health consequences that may continue the cycle of criminal activity. One of the more interesting theories of crime in the US is that it correlates with exposure to lead: (1) exposure to lead leads to all sorts of neurological problems, including increased aggressiveness;[23] (2) at the city level, high-crime areas correlate directly with increased levels of lead in the soil as compared to other parts of the same city with lower crime rates;[24] and (3) at the national level, steps taken to remove lead from our environment (gasoline, paint, etc.) have correlated with significant drops in crime in the US.[25]

But correlation is not causation, just because data looks to be connected doesn't mean that one factor causes the other. While there's disagreement about the possible connection between lead exposure and crime,[26] environmental causes—either physical environment or social environment such as family structure, access to certain community organizations, economic prosperity in your neighborhood, etc.—seem to play some role in crime, but what role it plays is difficult to pin down.

Poverty and crime is no different, especially in the US. Criminologist Barry Latzer has shown that not all ethnic groups in US had high crime when poor.[27] Poor German, Polish, and Jewish communities had low crime, but equally poor Irish, Italian, Mexican communities had high crime, while equally poor black American communities had even higher crime. As Irish and Italians got richer, crime dropped dramatically, not as much with black communities. Latzer thinks that there's a connection not just between poverty and crime, but between culture and crime. For black Americans, he thinks it's a cultural thing caused by historical alienation and a feeling that the deck constantly and consistently has been stacked against them. Crime is the response to this feeling. Explained in that way, it could be seen as rational.

The Rational Theory of Crime

Nobel laureate economist Gary Becker was among the first economists to realize that the tools of economics can be used not only to explain traditional "economic topics" such as trade or wealth, but also much of the rest of human behavior. He wrote extensively about the economics of discrimination, of the family and family roles, and in particular, about crime. He developed the "rational theory of crime"[28] and even developed a "rational theory of drug addiction."[29]

Becker's basic model of rational crime goes as follows: Imagine, as economists often do, people are self-interested utility maximizers. That is, presume they fundamentally care about promoting their own interests instead of the interests of others. When making decisions, they consider the possible payoffs and costs, and discount each outcome by the probability it would occur. If, say, placing a bet has an 80% chance of paying $100, and a 20% chance of losing $50, they'll place the bet. The expected utility of the bet is $70—a good bet!

Becker argues many criminal behaviors follow the same logic. Everyone is driven by a profit-motive. Their decisions about what to do, and even what kind of person to become, are explained by their desire to maximize their personal returns in light of the opportunities and constraints they face.

Let's take a first pass at this idea. Suppose I'm perfectly selfish. Imagine I can commit a petty theft which has an 80% chance of paying $1000. I have a 20% chance of getting caught, and suppose the penalty for getting caught is $500. In that case, the expected utility of theft is $700—a good bet!

Becker's theory is more complex and subtle than this, but that's the most basic form. Many criminals are weighing the possible payoffs of successful crime against the costs and penalties attached to getting stopped or caught. They're engaging in cost benefit analysis.

In its most basic form, the theory predicts that increasing penalties will reduce crime, as it changes the calculus. It also predicts that increasing the certainty of getting caught will greatly reduce crime. In fact, though, empirical work suggests the first prediction is mistaken but the second prediction is true. Longer sentences do not seem to deter crime much, but security measures which make crime more difficult and increase the probability of being identified or caught do.[30] We know that most people aren't perfectly selfish, though of course criminals may be more selfish than the average person.

Further, the moral psychologist Dan Ariely's work seems to contradict the rational theory of crime.[31] Ariely regularly runs experiments in which subjects have the opportunity to cheat—to lie to the experimenter—for money. He finds, as Becker might have expected, that when we lower the chance of getting caught, more subjects choose to cheat and they choose to cheat by higher amounts. But he also finds, contrary to what Becker might expect, that when the payoff to cheating gets higher, fewer people cheat, not more. Ariely hypothesizes that this is because most people both A) want to benefit from cheating and stealing but B) also want to think of themselves as honorable and good people. You can live with yourself if you lie, cheat, and steal a little—you're only aiming to be a pretty decent person, not perfect. But big lies, big cheats, and big thefts make you a bad person in your own eyes. Still, Ariely and others doing the same research generally run their experiments on undergraduates at various elite universities. Perhaps their results do not extrapolate to uneducated, non-elites growing up in squalid conditions.

But Becker's theory is more complex than we've let on so far. When we look deeper into the rational theory of crime, it can help explain certain subtler aspects of criminality. Consider the following questions:

1. Should I think short-term or long-term?
2. Should I invest in myself over the long-term to develop marketable skills?
3. Should I work to make my dispositions and behaviors highly conscientious, altruistic, and fair, or should I invest in developing a different—perhaps anti-social—personality set?

Imagine you grow up in the bad conditions we described at the beginning of this chapter. You lack the social and human capital to know about what kinds of personal investment strategies pay off. You have few opportunities easily available to you—especially if people discriminate against you because of your race or social position. You don't have people investing in you quite as heavily at a young age—in part because they lack the means, in part because they lack the knowledge, and in part because your bad conditions make you a high-risk investment. You don't invest much in yourself for those very same reasons. If you get caught and punished, you have less to lose than those who have more than you. In short: If you have a high degree of uncertainty in your future, low chances of future success, and low resources, then all things equal it makes sense for you and others to invest less in you and your development. You have more reason and less downside when you engage in higher risk, more criminal behaviors or develop criminal proclivities.

Consider question 3 in particular: When we make decisions about how to behave, we're also making decisions about what kind of person we're likely to be in the future. We can act in ways that change our dispositions. We can cultivate certain good or bad attitudes. We can reinforce our conscientiousness or reduce it. We can learn self-control or learn to be ruled by our tempers. And so on. Becker might say that to whatever degree your future virtue is in your control, whether you invest in making yourself one kind of person or another depends upon the likely payoffs of those investments in light of the costs and constraints you face.

Again, we're not making excuses. But we are saying it's understandable that crime is concentrated in poor areas, especially among the poor who lack strong community support networks or high levels of human capital. We know poverty is not guaranteed to cause crime. But when we see that crime is concentrated among the poor, and when we see the incentive structure and background constraints many poor people in poor communities face, we should see if reducing poverty and improving their conditions alleviates and reduces crime. Further—perhaps this doesn't need to be said—eliminating poverty and improving human capital are good for their own sake, even if they ended up having a minimal effect on crime. Worst case scenario is we improve social justice, if not criminal justice too.

Removing Barriers to Entrepreneurship and Economic Development

There is good evidence that entrepreneurship reduces both crime and poverty.[32]

For instance, the sociologist Karen Parker looked carefully at the crime drop in black communities through the late 1990s. She carefully controls for confounding factors, such as poverty rates and overall employment levels. She nevertheless finds that as the rate of black-owned businesses increases over time, the crime rate in the local area decreases. According to Parker, the explanation for this positive trend is two-fold: First, when local citizens start businesses in their home locales, they not only invest in these areas, but also create economic opportunities for others. They do so without displacing their neighbors. Second, they serve as role models for young people in their community, and help to create and sustain strong community ties and a culture of trust, which in turn reduce crime.

Criminality is a high-risk, usually low-reward kind of behavior. People who can easily get good jobs will tend to choose work over criminality. When they cannot do so—because there are no jobs available, because they face high levels of discrimination, or whatnot—criminality becomes more attractive as an alternative.

Political leaders seem to recognize this, and yet many American cities act as if they're positively hostile to local entrepreneurship. Consider each of the following problems.

According to the Small Business Administration, a federal agency, government regulations impose a disproportionately high cost on small businesses. Firms with fewer than 20 employees face about $10,600 in regulatory costs per employee. Larger firms—firms with 500 or more employees—enjoy economies of scale in dealing with regulatory costs, and thus face only about $7,800 in cost/employee.[33] Note that these are simply for *federal regulations*—state and local regulations impose additional costs but follow a similar pattern.

Complicated tax codes, regulatory regimes, and licensing rules naturally select for larger corporations. Regulations, tax codes, and complicated regulatory rules function like regressive taxes—they disadvantage the small. Some of these regulations are well-meaning, and some may be effective and necessary, but all things equal, red tape is barely a barrier for the multi-billion-dollar corporation but can stop small businesses from even forming.[34]

Now consider the red tape you face to open a business. Let's say you want to open a shop braiding hair. This kind of business requires little overhead. Well, good luck. In ten states, you'll be required to get a full-blown hairdresser or cosmetology license, which requires you to complete thousands of hours of classwork and training and pay tens of thousands of dollars in fees. In 15 states and Washington, DC, you'll instead need to complete only about 450 hours of coursework. Most of the coursework will be irrelevant.[35]

In most cities, similar requirements are imposed upon a wide range of other kinds of work. *The Atlantic* reports that in Connecticut, to have the right to install home entertainment systems, you must finish high school, buy a license, take a test, and complete a year-long apprenticeship.[36] In many states, the licensing requirements for tree trimmers are more onerous than those for EMTs! In Louisiana, eyebrow threading requires an expensive esthetician license.[37] There, even *florists* must sit for a written exam—by appointment only!—and pay $224 in fees.[38] New Jersey requires about three years of work before becoming a licensed locksmith.[39]

The Institute for Justice—a pro bono legal group which fights against government abuse of eminent domain and unfair restrictions on economic freedom—explains that the motivation behind these requirements was rarely public safety. Indeed, the empirical evidence shows these restrictions do not benefit the public.[40] Rather:

> Following the Civil War, southern governments enacted "black codes" designed to prevent newly emancipated blacks from engaging in trades they had learned as slaves. These efforts to deny basic economic liberty to blacks inspired federal civil rights legislation guaranteeing freedom of contract and private property rights, rights that were ultimately encompassed within the guarantee of "privileges or immunities of citizenship" under the Fourteenth Amendment.
>
> But in the 1873 Slaughter-House Cases, the Supreme Court ruled by a 5–4 vote that the Fourteenth Amendment does not protect an individual's right to pursue a trade or profession free from arbitrary or unequal government regulation. This decision, which remains on the books, opened the floodgates for the infamous "Jim Crow" laws, which severely impaired basic economic liberty for blacks.
>
> Licensing of cosmetologists commenced in 1920, and spread rapidly during the New Deal. Like many occupational licensing laws, cosmetology licensing was sought for protectionist purposes by practitioners within the affected industry. The National Hairdressers' and Cosmetologists' Association crafted and promoted a "model bill," ostensibly to protect health and safety, but with the intent and effect of limiting entry into an increasingly competitive occupation.[41]

Of course, the people behind such laws *say* they were for public safety. But their real purpose—and their actual effect—is two-fold. First, they were intended to reduce minority, in particular, *black*, access to certain jobs and trades. They work—after all, poor minorities are less likely to have access to the human and financial capital to complete the requirements. Second, they are intended to restrict competition in these jobs. That helps raise the wages of the people who end up with the jobs, but it also increases prices for everyone else, and prevents others from working. Just as microeconomics would predict, it hurts the losers more than it helps the winners. Economists both Left and Right largely agree that licensing laws—even licenses for *medical doctors*—tend to do more harm than good.[42]

If we want to reduce poverty and crime, one principal set of reforms we must implement is to reduce barriers to starting small businesses. We need to radically cut back the red tape and regulations we impose upon such businesses, keeping only those regulations we have overwhelming evidence are essential for protecting the public. We need to eliminate most licensing requirements for most trades, keeping only those we have overwhelming evidence are essential for keeping the public safe. We can't trust legislators to do the work—they are too susceptible to being bamboozled by rent seeking lobbyists, who want to manipulate the laws for their clients' benefits at the public's expense, all in the name of public safety. Accordingly, we may need to create independent commissions staffed by economists, and give them the power to veto regulations that don't pass the evidentiary test.

Eliminate Black Markets and Their Associated Crimes

Jason visits his drug dealer a few times a week. His drug dealer hires well-mannered, well-dressed young people, who greet him with a smile, and ask him how he'd like his drugs today. They offer a startling variety of beautiful preparations for the drug. They sell it in an attractive environment. They do what they can to make the drug buying experience as pleasurable and convenient as possible. Their prices are reasonable. There is no violence, and they never threaten the other drug dealers on the same street. Of course, Jason's drug dealer is Starbucks.

If you've ever seen a shop in a state where marijuana is legal, you realize that other drugs can be bought and sold the same way. In some states, marijuana is a risky product that may be laced with other drugs, sold by criminals working for violent suppliers. In others, marijuana is sold the way coffee is.

The same goes for alcohol—today at least. But it wasn't always like that. From 1919 to 1933, the US made alcohol illegal. People still drank. In fact, after a few years, they drank more, not less. People couldn't buy alcohol from safe and peaceful neighborhood supermarkets, so they bought it from smugglers and violent criminals who tried to create and maintain turf empires. Prohibition made the US Mafia legendary. Without alcohol prohibition, Al Capone would have been nothing more than a pimp.

In general, making drugs illegal does not make them go away. When you take something people want off the legal market, you thereby put it on the black market. Indeed, making drugs illegal often makes them more profitable to manufacture and sell drugs. Demand for drugs is relatively *inelastic*. That is, as the price of drugs increases, the demand for drugs does not decrease quite as rapidly. By making drugs illegal and thus reducing the number of suppliers, the government makes it possible to charge higher prices and make higher profits from drugs. The War on Drugs reduces market competition among drug suppliers. The few remaining drug suppliers can charge monopoly prices.

It also changes *who* supplies the drugs. Make a drug illegal, and you get the Mafia, the Mexican Cartels, or others supplying it. Make it legal, and you get

Starbucks or that nice wine shop down the street.[43] It also changes *how* people do the drugs. When a drug is illegal and thereby expensive, buyers need to get the most concentrated dose for a fast high, and sellers need to sell concentrated, overly powerful forms that are easy to conceal.

The drug warriors in the US don't target all users equally. Studies generally find that white and black Americans use drugs, including hard drugs, at roughly equal rates—though many studies instead find instead that white Americans are more likely to use drugs, more likely to sell drugs, and more likely to be involved in hard drugs than black Americans.[44] Nevertheless, black Americans are arrested for possessing and selling drugs at a far higher rate than white Americans. Black Americans use drugs less than white Americans, are more likely to be stopped, searched, and frisked, more likely to be prosecuted, more likely to be convicted, and finally tend to receive harsher sentences than white Americans for drug crimes. White Americans do and sell drugs as much or more than black Americans, and do and sell hard drugs as much or more, but the Drug Warriors target black Americans far more.[45]

In Chapter 3, we argued for each of the following principles of criminal law:

1. Just because something is immoral doesn't mean it should be illegal.
2. Criminalizing something must actually succeed in stopping it.
3. The benefits of criminalization must exceed the costs.
4. The body in charge of criminalization must act competently and in good faith.

The Drug War violates all four of these principles. Even if using drugs is a bad idea for many people, that doesn't by itself imply we should criminalize it. Criminalization doesn't do much to reduce drug use, and instead seems to push users to use harder, more concentrated, less pure, and more dangerous drugs. The social and economic costs of the Drug War exceed its benefits, in part because the fall out is so high, and in part because the Drug War enriches and emboldens organized crime. Finally, the Drug Warriors fight in a flagrantly racist way, thus violating the rule that they must act competently and good faith. The Drug War doesn't stop drug use, but it creates greater crime, economic blight, undermines community, and contributes to social decay. We fought the drugs and the drugs won. We've been shooting ourselves in the foot. It's time to stop.

Free Birth Control?

In the 1980s and the 1990s, conservative and progressive criminologists alike tended to pin the rise in violent crime on the rise in single-mother or single-parent homes. The argument seemed simple enough: There is a strong correlation between rates of single motherhood in a neighborhood and the local crime rate. Further, children raised in single-parent households are significantly more likely to be convicted of a crime, to be delinquent, and to have poor outcomes than children raised in two-parent households.[46] Crime was rising in the US as families were breaking down, and teen and single-parent households became more common. This story seemed to make sense of why, e.g., black crime rates were becoming higher from the 1960s through the early 1990s, even though black poverty was worse before then. In the 1950s and earlier, poor children benefitted from living with intact families; afterward, more poor children were growing up in broken families with lower levels of parental investment. Commentators left and right told this same story; the difference between them was where they placed the *moral* blame for the trend. (Conservatives might blame the poor for making bad choices; progressives would blame people in power for creating bad conditions that induced the poor to make such choices.)

When researching this book, we kept finding the same problem over and over: While lots of things are correlated with and predict crime, nothing quite seems to explain it. Two factors that go together over one period might come apart over another.

The single-parent argument faces the same problem as the others. The problem is that crime started dropping in the 1990s and has more or less continued dropping since. Yet the percent of households headed by single mothers, and the percent of children raised in single parent households, has remained steady or increased in that period.[47]

That's not to say that the single-parenting wasn't or isn't a problem. Rather, the issue that a huge number of factors contribute to crime, while other factors reduce it. To our surprise, in researching this book, it seems that there is no real consensus about *why* crime in the US dropped in the 1990s and after. Nevertheless, it's still the case today that children growing up in single-parent families are more likely to become criminals, and that the rate of single-parent households in a community is positively correlated with overall criminality.

Freakeconomist Steve Levitt and his co-author John Donohue famously argued that legal access to abortion after Roe v. Wade significantly reduced crime in the 1990s.[48] The idea here is that in the absence of access of abortion, more kids would have been born into bad circumstances, and then would have come to the age of criminality around the mid 1990s. But thanks to abortion rights, those kids simply weren't born. However, other economists vigorously dispute their results, claiming for instance, Donohue and Levitt had a coding error or messy data, or that they had failed to control for other confounding variables.[49]

At any rate, there remains some sort of persistent connection between single-parent households and crime. Calm down, Murphy Brown; we're not saying all single-parent households are bad and all two-parent households are good. (Know that one of us grew up in a single-parent household, before you get too offended.) And just how strong the "effect size" is up for debate. But, still, reducing the incidence of single parent households means reducing the number of children raised in conditions which make it more likely they'll become criminals later.

One area to explore, then, is whether there are policy tools to reduce the incidence of single-motherhood. Perhaps better sex ed would be enough. But more radically, perhaps governments could experiment with providing tax-financed birth control, such as providing the pill for "free." Conservatives may balk at that—why should the taxpayers have to pay for your sex life?—but the argument here isn't the progressive one that women have a human right to state-financed oral contraceptives. Rather, it's that this is a way of nipping the crime problem in the bud. Even more radically, we might experiment with government-financed "free" abortions. As we write this, Ireland—which has recently legalized abortion—is poised to provide abortion services for "free."[50]

Better Schools?

Children from disadvantaged backgrounds tend to go bad schools. They get disciplined harshly and face criminal penalties for what would have been detention-worthy infractions in richer school districts. Police are on hand, ready to intervene when kids violate zero tolerance policies and strict school disturbance laws. Despite some schools having very high spending per student—e.g., in Washington, DC, over $27,000 per pupil[51]—conditions are bad and outcomes are poor. The result: the much dreaded "school-to-prison pipeline."[52]

One major—and often highly politicized debate—right now concerns whether giving parents increased power to choose where to go to school would help reduce crime. In OECD countries, governments provide free schooling, but parents have significant power to choose which public schools their children will attend, and can often receive vouchers or public funds to attend private or even religious schools.[53] In the US, though, this is for some reason a highly contentious left-right issue, with so-called progressives often opposing copying the school choice policies of the left-leaning European countries they otherwise claim to admire. Our best guess is that this ideological disconnect is not because American progressives know something European progressives don't, but rather is a way for American progressives to signal that the teachers' unions are part of the Democratic alliance. The US is unusual in that in most places, you go to the local public school your government assigns you, and get little say in going someplace better.

The logic of choice is simple. Consider an analogy:

1. Imagine we imposed a law that said you must eat every meal at your one local restaurant. You're not allowed to eat elsewhere unless you can pay

$30,000 a year for the privilege. The restaurant owners get paid directly from your property taxes. You can complain as much as you like, and every few years, voters can even force the restaurant to get new managers.

2. Imagine instead there are lots of restaurants, and you may eat at whichever one you believe offers the best quality.

Under which situation, 1 or 2, would you expect higher quality meals? Most people realize that when it comes to almost any other service—food, car dealerships, clothing stores—or whatnot, monopolies lead to poor quality. But for some reason, they ignore this logic when it comes to public schools. If you suggest public schools should compete for students and parents should have the freedom to pick the best school for their kids—even with government footing the bill—you get accused of being a "neoliberal shill," whatever that means.

In the US, school choice is—in a way—almost universal for the rich, upper-middle, and middle classes. They can not only afford to send their kids to private and parochial schools, but also usually have the means to choose to move to neighborhoods attached to the best public schools. Higher quality public schools drive housing prices up, which in turn price the poor out of the neighborhood, ensuring their kids go elsewhere. It's only the American poor who lack the capacity for effective school choice.

Whether school choice improves academic outcomes is not our interest here. Instead, we want to know: How does school choice affect criminality and arrest rates?

David Deming examined the Charlotte-Mecklenburg school district in North Carolina, which, in 2002, created an open enrollment plan allowing parents to enroll their children at any school in the district. Of course, some schools are more in demand than others, and soon were oversubscribed. The district used a lottery to allocate slots at these oversubscribed schools. From a social scientific standpoint, lotteries are wonderful, because they introduce randomness into who gets to attend, and thus create a natural experiment. Deming can then meaningfully compare two groups of students: A) the students who won the lottery and go to go to the school their parents selected vs. B) the students who lost the lottery and were stuck at their less preferred options. Deming found that students in group A were later significantly less likely to be arrested for crimes than those in group B, and the effect was *especially strong* for students who were *ex ante* at high risk for crime. Indeed, for high risk students, winning the lottery effectively cut the expected social costs of their crimes in half, cut their expected days served in jail in half, and significantly reduces their risk of arrest, especially for drug crimes.[54]

Economist Roland Fryer and his co-author Will Dobbie did a similar study, examining the effects of charter schools in Harlem, which also used a lottery system to allocate students. They find not only that charter schools improved academic performance, but also that they lead to a 10.1 percentage point drop in teen pregnancy among females and a 4.4 percentage point drop in incarceration rates among males. They also found significant improvement in students' physical and mental health, and a large reduction in their general levels of risky behavior.[55]

Economists Julie Cullen, Brian Jacob, and Steve Levitt examine a similar program in Chicago public schools. They find less evidence of significant improvements in student's academic outcomes. However, they nevertheless find that students who win the lotteries are disciplined at school less, have lower arrest rates, and lower incarceration rates, especially if the students are placed into a previously identified high-achieving school.[56]

School choice seems to reduce crime in general, but the bad news is that the lottery winners win partly at the expense of the losers. It's not purely zero-sum, since the good schools often generally end up having more students than the bad schools. Also, there is evidence that introducing school choice makes the worst performing schools perform better—they start shaping up in response to competition.[57]

For school choice to be most effective, then, as a way of reducing crime on net, we need a genuinely competitive system. This might mean shutting down the worst schools—the schools that parents continue to rank as their last choices. It might mean instead firing and replacing the administrative and teaching staff at those schools and using replacements. It means having a range of charters which must continue to perform well to stay in business.

School choice works, in the sense that parents are able to pick the better schools and generate better outcomes for their children. The problem is that parents don't have enough choice. The lottery losers get thrown in the bad schools. We need to expand school choice to create a system where no one gets stuck at the bad school.

As an analogy, suppose your town provides free medical care. There are three doctors, Rodrick, Smith, and Thompson. Rodrick has the reputation of being better than Smith, who is reputed to be better than Thompson. As of now, you are stuck going to the doctor closest to you. It's possible, a priori, that no one is actually better—maybe Rodrick just already has the healthiest patients, because he works in the richest, healthiest neighborhood.

Suppose, however, your town introduces a reform which allows you to "choose" your doctor. You can rank the doctors, and they'll try to give you your topped ranked doctor, if there's space. However, Rodrick is soon oversubscribed, and Thompson undersubscribed, because most people want to go to Rodrick and not Thompson. The town then has to use a lottery to determine who gets who, though Rodrick still ends up with more patients than Thompson. We then compare the lottery winners (who have Rodrick) to the lottery losers (who get Thompson), and find their health outcomes are indeed better. The people who go to Thompson are worse off, though Thompson starts upping his game in response to being everyone's last choice. Now we know Rodrick really was the better doctor, and letting people choose doctors does indeed result in better health.

The implication here isn't just that Rodrick is better, and that giving people choice leads to better outcomes. The implication is that we need to make choices effective. That means firing Thompson—if he doesn't improve enough—and replacing him. If the town keeps Thompson around, then they're condemning the lottery losers to bad outcomes.

Why Be Hopeful?

This chapter, like much of this book, may give you reasons not to be hopeful. Since it's not clear what the connection is between poverty and crime, it's not unreasonable to think that even if we had unlimited financial resources we might not be able to figure out the best path forward. And, of course, resources are not unlimited. Given limited resources and reasonable concerns about even well-intended policies having unintended, negative consequences, what should we do? Are there places where we have seen dramatic turnarounds quickly, and, if so, how were those turnarounds achieved?

If you want to be hopeful, look no further than the East Lake neighborhood in Atlanta. In 1971, the City of Atlanta built East Lake Meadows in the neighborhood, a notorious public housing development that had become known as "little Vietnam" because of the level of crime and violence in the community.[58] Just how bad was East Lake? Very bad.[59] The crime rate was 18 times the national average and the average family could expect to be the victim of three violent felonies a year. Beyond the crime, the average family income was $4,000 per year, nearly 60% of families were on welfare, only 5% of children in the community could pass the state math test at the appropriate level and only 30% graduated high school, and the employment rate was an abysmal 14%.

The situation for East Lake changed dramatically in 1995, when a private group led by local real estate developer Tom Cousins partnered with the City of Atlanta to tear down East Lake Meadows and rebuild the community. Driven by a "cradle to college" philosophy, they rebuilt the community with mixed income housing (where poor and middle-income people lived together), two public schools, parks, ballfields, and otherwise turned it into a place where people would want to live. They gave the people who lived there something to take pride in; something to take care of; and, perhaps most important, a place where their children could have a chance to live thriving, fulfilling, and safe lives. Today, over 70% of East Lake's residents are employed, crime has plummeted, and the high school graduation rate is nearly 100%.

This dramatic turnaround didn't come quick and didn't come cheap. Cousins is one of the wealthiest people in Atlanta and invested much of his personal fortune into restoring this community. One of the primary features of the community is East Lake Golf Club, which Cousins purchased in 1995 and restored. All of the profits from the East Lake Golf Club go to the East Lake Foundation, which supports the East Lake community. To generate funds for the Foundation, he convinced the leaders of 40 large US companies to purchase $50,000 corporate memberships to the club, as well as to donate $200,000 each to support the East Lake Foundation. Now, East Lake Golf Club is the permanent home of the PGA Tour's Tour Championship, generating about $2 million per year for the Foundation to support the community.

In hopes of replicating the success of the East Lake private-public partnership in other cities around the country, Cousins, along with investor Warren Buffet and hedge fund manager Julian Robertson, helped establish Purpose Built Communities in 2009. The non-profit aims to support similar development initiatives in communities with similar problems as East Lake. In 2019, Purpose Built Communities had established network partners in 16 other cities: Birmingham (AL), Columbus (OH), Grand Rapids (MI), Indianapolis (IN), New Orleans (LA), Orlando (FL), Rome (GA), Tulsa (OK), Charlotte (NC), Fort Worth (TX), Houston (TX), Kansas City (KS), Omaha (NE), Raleigh (NC), Spartanburg (SC), and Wilmington (DE).

Success in East Lake did not come easy and did not come cheap. But it did come. While it remains to be seen if these other communities can replicate the success of East Lake, the initial data is very promising. At the very least, the story of East Lake should give us hope that struggling communities can be turned around, crime can be reduced significantly, and opportunities for education and financial stability can be created. But success requires us not only to commit the appropriate amount of financial resources, but also to identify important community players—people who have benefitted from the opportunities and important players in the community step up and take responsibility to lead these turnarounds.

Notes

1 US Department of Justice 2017c.
2 Horwitz 2015.
3 Harris and Shaw 2000.
4 National Gang Center 2013
5 Crime and Justice News 2018.
6 Milanovic 2010.
7 Latzer 2013.
8 US Federal Bureau of Investigation 2018.
9 Kaste 2018.
10 Statista 2018.
11 Allen 2018.
12 Wikipedia 2019.
13 Associated Press 2019.

14 Gleaner Staff 2019.
15 Schrank 2019.
16 Lane 2019.
17 Detroit Free Press Staff and Wire Services 2019.
18 Anderson 2019.
19 Verner 2019.
20 City of New Orleans 2019.
21 Washington Post 2018b.
22 Surprenant 2019.
23 Naicker 2018; Nkomo 2018.
24 Hawthorne 2015.
25 Drum 2016.
26 Lind and Lopez 2016.
27 Latzer 2016.
28 Becker 1968.
29 Becker and Murphy 1988.
30 Cook and Wilkins 2016.
31 Ariely 2012.
32 Bruton, Ketchen Jr., and Ireland 2013; Haughton 2013; Parker 2015.
33 Crain and Crain 2010.
34 Munger 2017.
35 Institute for Justice 2014.
36 Friedersdorf 2017.
37 Mcconnaughey 2016.
38 State of Louisiana Department of Agriculture & Forestry 2019.
39 State of New Jersey Office of the Attorney General 2019.
40 Kleiner 2017.
41 Institute for Justice 1991.
42 Svorny 2004.
43 Miron 1999.
44 Langan 1995; McCabe et al. 2007; Ingraham 2014; Lopez 2016; Rosenberg, Groves, and Blankenship 2017; Hamilton Project 2019.
45 Alexander 2010.
46 Antecol and Bedard 2002.
47 Cohen 2012; Rector 2014.
48 Donohue and Levitt 2001.
49 Joyce 2004; Foote and Goetz 2008.
50 Cionnaith 2018.
51 McShane 2012.
52 Heitzeg 2009.
53 Organisation for Economic Co-operation and Development 2017.
54 Deming 2011.
55 Dobbie and Fryer 2015.
56 Cullen, Jacob, and Levitt 2006.
57 Egalite 2016.
58 Schank 2017.
59 Pitts 2007.

7

CHANGING THE RULES

Changing the Incentives

This book has been a lot of doom and gloom, and for good reason. But there are reasons to be hopeful, especially if we have correctly diagnosed the causes of the problems we see related to policing and punishment in the US. Camden, New Jersey is one such turnaround story. Between 2000 and 2014, Camden was frequently ranked as one of the most dangerous cities in the US, and three times as *the* most dangerous city, in terms of per capita violent crime.[1] But in 2015, crime, especially violent crime, started to fall dramatically. In 2018, as compared to 2012, property crimes were down 45% and homicides were down 67%.[2] Not only is Camden no longer one of the most dangerous cities in the country, but also it has become a model for other communities with similar problems.

So, what happened? In 2013, Camden received national attention by taking the drastic step of disbanding its police department—the Camden Police Department. In its place, they worked with the state and county officials to create the Camden County Police Department, rehiring many of the old police officers, but implementing new policies. While public comments from Camden city officials have credited the turnaround on the reorienting of policing strategy towards "community policing," the actual explanation of Camden's success may be more straightforward.

When the Camden Police Department was disbanded, it also eliminated the police union and its union contracts.[3] One advantage of eliminating these contracts was that the department was able to put more officers on the streets for the same overall budget amount. How did they accomplish this? Union contracts are expensive, in both the obvious ways (higher salaries and more benefits) and not so obvious ways. For example, one provision of these contracts was that various non-policing desk jobs had to be staffed by trained police officers. These officers were then paid their normal police salaries, which were considerably higher than the market rate for, say, hiring a receptionist.[4] Making minor changes like this throughout the department allowed the department's budget to remain level while putting significantly more officers on the streets.

More police on the street has been shown to reduce crime.[5] Perhaps the most easy-to-grasp statistic: In 2018, Princeton University economics researcher Steven Mello found that one additional police officer per 10,000 residents reduces crime victimization costs by \$35 per person.[6] Put differently, a city of 70,000 residents (like Camden) that puts seven more police officers on the street will see a decrease in victimization cost of around \$245,000, or numbers right in line with what Camden experienced.

The basic lesson of institutional economics is that constraints shape institutions which determine incentives which shape behavior. Bad institutional design creates the wrong mix of incentives, which leads flawed human beings like all of us to act in systematically dysfunctional ways. The United States has an unusually bad criminal justice system, but to explain that, we don't need to —nor is it useful—to posit that Americans are unusually bad people.

Good rules align individuals' self-interest with the public good. An ideal institutional structure, in criminal justice, would be one where all the parties involved get rewarded every time they promote whatever justice requires and get penalized whenever they make a mistake. But, as we've seen over the past six chapters, there's no obvious way to do that. Government agents are supposed to answer to voters, but voters are incentivized to be ignorant, irrational, and emotional. Accordingly, politicians and their underlings have every incentive to do things that *sound good* to dummies rather than things that actually work. They have no incentive to figure out what really causes crime or what the best ways to deal with it are. They can serve their own interests by catering to voters' prejudices. The bureaucrats deeply imbedded in the criminal justice can serve their own interests by passing off costs and by using criminal justice as a means of expropriating revenue from citizens directly or from taxes. At every turn, the key players not only can get away with making bad choices, but also will often be rewarded for doing so.

So it goes. But the good news is that we are not doomed. Other countries do what we do better, and we can copy their examples. Others do certain things worse, and we can learn from their mistakes.

In this chapter, we propose a wide range of possible reforms, each aimed at specific problem. Some are more speculative than others. Of course, even if our proposed reforms work, there remains a big problem: Few people in power have a stake in implementing these reforms, and voters have little stake in knowing about them and supporting politicians who would implement them. We face the problem institutional economists almost always face—even if you know which institutions work better, you need to get the people working in the current institutions to make the change. So, we'll end by reflecting on some possible ways to actually get these changes made.

End Policing for Profit

For most problems related to policing and punishment for profit, practical reform requires realigning incentives. For fines and forfeitures, identifying the theoretical solution is relatively easy, even if it is difficult to bring that solution about in practice. Many of the problems identified in the previous chapters could have been avoided if police departments and municipalities did not profit financially from issuing citations or seizing property. That doesn't mean that they would stop issuing citations or seizing property when appropriate, but rather that any fines paid or property seized would not go to them for financial support.

Where could it go? There are a variety of options. It could be returned to the taxpayers, directed to legitimate charities, or directed to accounts for victim restitution. These present their own perverse incentives, but they present less perverse incentives than the current system.

In July 2017, for example, there was significant discussion in Colorado about a proposed ballot measure that would accomplish this goal of redirecting fine revenue.

> Instead of the fining agency keeping that money, it first would go to reimburse a victim for any financial losses. If there is no victim, such as in a speeding incident, the money would go to a charity of the fine payer's choice.[7]

Although proposals like this one in Colorado are certainly a step in the right direction, we should be wary of potential rent-seeking or abuse with a policy that directs fine money to charities. In 2017, for example, the DOJ ended a fine settlement practice enacted under the Obama administration that allowed payments to be made directly to certain community and legal aid organizations, instead of making the payments to the Treasury Department (Walsh and Reilly 2017). To encourage settlement amounts to be paid to these community and legal aid organizations, any payments made to them received a 2 for 1 credit towards the settlement amount. So, if a bank settled with the DOJ for $100 million, they could pay $50 million to the qualifying organizations and their settlement obligation would be met.[8] It is easy to see how a program like this one, where the government is picking winners and losers by determining which organizations are able to receive settlement funds and which are not, is ripe for abuse.

There are other good options for redirecting fine funds. For example, instead of allocating fine revenue in a manner consistent with the Colorado proposal, the entire amount could be sent to a victim restitution fund, established and maintained in such a way so that no one profits from lobbying for more fines. All real crimes have victims. One way to make sure victims are restored as much as possible to the condition they were in before the crime is to have a healthy restitution fund available for support. Our point here is not to advocate for one solution in particular, but to show the direction that policy solutions must trend towards. Many solutions could adequately address the problems connected to the collection and use of fine revenue. For all of these solutions, the aim is not to return money to taxpayers or to build a restitution fund, but rather to eliminate the added financial incentive to fine individuals or seize their property. No one should profit from crime. That includes the state.

Stop Electing Prosecutors and Judges

Legal theorist Ronald Wright writes:

> In the United States, we typically hold prosecutors accountable for their discretionary choices by asking the lead prosecutor to stand for election from time to time.
>
> This is not true in most places around the globe. In the various civil law systems in other countries, the idea of electing prosecutors is jarring. In the civil law depiction of the public prosecutor's job, training and experience hold criminal prosecutors accountable to public values and legal standards. Prosecutors in a civil law tradition perform a ministerial function as they progress through a career-long bureaucratic journey. He or she simply assembles and evaluates the available evidence; if that evidence meets the relevant standard of proof to support a conviction for each element of a crime, the prosecutor has the duty to initiate a prosecution. This lawyerly evaluation—nothing more and nothing less—constitutes the prosecutor's job.[9]

Wright goes on to examine how prosecutor elections work. The answer: they don't. Prosecutors running for election are rarely contested. They rarely advertise their conviction rates per se, but rather advertise more specific numbers, such as the rate of jury trials they win. (Remember: most convictions occur through plea bargains, not through jury trials.) They make symbolic arguments about priorities and goals.

In the European model, prosecutors generally work for independent agencies who answer only indirectly to the legislature. The analog in the US would be, say, the FBI. Prosecutors answer to their bosses and try to move up the bureaucratic ladder. They are not selected by voters. In the American model, lower-level prosecutors may be hired by the district attorney, but the

DA and many other higher-level prosecutors stand for election. In many parts of the US, judges also stand for election, something unheard of in most of the world.

A priori, there was no reason to think the European model would work better than the American model. A bureaucracy insulated from voters and only occasionally checked by the legislature can develop its own priorities at the expense of the public interest. Offices chosen by voters could in principle lead to citizens picking the best candidate. But we've had hundreds of years of experience with both models, and it turns out that in practice, the problems created by voters' rational ignorance and rational irrationality outweigh the problems of unchecked bureaucracy.

Required Rotation of Public Defenders and Prosecution

Another idea, one compatible with the previous, is to eliminate the professional prosecutorial class.

The US promises defendants a fair trial, and promises that representation will be provided if they cannot afford it. But it doesn't keep these promises.

We understand it seems perverse at first glance that a person who actually murdered others should get high quality legal representation, with the bill footed by innocent taxpayers. The main reason it's a good idea, though, is that we want to make it difficult in general for the state to wield its awesome power against citizens. We put impediments to state power not to protect the guilty but to protect the innocent. If the state were staffed by angels, no such protections would be needed.

Right now, the deck is stacked in favor of prosecution. Prosecutors receive lighter caseloads. The police and the forensics departments work, in effect, for them—they help produce evidence for the purposes of achieving conviction. Public defenders receive far fewer resources, lower pay, and little to no assistance from other government agencies. In many jurisdictions, public defenders are simply private attorneys who agree to represent clients for a small fee. The pay is bad, and their incentive is usually to recommend taking a quick plea bargain. As we saw in Chapter 2, prosecutors and elected judges further have an incentive to gather high conviction rates and long sentences, to be seen as "tough on crime."

One possible strategy to fix this problem is to change the career track of some government employees. Instead of having a pool of prosecutors, we have instead a pool of public attorneys, with equal pay and equal access to resources. In any given case, a public attorney could be assigned to either a prosecutorial or defense role. Promotions might be based on winning, but in this case, any attorney up for promotion will want to garner "wins" as defense, not just as a prosecutor.

No Government Prosecutors, Period

An even more radical variation of this idea dispenses with government prosecution altogether. The government could instead have a pool of privately employed lawyers who have pre-qualified and announced their willingness to serve in these cases. When police arrest someone for a crime, the government could select a prosecuting and defensive attorney team from this pool, offering fees in proportion to the complexity of the case. (Of course, we must be careful to structure payments in a way that avoids either incentivizing both sides to settle too quickly or to drag the entire thing out) The government could incentivize each side to win by offering a cash bonus to the winning side. Further, as a control mechanism, there could be a rule that if a conviction is subsequently reversed on appeal, the winning prosecutor must pay back his bonus.[10]

Under this system, we eliminate the problem of career prosecutors who hope to build their credentials on conviction rates. We reduce the degree of collusion between prosecutors and forensics and the police. We rather ask private civilians to step up and serve justice, and the civilians in question will rotate between the prosecutor and defensive role.

Elect Judges and DAs, but Use a Different Method

An alternative method of selecting prosecutors, judges, and the like is to keep things democratic, but then give the participants in the democratic decisions an incentive to choose wisely.

Many contemporary political theorists think we can borrow a method from ancient Athens to do just that. The idea is called "deliberative polling." Here's how it works: First, we randomly select, say, 50 citizens. They and only they are summoned, as in jury duty, to serve on a deliberative committee, which will review and select applicants for these jobs. There may be some oversight —perhaps some citizens will be released to do hardship or rejected due to clear and demonstrable prejudice or conflicts of interest. Those that pass muster will be paid fair wages to spend time examining the applicants' records, and they and only they will decide who will be appointed.

The upside of the method is that it remains democratic—everyone has an equal basic chance of being selected, and the randomness prevents money or privilege from giving some more say than others. Further, because there are fewer citizens voting, individual votes now have significant efficacy, and citizens then acquire some incentive to use their votes wisely. Further, because they must deliberate together, it's possible they will learn from one another, become more open-minded, and make wiser decisions.

That said, this system has some serious drawbacks. One is that, depending on how it's administered, it may end up being more expensive than other methods of selecting prosecutors and judges. Sure, elections are expensive, but these elections tend to be packaged with other existing elections, and so the marginal cost of administering the elections are relatively low. That said, it may cut down on campaign spending and be a net gain.

But there are other problems. Deliberation often backfires and makes things worse, especially when citizens are asked to deliberate about sensitive political issues upon which their political parties have already taken a side.[11] Further, it's unclear whether citizens would know enough to ask hard questions about how to evaluate prosecutors. If they haven't read books and articles educating them about the problems of criminal justice, they may just select the DAs with the highest conviction rates, unaware of the problems this causes.

Fair Notice

Western liberal democracies supposedly instantiate something called "the rule of law." One of the major tenets of the rule of law is that the laws and regulations to which we are subject should be public, clear, and knowable. Ordinary citizens are supposed to be able to know ahead of time what the rules are, and whether various kinds of behavior are violations of the law or not.

Consider a speed limit sign that just said, "Drive safely." Good people in good conscience could not easily know whether their driving behavior falls on either side of that law. Sure, there are behaviors that no reasonable person could regard as safe, and there may even be some that no reasonable person could regard as unsafe. Still, a wide range of common driving behaviors and speeds would fall in the middle "Who knows?" category. Badly incentivized traffic cops or prosecutors would have far too much discretion to assign meaning on an ad hoc basis. A person cannot really know ahead of time whether they are doing something that would subject them to criminal prosecution. They are subject to the rule of men, not the rule of law.

In *Three Felonies a Day*, Harvey Silverglate documents at great length how a huge range of federal regulations are written in impossibly vague and convoluted language. Some regulations and laws are so complex that understanding them requires specialized legal knowledge. Large corporations can afford to hire legal teams to monitor compliance; everyone else better just hope they don't break the relevant laws (out of the 175,000 pages of federal regulations to which they are subject). Many laws are so vague that even specialist lawyers, let alone lay citizens, cannot predict ahead of time which behaviors run afoul of the law.

Martha Stewart was never charged with, let alone convicted for, insider trading. Indeed, it's clear now that she does not qualify as an "insider" even on the wrongfully vague law.[12] After being publicly accused (if not charged), Stewart made a number of public statements where she asserted her innocence. The SEC decided that this constituted obstruction of justice and securities fraud, claiming that she was just manipulating her stock. As Silverglate carefully documents, no one ahead of time could have known the SEC would interpret her behavior that way—they expanded their definition to include her behavior on the spot, as it suited them.[13]

The United States has a serious problem. Prosecutors and bureaucrats—who have financial, self-interested incentives to nail people—especially high profile people—regardless of guilt—get to decide what the law means, and often just get to decide what the law is. Normal people can't understand the law and don't have time to learn it even if they could understand it. What can be done about that?

Here are some ideas:

1. Just as mortgage companies are now required to disclose the terms of a loan in plain and simple language, so the government must now take on the burden of disclosing the law in similarly plain and simple language, complete with clear examples. It won't be enough simply to publish the laws in the impenetrable federalregister.gov. It must instead take it upon itself to send each citizen an account of the laws that apply to them as citizens, and to each business the laws that apply to it.

2. Before someone can be charged, there must be a citizen review process. Grand jurists are given the law, and then given a wide range of behaviors, including not only the behaviors attorneys are thinking of prosecuting as crimes, but also a range of other related behaviors. Unless a supermajority of the grand jurists agrees the behavior in question is *clearly* a violation of that law, then no charges can be made.

3. During a trial, we repeat that process. Before even hearing the case, jurors are given the law, and then given a wide range of behaviors, including not only the behaviors attorneys are thinking of prosecuting as crimes, but also a range of other related behaviors. Unless a supermajority of the jurors agree the behavior in question is *clearly* a violation of that law, then the charges are automatically dropped.

In both 2 and 3, the grand jurors and jurors vote to assess whether law as written is clear and precise, and whether charges *clearly* fall within the confines of that law. If not—if the law is in a gray area or is not obvious—then the charges are automatically dropped.

Eliminate Cash Bail

We began Chapter 4 with the story of Charles and Cynthia Jones, a husband and wife in New Orleans who were going to have their lives severely disrupted if not for the intervention of the New Orleans Bail Fund. In Chapter

5, we talked about the large number of people who are sitting in our local jails while they await trial—462,000, or one out of five of all incarcerated people in the US. Over half of these people could get out of jail if they had the financial means, but they're simply too poor to bail themselves out.[14] And we're not talking about needing hundreds of thousands of dollars. In most of these cases, a few hundred dollars would do it.

District attorneys argue that the reason why cash bail is necessary is to keep dangerous people off the streets and otherwise make sure that defendants return for their court dates.[15] But studies examining the effects of cash bail on a community have shown that it actually makes people less safe. People who are unable to bail themselves out while awaiting their trials are more likely to become and remain unemployed, as well as more likely to have other arrests down the road as a result.[16]

There's also no evidence showing that assigning cash bail makes it more likely for defendants to appear for their court dates. New Jersey passed sweeping bail reform measures in 2014,[17] implementing them in 2017. Since these measures were implemented violent crime is down by more than 30%,[18] pre-trial detention is down by 44% or about 6,000 people at any given time,[19] and there was a statistically insignificant percentages change in the number of defendants who failed to appear for their court dates.[20] In Philadelphia, newly elected district attorney Larry Krasner unilaterally stopped requesting cash bail for a wide range of offenses. The result was an immediate 22% decrease in the number of defendants who had to spend at least one night in jail with no change to the failure-to-appear rate or recidivism.[21]

So why do we have it? Follow the money. In the US, the bail bonds industry generates over $2 billion (yes, billion) a year,[22] money made mostly from the pockets of our nation's poor. Over a recent five-year period in Maryland, families of accused individuals who later went on to be exonerated or have their charges dropped paid over $75 million in non-refundable bail-bond payments.[23] Over a recent 18-month period, bail companies in Mississippi took in over $43 million in non-refundable payments.[24] These numbers become worse when examining the racial disparities. In New Orleans in 2015, $4.7 million in non-refundable bail payments were made to free fewer than 5,000 accused individuals before their trials. $3.95 million or 84% of these payments were made by black families.[25] It's time we end the practice of cash bail and the commercialization of bail—something that only exists in two countries, the US and the Philippines.[26]

Bring Back *Mens Rea*

One of the major changes in criminal law over the past 60 years, especially in drug crime and white collar crimes, is the gradual elimination through a thousand cuts of the concept of *mens rea*. The idea here is that to convict a person of crime, it is not enough that they did something which technically breaks a rule or regulation. They must *intend* to do so—they must have be an "evil-meaning mind with an evil-doing hand."[27] "*Mens rea*" refers to that evil-meaning mind.

Today, because there are simply so many laws and regulations in place, and so many of them are vague and open to various interpretations, many people charged with crimes often didn't know (and couldn't have known) that what they were doing was illegal. Here, we're not talking about people who know they're acting badly but aren't aware of the specific law they're violating. Rather, in the cases we're concerned with the supposedly illegal action was likely the most reasonable and what any normal person could or would have done under the circumstances.

The most egregious example we came across, brought to our attention by Senator Rand Paul, was the US government's prosecution of Honduran businessman David McNabb, and three US citizens—Robert Blandford, Abbie Schoenwetter, and Diane Huang—who bought McNabb's frozen seafood and distributed it to restaurants like Red Lobster.[28] In 1999, the National Marine Fisheries Service received an anonymous tip that McNabb was importing lobsters into the US that supposedly failed to meet the size requirements to export lobsters under Honduran law. When the 70,000lbs of frozen lobster arrived in Alabama, NMFS agents seized the shipment and held it for months as they tried to identify some Honduran law that had been broken. That's right, US federal agents were looking to prosecute US citizens for accepting frozen seafood from a Honduran seafood supplier that may have been sourced or shipped in a manner that violated Honduran—not US—law.

They settled on three supposed violations: (1) a prohibition on harvesting lobsters with tails shorter than 5.5 inches, (2) a prohibition on harvesting or destroying marine eggs, and (3) a regulation that frozen seafood should be packed in cardboard boxes. The purpose of charging the four with these violations was to attach more serious charges. If, for example, importing frozen lobsters in plastic bags was illegal, then planning to import them was criminal conspiracy, actually importing them was smuggling, and paying for them was money laundering.

This case actually went to trial. During the trial, the four defendants produced numerous documents from Honduras—including a letter from the attorney general—to confirm that the prohibition on harvesting lobsters with smaller tails was never signed into law and that the prohibition on marine eggs meant to apply to things like turtle eggs, not fish or lobsters that may be carrying eggs. As for packing frozen seafood in cardboard boxes? That was merely a suggestion. Despite the lack of criminal intent—and even the lack of committing a crime by Honduran law, never mind US law—all four were convicted—yes, convicted!—on a general verdict. McNabb, Blandford, and

Schoenwetter were each sentenced to eight years in federal prison, while Huang was sentenced to two years in prison.

Even if you believe that a federal prison sentence is appropriate for someone who packs frozen seafood in plastic bags instead of cardboard boxes, it seems entirely unreasonable to think that this punishment—or any punishment—is appropriate for someone who has no knowledge of the law and has no reason to believe that what he is doing is bad or illegal. One way to resolve this problem is to restore a stronger version of the *mens rea* requirement for criminal convictions. That is, in order for someone to be convicted of a crime, the prosecution must prove that he (1) had intent to do something he could reasonably recognize as illegal, or (2) the applicable law was easily knowable to the defendant, and he could have (or should have) easily known ahead of time he was breaking that law.

Change Who Pays for Prison

For prison policy, aligning incentives with appropriate public goals is a bit more complicated. People are incarcerated at the local, state, and federal level. They are incarcerated in facilities as far ranging as those holding juveniles to those serving entirely families who have been detained. How people end up in each of those facilities, at any of the different levels, varies greatly.

Take state prisons, which currently house the majority of US inmates. State prisons house people who have been arrested by local police and sentenced by local judges, but do their time at a facility paid for by the state (and often subsidized by the federal government). As a result, local municipalities do not bear the cost of sending people to state prison—the state pays for it. But if a municipality opts for a rehabilitation program or alternative punishment arrangement, in most cases those costs are not paid by the state but by the municipality. It's no surprise that for many municipalities, the first and only option to punish offenders is sending them to state prison.

Want to send fewer people to prison? Change the financial incentives.

One possible change would be to require local municipalities to pay a higher percentage of the costs of incarcerating criminals from their jurisdiction. Perhaps it makes sense not to make them bear the full costs, as poor areas might have higher crime but insufficient tax revenues to cover all their various functions. We might have little choice but to have high-income and low-crime towns subsidize criminal justice in low-income but high-crime areas. However, we should at least make it so that sending criminals to state or county prison is not significantly cheaper for a municipality than putting up preventative measures—such as more police on the streets. (An even more radical version of this proposal would be to have all policing paid for at the state level, though this creates some of its own problems.)

Another would be for states to pay the per person costs of rehabilitation programs or other incarceration alternatives. Not only are incarceration alternatives more successful at preventing future bad behavior, but also they often cost less. A 2016 report from the Brennan Center for Justice showed that we could save over $20 billion (yes, billion) nationwide by moving to more effective alternatives.[29] State-level studies have shown similar impact.[30]

Competitive Prisons

As we discussed at length in Chapter 4, American prisons are terrible. We argued we should use prisons far less—incarceration should be used as a punishment only in special cases, and pre-trial detention should be used only in truly exceptional cases. But is there a way to make prisons—however often they're used—better?

Wringing our hands and complaining about conditions doesn't seem to help. Getting voters on board with pushing for more serious oversight seems impractical. As we discussed in Chapter 2, voters have little incentive to think carefully about this issue or to care much about prisoners. Everyone knows prison conditions are awful and hardly anyone cares. Voters are not willing to spend *more* to make prisons better when that money could be spent on schools, roads, or veteran care.

The Australian Prison Ship from Chapter 2 provides an analogous case here. Regulation didn't work. Trying to hire nicer ship captains didn't work. Requiring ships to employ medical doctors didn't work. What fixed the problem was changing how the captains were paid. Changing the behavior means changing the incentives.

Right now, the problem both public and private prisons face is that the *customer* is not the recipient of the "service." The customer is the one who pays —in this case, the government directly and taxpayers indirectly. The inmates consume the service, but don't pay. The customer has an incentive to cut costs and little incentive to care about quality.

If we could make the prisoners the customers, that could fix things. Consider this proposal: Imagine if prisoners could *choose* their own prisons and prisons had to compete to get prisoners. Every year, each prisoner is given a tax-financed voucher to spend on prison. The prisoner is given plenty of time to research various competing prisons, each of which can advertise its amenities, recidivism rates, conditions, and so on. Prisoners then select a prison for their year, and the prison in question gets their voucher. While both public and private prisons in this system would all things equal want to cut costs, they'll have to compete on quality to win prisoners. If prisoners can talk with each other and share their experiences, then prisons will have public reputations and won't be able to dupe potential customers for long.

Competitive measures like this work in almost every other market. It would sure be surprising if they didn't work for prisons. Of course, the danger in the real world is the same danger we face with school vouchers—the entrenched powers may overregulate the private prisons and offer too little in voucher money, perhaps with the deliberate goal of sabotaging the competition.

If all prisons receive the same payment, they'll compete on quality. But we might even consider allowing them to compete on price. For instance, suppose a standard voucher is $31,000.[31] If every prison costs $31,000, they will only be able to compete with each other by offering better amenities and conditions. But suppose we make the following deal with prisoners: You get $31,000 a year to spend. But if you select a less expensive prison, thereby saving taxpayers' money, you get to keep half the savings, which you can either A) give to family members or dependents now, or B) save for your eventual release. In this system, prisons compete on quality *and* price, and prisoners can make personal choices about the quality vs. price tradeoff.

When we've presented these ideas, to our surprise, the main negative reaction we have gotten is this: Our proposal will make prisons *too nice*. They won't be sufficiently punitive to qualify as punishments. But, we think, the primary point of prisons shouldn't be to punish. If all we want to do is punish people, there are far better, cheaper, and less destructive ways of punishing them. Instead, the purpose of prison should be to remove demonstrably dangerous people from society. (Indeed, we argued that *only* such people should be imprisoned—people who have done some wrong but do not represent an ongoing threat should not be imprisoned.)

Reduce Plea Bargaining

Approximately 95% of criminal cases that end in a conviction never go to trial.[32] They instead end with a plea bargain: an agreement between the prosecution and defense where the defendant pleads guilty (or pleads no contest) in exchange for having a portion of the charges dropped or having the one or more of the charges reduced to a less serious offense. Why so many pleas? Two practical reasons: (1) Most prosecutors get elected based on their high conviction rate. Pleas count as convictions. You can see the incentive here on the side of the prosecutor—it's a no-risk win! (2) Without such a high number of plea deals, the legal system would grind to a halt.[33] Our judicial system is already clogged with cases to the point that we're close to dysfunction. If a significant percentage of plea deal cases went to trial, it's tough to see how most defendants' right to a speedy trial could be preserved.

The problem with pleas isn't just their volume. Prosecutors have discretion as to what deals they can make, and research has found significant racial bias in what offers are made. The most in-depth study to date, conducted by Carlos Berdejó of Loyola Law School in Los Angeles, analyzed 30,807 cases in Wisconsin over a seven-year period.[34] Berdejó found that in felony cases, white defendants were 25% more likely than black defendants to receive an offer where the most serious charge they were facing was dropped or reduced. In misdemeanor cases, white defendants were 75% more likely than black defendants to have all charges that carried a punishment of imprisonment dropped or reduced to a lesser charge where jail time wasn't a possibility. Berdejó concluded that these figures suggest that prosecutors are likely using race as a proxy for "a defendant's latent criminality and likelihood to recidivate."

In additional to racial inequities, the widespread use of plea bargains encourages innocent people to admit to crimes they either did not commit or likely would not have been convicted of. Why? The National Association of Criminal Defense Lawyers calls it the "trial penalty."

> The "trial penalty" refers to the substantial difference between the sentence offered in a plea offer prior to trial versus the sentence a defendant receives after trial … To avoid the penalty, accused persons must surrender many other fundamental rights which are essential to a fair justice system.[35]

Consider the case of Christian Allmendinger, who was accused of a life insurance policy scheme.[36] Allmendinger's alleged partner in crime—Brent Oncale—pled guilty to what they were accused of doing and received a sentence of ten years in prison, which then got reduced to five years after agreeing to testify against Allmendinger. But Allmendinger took his case to trial, was found guilty, and sentenced to 45 years in prison.

When Oncale pled guilty, it's likely that he had, in fact, done what prosecutors alleged. But many people who plead guilty are not, in fact, guilty of what they've been charged with or any crime at all. According to the National Registry of Exonerations, 15% of all people proven to be innocent after a guilty conviction pled guilty to that crime. For people exonerated of manslaughter, that number rises to 49%; for drug crimes, the number is a staggering 66%.[37] Why would anyone agree to plead guilty to a crime he didn't commit? For many people in this position, the cost of taking their case to trial was simply too high. Not only would they be facing a situation like Christian Allmendinger—ten years if you take a plea versus 45 years if you roll the dice and go to trial—but also many of these people don't have the financial resources to bail themselves out or otherwise conduct a proper defense. They face a situation where the deck will be stacked against them at trial, they'll have to wait in jail until their trial date (which sometimes can be a year or two off in the distance), and if they lose they're looking at a far more severe penalty than if they would have agreed to do the time in the first place.

The challenge is that effectively reducing plea bargaining is a collective action problem. The only way to do it effectively is to have more defendants reject pleas and take their cases to trial. But this strategy works only if a significant enough number of defendants make this decision to cause the type of resource strain on the courts and prosecutor's office that would require some type of positive action. Further complicating the matter is that defense attorneys are under an ethical obligation to their clients to explain the ramifications of choosing to accept or not accept the plea, including what they face if they don't accept. So, if our client is facing a drug charge and he has been offered a plea of time served or the threat of ten years in prison if he takes his case to trial, there's no way we can encourage him to have his day in court. But the guy who is facing a possible 30-year sentence for manslaughter who has been offered a plea of 20 years? He's an excellent candidate, and there are certainly more than enough of these cases to go around.

Mandatory Notification of Right of Jury Nullification

In the common law tradition, juries often acted as judges both of facts and of the law itself. "Jury nullification" refers to when a jury finds a defendant not guilty, even though it believes beyond a reasonable doubt that defendant did in fact break the laws, because:

1.   The jury thinks the law itself lacks authority,
2.   The jury believes the law is inhumane or unjust,
3.   The jury believes it is inappropriate to enforce the law in this case, and/or
4.   The jury believes the defendant should not be punished for breaking the law.

Jury nullification remains legal, but it's a secret. Many jurisdictions forbid activists from passing out pamphlets advocating nullification near courthouses; they claim this constitutes "jury tampering.". Judges and prosecutors will routinely dismiss jurors who admit they would even consider nullifying a law. If a particular juror hangs a jury, the judge might interview the juror at length; if the judge determines the juror is trying to nullify the law, they will dismiss the juror and use an alternate.

We recommend pushing jury nullification with a vengeance. The point of jury nullification is to expand the "checks and balances" on government power. We the People interact with the criminal law as jurors. As jurors, our incentives are different from our incentives as voters. We're now conscripted into hearing the facts of a case, and our individual votes matter a great deal. We cannot count on voters providing a check on the misuse or abuse of criminal law, but we can count on jurors doing *some* work.

During every trial, before the jurors retreat to deliberate, the judge should say:

> You, the jury, represent all the citizens of [your jurisdiction]. You have the right and responsibility to judge not merely the facts of this case, but the law itself. Even if you believe that the defendant did break the law, you may issue a verdict of not guilty if you believe that the law is unjust, that the law is unconstitutional, that the punishments attached to the law are unjust, or if in this case, finding the defendant guilty would be inhumane or unwarranted.

Once so instructed, the jury would be able to freely deliberate whether to nullify the law in question. When the jury delivers their verdict, they could announce, "We the jury find the defendant not guilty by nullification."

We suggest that nullification go beyond the single case. We are not sure the best way to operationalize this idea, but the general recommendation is this: If juries continually nullify a particular law, at some point, this should lead to an automatic repeal of that law. For instance, suppose a majority of juries in Kansas in a 365-day period routinely nullify charges against marijuana dealers. If so, then the law criminalizing marijuana dealing should automatically be repealed, and all those currently convicted of that charge should have those convictions eliminated and their punishments, if ongoing, reduced.

Change How Judges/Juries Punish—Athenian Model

Most college students who take an introduction to philosophy course read Plato's *Apology*, a philosophical dialogue that portrays the trial of the Greek philosopher Socrates. After Socrates is found guilty of impiety and corrupting the youth, the sentencing phase begins. Modern judicial systems that have clearly defined punishments or a range of punishments for each violation of the law. But in the Athenian model of trial punishment presented by Plato, both the prosecution and the defense must offer an option for an appropriate punishment and it is the jury that decides between those two options. In the trial of Socrates, the prosecution's suggested punishment was death and Socrates suggested "punishment" was that he be allowed to feast in the Prytaneum, a city hall where distinguished citizens or guests were celebrated. Socrates's jury chose death.

It would be hard for the two of us with our philosophy PhDs to write a book without making reference to at least something significant in the history of philosophy. In most cases, such examples could be dismissed as quaint but otherwise not suitable given how much the world has changed between then and now. But adopting this Athenian model of punishment selection might help address a number of sentencing problems we see in the US today. Imagine what would happen if a judge or jury had to decide between two punishments, one suggested by the prosecution and one by the defense. The most obvious result is that all statutory punishments, including things like mandatory minimums, would be gone. This change would have a cascade effect across the judicial system, especially if we mandated that defense's punishment suggestion was to be implemented unless unanimous jury or supermajority jury decided in favor of the prosecution's punishment.

On the positive side, it would force prosecutors to think more carefully about what punishment would be appropriate given the circumstances of the crime. They would then have to convince a jury, going in to details like risk to the community, effectiveness of the punishment, cost, comparisons with similar offenders, etc. It would also encourage citizens more generally to think about what punishments are most appropriate. Right now, trials focus mostly on proving guilt, with the punishments predetermined based on guilt. Juries don't even know what the punishment will be when they determine someone's guilt or innocence. While these two things are disconnected in our justice system, that seems to be an obstacle to just outcomes, not something that encourages them.

Not only would prosecutors need to think more carefully about what punishments would be most appropriate, but it would also affect how they approached cases more generally. If we adopted this approach, you'd likely see a significant reduction in the number of cases resolved by plea bargain. Right now, the leverage lies entirely with the prosecution. When someone commits a crime now, even something minor, the prosecution's strategy is to try to charge that person with as many crimes as possible and threaten extremely severe penalties in hopes of having them plea to something. That's a win for the prosecutor, but not a win for justice.

This change would not be without its potential problems. Perhaps you are concerned that this approach to punishment will exacerbate racial disparities in the justice system or that it will clog up the justice system because fewer people will take plea bargains. While the concern for racial disparities is real, there's no reason to think that this approach to sentencing will make these disparities worse. If anything, on an individualized basis, defense attorneys could argue that prosecutors are racists if they seek harsher sentences for black defendants who have been convicted of the same crimes as white defendants, making it more likely that the jury will go against the prosecutor's punishment option. As for clogging the courts, we see this as a possible feature, not a bug. It is not clear that justice is served when roughly 95% of cases end with a plea bargain. Prosecutors would need to decide if it's worth going after minor offenders, and we may need to rewrite laws to eliminate non-harm crimes. We see both of these moves as a step in the right direction.

Conclusion

The American criminal justice is a mess. It's not a mess caused primarily by racism, by inequality, by poverty, or social and familial breakdown, though these problems in various ways contribute and in other ways are *caused* by the problems in the criminal justice system. Rather, a large amount of what makes the American system especially dysfunctional compared to other liberal democracies has to do with perverse incentives created by the way different bureaucracies and offices are funded, by how various officers and politicians win office, and by various rents created inside the locality to county to state to federal divisions.

Fixing the problem means fixing the incentives. In many cases, that means changing the rules about how different people win office, about how things are funded, or about who pays for what. In some cases, it means a more radical rethinking about what criminal justice systems should do. Many problems could instead be dealt with as torts—you hurt someone, you pay *them* restitution, rather than you hurt someone, we all pay to punish you. Too many things are criminalized, period. The system is too complex and some people benefit from the complexity—at the expense of justice. And, finally, incarceration should be a last resort, used only in special cases where certain wrongdoers are ongoing threats. It should not be the default form of punishment.

Our proposals are realistic in one sense and unrealistic in another. They are realistic in the sense that they do not, as far as we can tell, contain built-in bad incentive problems. They do not require a fundamental change in human nature or a sudden influx of good will and altruistic fellow-feeling. If these institutions or policy changes were put in place, they would not in turn incentivize actors to behave the opposite of how we'd hope. But they are unrealistic in the more limited sense that right now, there is little willpower to implement them. Voters are not much peeved by the fact that one in 100 American adults are behind bars, or that our criminal sentences are much harsher than those of our peer countries. Politicians have little incentive to tell voters the truth or run on campaigns promising reforms.

So, there is a barrier to reform, we don't know how to fix that. There's no good general theory of social change available which tells us why some movements for reform succeed while other problems persist for decades with no change. Our best hope is that the ideas present in this book get into the hands of the right people in the right place at the right time … whoever they are. Or, perhaps more plausibly, that they spread over time, so that in the future people are marginally more likely to vote the right way and reward leaders who promise the right reforms.

Notes

1 May 2015.
2 Fox 29 News 2019.
3 Laday 2014.

4 Holder 2018.
5 Donohue and Ludwig 2007; Lin 2009; Lehman 2018; Yglesias 2019.
6 Mello 2018.
7 Ashby 2017.
8 Higgins 2016.
9 Eagly 2010.
10 Thanks to John Hasnas for suggesting this appeal rule.
11 Brennan 2016.
12 Silverglate 2009, 120.
13 Silverglate 2009, 114–22.
14 VanNostrand 2013; Subramanian et al. 2015; City of New York, New York— Independent Budget Office 2017.
15 Roy 2019; Vargas 2019.
16 Criminal Justice Reform Clinic at UCLA 2007.
17 State of New Jersey 216th Legislature 2014.
18 Ibarra 2018.
19 Parmley 2019.
20 New Jersey Judiciary 2018.
21 Ouss and Stevenson 2019.
22 Kight 2018.
23 White 2017.
24 Neff 2018.
25 White 2017.
26 Jacobson 2018.
27 Silverglate 2009, xxxv.
28 Paul 2013, Chapter 10.
29 Eisen et al. 2016.
30 Martin and Grattet 2015; Bischoff 2017; Kollmann 2018, et al.
31 This is the standard cost to house one prisoner for one year in the US, though rates vary dramatically, with costs twice that or more in some places. Mils 2017.
32 Goode 2012.
33 Milliken 2010.
34 Berdejó 2018.
35 National Association of Criminal Defense Lawyers 2018.
36 Pavlo 2018.
37 National Registry of Exonerations 2015.

BIBLIOGRAPHY

Achen, C., and L. Bartels. (2016), *Democracy for Realists*, Princeton, NJ: Princeton University Press.

Adelson, J. (2017), "LaToya Cantrell Campaign Now Says All Traffic Cameras, Not Just New Ones, Would Be Suspended if She's Elected," *New Orleans Advocate*, published July 19, 2017, at: www.theadvocate.com/new_orleans/news/politics/elections/article_4937e22a-6ca4-11e7-85df-93d3e58f3446.html.

Aharoni, E., H. Kleider-Offutt, S. Brosnan, and J. Watzek. (2019), "Justice at Any Cost? The Impact of Cost-benefit Salience on Criminal Punishment Judgements," *Behavioral Sciences & the Law* 31(1): 38–60.

Alexander, M. (2010), *The New Jim Crow*, New York: The New Press.

Allen, M. (2018), "Police-reported Crime Statistics in Canada, 2017," *Statistics Canada*, See: www.150.statcan.gc.ca/n1/pub/85-002-x/2018001/article/54974-eng.htm accessed 4/25/2019.

Alper, M., M. Durose, and J. Markman. (2018), "2018 Update on Prisoner Recidivism: A 9-year Follow-up Period (2005–2014)," *Bureau of Justice Statistics*, See: www.bjs.gov/index.cfm?ty=pbdetail&iid=6266 accessed 4/24/2019.

Althaus, S. (2003), *Collective Preferences in Democratic Politics*, New York: Cambridge University Press.

Anderson, J. (2019), "Majority of Baltimore Homicide Victims in 2018 Were Shot in the Head, Analysis Shows," *The Baltimore Sun*, See: www.baltimoresun.com/news/maryland/crime/bs-md-sun-investigates-homicides-20190102-story.html accessed 4/25/2019.

Andrzejewski, A. (2016), "War Weapons for America's Police Departments: New Data Shows Feds Transfer $2.2B in Military Gear," *Forbes*, See: www.forbes.com/sites/adamandrzejewski/2016/05/10/war-weapons-for-americas-local-police-departments/#7b810c8f4af4 accessed 4/17/2019.

Antecol, H., and K. Bedard. (2002), "Does Single Parenthood Increase the Probability of Teenage Promiscuity, Substance Use, and Crime?" *Journal of Population Economics* 20: 55–71.

Arceneaux, K., and R. M. Stein. (2006), "Who Is Held Responsible When Disaster Strikes? The Attribution of Responsibility for a Natural Disaster in an Urban Election," *Journal of Urban Affairs* 28: 43–53.

Ariely, D. (2012), *The Honest Truth about Dishonesty*, New York: Harper.

Arnsdorf, I. (2016), "Private Prison Company GEO Hires Three Firms," *Politico*, published October 12, 2016, at: www.politico.com/tipsheets/politico-influence/2016/10/private-prison-company-geo-hires-three-firms-216823.

Ashby, C. (2017), "Libertarian Wants End to Governments' Ability to Profit from Fines," *The Daily Sentinel*, published July 9, 2017, at: www.gjsentinel.com/news/articles/liber tarian-wants-end-to-governments-ability-to-pr.

Associated Press. (2017), "At $75,560, Housing a Prisoner in California Now Costs More than a Year at Harvard," *Los Angeles Times*, See: www.latimes.com/local/lanow/la-me-prison-costs-20170604-htmlstory.html accessed 4/15/2019.

Associated Press. (2019), "El Salvador Murder Rate Falls, though Still among Deadliest," See: www.boston25news.com/news/el-salvador-murder-rate-falls-though-still-among-deadliest/898165245 accessed 5/1/2019.

Aubrey, A. (2015), "Whole Foods Says It Will Stop Selling Foods Made with Prison Labor," *NPR.org*, published September 30, 2015, at: www.npr.org/sections/thesalt/2015/09/30/444797169/whole-foods-says-it-will-stop-selling-foods-made-by-prisoners.

Baker, A., et al. (2015), "Beyond the Chokehold: The Path to Eric Garner's Death," *New York Times*, published June 13, 2015, at: www.nytimes.com/2015/06/14/nyregion/eric-garner-police-chokehold-staten-island.html.

Balko, R. (2013), *The Rise of the Warrior Cop*, New York: PublicAffairs.

Balko, R. (2014), "Once Again: Police Work is NOT Getting More Dangerous," *The Washington Post*, See: www.washingtonpost.com/news/the-watch/wp/2014/10/02/once-again-police-work-is-not-getting-more-dangerous/?utm_term=.4266e4b2655a accessed 4/17/2019.

Barshad, A. (2017), "Infamous Cop Louis Scarcella Gets a Hero's Reception," *Intelligencer Magazine*, See: http://nymag.com/intelligencer/2017/10/infamous-cop-louis-scar cella-gets-a-heros-reception.html accessed 4/15/2019.

Barstow, D., and D. Wilson (2006), "Charles of Rape against 3 at Duke are Dropped," *New York Times*, See: www.nytimes.com/2006/12/23/sports/23duke.html accessed 4/15/2019.

Bartels, L. (2003), "Democracy with Attitudes," in *Electoral Democracy*, eds. G. Rabinowitz and M. B. MacKeun. New York: Oxford University Press, pp. 48–82.

BBC. (2019), "World Prison Populations," See: http://news.bbc.co.uk/2/shared/spl/hi/uk/06/prisons/html/nn2page1.stm accessed 3/28/2019.

Beale, C. (1996), "Rural Prisons: An Update," *Rural Development Perspectives* 11: 25–27.

Becker, G. (1968), "Crime and Punishment: An Economic Approach," *The Journal of Political Economy* 76: 169–217.

Becker, G., and K. Murphy. (1988), "A Theory of Rational Addiction," *Journal of Political Economy* 96: 675–700.

Bedau, H. A., and E. Kelly (2015), "Punishment," *Stanford Encyclopedia of Philosophy*, ed. E. N. Zalta. See: http://plato.stanford.edu/entries/punishment/ accessed 9/28/2019.

Benatar, D. (1998), "Corporation Punishment," *Social Theory and Practice* 24: 237–260.

Berdejó, C. (2018), "Criminalizing Race: Racial Disparities in Plea Bargaining," *Boston College Law Review* 59(4): 1187–1249.

Betaud, J.-P. (1988), *The Army of the French Revolution: From Citizen-Soldier to Instrument of Power*, Princeton, NJ: Princeton University Press.

Bhattacharjee, A., J. Dana, and J. Baron. (2017), "Anti-Profit Beliefs: How People Neglect the Societal Benefits of Profit," *Journal of Personality and Social Psychology* 113: 671–696.

Bischoff, L. (2017), "Ohio Now Spends about $2B Annually on Corrections," *Dayton Daily News*, See: www.daytondailynews.com/news/state–regional-govt–politics/prisons-high-cost-fuels-search-for-alternatives/1tu8waMeeTNolUvFOTor4H/ accessed 6/14/2019.

Bottari, M., and J. Persson (2014), "Inmates Die in Droves after Governor Rick Scott Outsources Prison Healthcare," *PR Watch*, published October 16, 2014, at: www.prwatch.org/news/2014/10/12621/inmates-die-droves-after-governor-scott-outsources-prison-healthcare.

Bozelko, C. (2017), "Give Working Prisoners Dignity – And Decent Wages," *National Review*, published January 11, 2017, at: www.nationalreview.com/article/443747/prison-labor-laws-wages-make-it-close-slavery.

Brennan, J. (2004), "Marijuana," in *Social Issues in America*, ed. J. Ciment. Armonk, NY: M. E. Sharpe, pp. 1044–1054.

Brennan, J. (2011), "The Right to a Competent Electorate," *Philosophical Quarterly* 61: 700–724.

Brennan, J. (2016), *Against Democracy*, Princeton, NJ: Princeton University Press.

Brennan, J., and L. Hill. (2014), *Compulsory Voting: For and Against*, New York: Cambridge University Press.

Brennan, J., and P. Jaworski. (2016), *Markets without Limits*, New York: Routledge.

Bridges, T. (2019), "Cantrell's Quest for More Infrastructure Dollars Centers on $160 Million in Tourism Taxes," *New Orleans Advocate*, published January 12, 2019, at: www.theadvocate.com/new_orleans/news/article_ef7a61b6-1604-11e9-a552-2f2ab9a5995b.html.

Bruton, G. D., D. J. Ketchen, Jr., and R. Duane Ireland. (2013), "Entrepreneurship as a Solution to Poverty," *Journal of Business Venturing* 28: 683–689.

Bureau of Justice Statistics. (2017), "Drugs and Crime Facts," published September 26, 2017, at: www.bjs.gov/content/dcf/duc.cfm.

Burnett, S. (2014), "SWAT Teams Treat U.S. Neighborhoods 'Like a War Zone,'" *Time*, See: http://time.com/2916554/aclu-police-militarized-report-swat-war-comes-home/ accessed 4/17/2019.

Calacal, C., and D. Petrohilos (2016), "How Dangerous is it to Be a Cop? Here's What the Data Says," *Think Progress*, See: https://thinkprogress.org/how-dangerous-is-it-to-be-a-cop-heres-what-the-data-says-c07f6a58d8fc/ accessed 4/17/2019.

Campaign Legal Center, et al. v. Federal Election Commission. (2018), "United States District Court for the District of Columbia, Filed June 7, 2018," See: www.fec.gov/resources/cms-content/documents/clc_dc_opinion_060718.pdf accessed 4/30/2019.

CBS News. (2009), "Feds Seize Madoff Penthouse, Wife Evicted," published July 2, 2009, at: www.cbsnews.com/news/feds-seize-madoff-penthouse-wife-evicted/.

Celona, L., et al. (2014a), "Gunman Executes 2 NYPD Cops in Garner 'Revenge'," *New York Post*, published December 20, 2014, at: http://nypost.com/2014/12/20/2-nypd-cops-shot-execution-style-in-brooklyn/.

Celona, L., et al. (2014b), "Arrests Plummet 66% with NYPD in Virtual Work Stoppage," *New York Post*, published December 29, 2014, at: http://nypost.com/2014/12/29/arrests-plummet-following-execution-of-two-cops/.

Chong, D. (2013), "Degrees of Rationality in Politics," in *The Oxford Handbook of Political Psychology*, eds. D. O. Sears and J. S. Levy. New York: Oxford University Press, pp. 96–129.

Cionnaith, F. (2018), Abortion Services Will Be Free, Harris Confirms, *Irish Examiner*, See: www.irishexaminer.com/breakingnews/ireland/abortion-services-will-be-free-harris-confirms-870089.html accessed 5/1/2019.

City of Atlanta, Georgia. (2017a), "City of Atlanta Fiscal Year 2017 Adopted Budget," retrieved September 25, 2017, from: www.atlantaga.gov/Home/ShowDocument?id=23122.

City of Atlanta, Georgia. (2018), "City of Atlanta Fiscal Year 2019 Adopted Budget," retrieved February 15, 2019, from: www.atlantaga.gov/home/showdocument?id=35822.

City of Casper, Wyoming. (2018), "Casper Police Officer Involved Shooting," *City of Casper, Wyoming*, See: http://casperwy.gov/news/news/city_newsroom/casper_police_officer_involved_ shooting accessed 4/15/2019.

City of Chicago, Illinois. (2016), "City of Chicago – 2017 Budget Overview," retrieved September 25, 2017, from: www.cityofchicago.org/content/dam/city/depts/obm/supp_info/2017%20Budget/2017BudgetOverviewFinal.pdf.

City of Chicago, Illinois. (2018), "City of Chicago – Annual Financial Analysis 2017," retrieved February 15, 2019, from: www.chicago.gov/content/dam/city/depts/obm/supp_info/2017%20Budget/AFA_2017.pdf.

City of Detroit, Michigan. (2016), "City of Detroit 2016–2017 Budget in Brief," retrieved September 25, 2017, from: www.detroitmi.gov/Portals/0/docs/budgetdept/Budget%20in%20Brief%20Final%20-%2010%2025%2016_1.pdf?ver=2016-11-18-113645-100.

City of Houston, Texas. (2016), "City of Houston Adopted Operating Budget for the Period July 1, 2016 to June 30, 2017," retrieved September 25, 2017, from: http://houstontx.gov/budget/17budadopt/FY2017_Adopted_Budget.pdf.

City of Mobile, Alabama. (2017), "2017 Budget Message, City of Mobile, Alabama," retrieved September 25, 2017, from: www.cityofmobile.org/citycouncil/images/news/combined_fy2017_proposed_budget.pdf.

City of New Orleans, Louisiana. (2016), "2017 Annual Operating Budget – City of New Orleans," published October 17, 2016, at: www.nola.gov/mayor/budget/documents/2017-budget/2017-proposed-operating-budget-book/.

City of New Orleans, Louisiana. (2017), "City of New Orleans, Louisiana, Comprehensive Annual Financial Report, December 31, 2017," retrieved February 15, 2019, from: http://app.lla.state.la.us/PublicReports.nsf/0/E14959D404DB10A8862582DA00734CB3/$FILE/0001A34E.pdf.

City of New Orleans, Louisiana. (2018), "2019 Annual Operating Budget," published October 24, 2018, at: www.nola.gov/nola/media/Mayor-s-Office/Files/2019-Adopted-Budget-Book_File.pdf.

City of New Orleans, Louisiana. (2019), "Electronic Police Report 2018," See: https://data.nola.gov/Public-Safety-and-Preparedness/Electronic-Police-Report-2018/3m97-9vtw accessed 5/1/2019.

City of New York, New York – Independent Budget Office. (2017), "Letter from Ronnie Lowenstein, Director, to Honorable Rory Lancman, New York City Council," See: https://ibo.nyc.ny.us/iboreports/pretrial-detention-rates-may-2017.pdf accessed 5/3/2019.

City of Waldo, Florida. (2015), "City of Waldo – General Fund Budget 2015," retrieved September 25, 2017, from: http://waldo-fl.com/files/15Budget.pdf.

City of Waldo, Florida. (2016), "City of Waldo – General Fund Budget 2015," retrieved September 25, 2017, from: http://waldo-fl.com/files/16Budget.pdf.

Cohen, G. (2003), "Party over Policy: The Dominating Impact of Group Influence on Political Beliefs," *Journal of Personality and Social Psychology* 85: 808–822.

Cohen, P. (2012), "Single Moms Can't Be Scapegoated for the Murder Rate Anymore," *The Atlantic,* See: www.theatlantic.com/sexes/archive/2012/11/single-moms-cant-be-scapegoated-for-the-murder-rate-anymore/265576/ accessed 5/1/2019.

Conly, S. (2012), *Against Autonomy: Justifying Coercive Paternalism*, New York: Cambridge University Press.

Cook, G., and T. Wilkins. (2016), "Father Shot 2 Officers Who Mistakenly Served Warrant at His Home," *NBC Washington,* See: www.nbcwashington.com/news/local/Father-Shot-2-Officers-Who-Mistakenly-Served-Warrant-at-His-Home-493885861.html accessed 5/1/2019.

Copeland, J. (2012), "Alan Turing: The Codebreaker Who Saved 'Millions of Lives,'" *British Broadcasting Corporation*, See: www.bbc.com/news/technology-18419691 accessed 4/23/2019.

CoreCivic. (2016), "CoreCivic Extends Contract for the McRae Correctional Facility," *Globe Newswire*, published November 15, 2016, at: http://globenewswire.com/news-release/2016/11/15/890117/0/en/CoreCivic-Extends-Contract-for-the-McRae-Correctional-Facility.html.

Corizon. (2017), "About Corizon Health," retrieved on July 15, 2017, from: www.corizonhealth.com/About-Corizon/Locations.

Council of the City of New York, Department of Finance. (2016), "Report on the Fiscal 2017 Executive Budget," published May 24, 2016, at: http://council.nyc.gov/budget/wp-content/uploads/sites/54/2016/05/836-DOF.pdf.

Cowen, T., and A. Tabarrok. (2014), *Principles of Economics*. New York: Worth Publishers.

Crain, N., and W. M. Crain. (2010), "The Impact of Regulatory Cost of Small Firms," See: www.sba.gov/sites/default/files/The%20Impact%20of%20Regulatory%20Costs%20on%20Small%20Firms%20(Full).pdf accessed 5/3/2019.

Crime and Justice News. (2018), "Violent Crime in Rural Areas Rises above U.S. Average," *The Crime Report,* See: https://thecrimereport.org/2018/05/14/rural-violent-crime-rate-rises-above-u-s-average accessed 4/25/2019.

Criminal Justice Reform Clinic at UCLA. (2007), "The Devil in the Details: Bail Bond Contracts in California," *Prison Policy,* See: https://static.prisonpolicy.org/scans/UCLA_Devil%20_in_the_Details.pdf accessed 5/3/2019.

Cullen, J. B., B. A. Jacob, and S. Levitt. (2006), "The Effect of School Choice on Participants: Evidence from Randomized Lotteries," *Econometrica* 74: 1191–1230.

Curry, C. (2015), "Whole Foods, Expensive Cheese, and the Dilemma of Cheap Prison Labor," *Vice*, published July 21, 2015, at: https://news.vice.com/article/whole-foods-expensive-cheese-and-the-dilemma-of-cheap-prison-labor.

D. K. (2014), "Trigger Happy," *The Economist*, See: www.economist.com/democracy-in-america/2014/08/15/trigger-happy?fsrc=scn/tw/te/bl/triggerhappy accessed 4/17/2019.

Dearen, J. (2014), "Infamous Speed Trap Town Investigated over Tickets," *The San Diego Union-Tribune*, published September 2, 2014, at: www.sandiegouniontribune.com/sdut-waldo-suspends-2-police-chiefs-after-quota-claims-2014sep02-story.html.

Deming, D. J. (2011), "Better Schools, Less Crime?" *The Quarterly Journal of Economics* 126: 2063–2115.

Department of Homeland Security. (2018), "US Immigration and Customs Enforcement, Budget Overview, Fiscal Year 2019," retrieved February 15, 2019, from: www.dhs. gov/sites/default/files/publications/U.S.%20Immigration%20and%20Customs% 20Enforcement.pdf.

Desilver, D. (2013), "A Minority of Americans Own Guns, but Just How Many is Unclear," Pew Research Center, June 4, www.pewresearch.org/fact-tank/2013/06/04/a-minority-of-americans-own-guns-but-just-how-many-is-unclear/ accessed 4/25/2019.

Detroit Free Press Staff and Wire Services. (2019), "Number of Detroit Homicides Falls for 2nd Consecutive Year," *Detroit Free Press,* See: www.freep.com/story/news/local/michigan/detroit/2019/01/02/homicides-2018/2461980002/ accessed 4/25/2019.

Dobbie, W., and R. Fryer, Jr. (2015), "The Medium-term Impacts of High-achieving Charter Schools," *Journal of Political Economy* 123: 985–1037.

Doman, M., S. Hutcheon, D. Welch, and K. Taylor. (2018), "China's Frontier of Fear," *ABC News*, (Australia). See: www.abc.net.au/news/2018-11-01/satellite-images-expose-chinas-network-of-re-education-camps/10432924 accessed 4/21/2019.

Donohue, J., and J. Ludwig. (2007), "More Cops," *Brookings*, See: www.brookings.edu/research/more-cops/ accessed 5/2/2019.

Donohue, III, J. J., and S. D. Levitt. (2001), "The Impact of Legalized Abortion on Crime," *The Quarterly Journal of Economics* 116: 379–420.

Doob, A., and C. Webster. (2003), "Sentence Severity and Crime: Accepting the Null Hypotheses," *Crime and Justice* 30(2003): 143–195.

Drug Policy Alliance. (2018), "From Prohibition to Progress: A Status Report on Marijuana Legalization," retrieved August 12, 2018, at: www.drugpolicy.org/legalization-status-report.

Drum, K. (2016), "Lead: America's Real Criminal Element," *Mother Jones*, See: www.mother jones.com/environment/2016/02/lead-exposure-gasoline-crime-increase-children-health/ accessed 5/1/2019.

Drummond-Ayres, B. (1997), "Jury Decides Simpson Must Pay $25 Million in Punitive Award," *The New York Times*, See: www.nytimes.com/1997/02/11/us/jury-decides-simpson-must-pay-25-million-in-punitive-award.html accessed 4/23/2019.

Duff, A. (2013), "Legal Punishment," *Stanford Encyclopedia of Philosophy*, ed. E. N. Zalta, See: http://plato.stanford.edu/entries/legal-punishment/ accessed 9/28/2019.

Durlauf, S., and D. Nagin. (2011), "Imprisonment and Crime," *Criminology & Public Policy* 10(1): 13–54.

Eagle Pass News Leader. (2018), "Texas Police Officer Pulls Gun on Kids Cursing at Him," *Eagle Pass News Leader*, See: www.epnewsleader.com/feed/video-texas-officer-pulls-gun-on-kids-cursing-at-him accessed 4/15/2019.

Eagly, I. V. (2010), "Local Immigration Prosecution: A Study of Arizona Before SB 1070," *UCLA Law Review* 58: 1749.

Egalite, A. J. (2016), "The Competitive Effects of the Louisiana Scholarship Program on Public School Performance," Technical Report. Louisiana Scholarship Program Evaluation Report# 4. *School Choice Demonstration Project*.

Eisen, L. B., J. Austin, J. Cullen, J. Frank, and M. Chettiar. (2016), "How Many Americans Are Unnecessarily Incarcerated?" *Brennan Center for Justice*, See: www. brennancenter.org/publication/how-many-americans-are-unnecessarily-incarcerated accessed 6/14/2019.

Eliahou, M., and C. Zdanowicz. (2018), "A Texas Police Officer Pulled His Gun on a Group of Kids. Now, He's Doing Desk Duty," *CNN*, See: www.cnn.com/2018/07/09/us/texas-police-pulls-gun-on-kids-trnd/index.html accessed 4/15/2019.

Emshwiller, J., and G. Fields. (2011), "Many Failed Efforts to Count Nation's Federal Criminal Laws," *The Wall Street Journal*, See: www.wsj.com/articles/SB10001424052702304319804576389601079728920 accessed 4/23/2019.

Erison, C., M. Lodge, and C. S. Taber. (2014), "Affective Contagion in Effortful Political Thinking," *Political Psychology* 35(2014): 187–206.

Fang, L. (2014), "The Real Reason Pot is Still Illegal," *The Nation*, published July 2, 2014, at: www.thenation.com/article/anti-pot-lobbys-big-bankroll/.

Farrington, D. P., P. A. Langan, and M. Tonry. (eds.) (2004), *Cross-National Studies in Crime and Justice*, Washington, DC: US Bureau of Justice Statistics (NCJ 200988).

Farrington, D. P., P. A. Langan, and P. O. Wikström (1994), "Changes in Crime and Punishment in America, England, and Sweden between the 1980s and 1990s," *Studies on Crime and Crime Prevention* 3 (1994): 103–131.

Federal Bureau of Investigation (FBI). (2017), "What We Investigate," retrieved September 27, 2017, from: www.fbi.gov/investigate/white-collar-crime/asset-forfeiture.

Ferreira, S. (2017), "Portugal's Radical Drugs Policy is Working. Why Hasn't the World Copied it?" *The Guardian,* See: www.theguardian.com/news/2017/dec/05/portugals-radical-drugs-policy-is-working-why-hasnt-the-world-copied-it accessed 4/23/2019.

Feuer, A. (2017), "Despite 7 Scrapped Convictions, Prosecutors Say Ex-Detective Broke No Laws," *The New York Times*, See: www.nytimes.com/2017/05/25/nyregion/louis-scarcella-murder-dismissals.html accessed 4/15/2019.

Fleetwood, B. (2017), "Police Work isn't as Dangerous as You May Think," *Huffington Post*, See: www.huffingtonpost.com/blake-fleetwood/how-dangerous-is-police-w_b_6373798.htm, accessed 4/17/2019.

Flounders, S. (2011), "The Pentagon and Slave Labor in U.S. Prisons," *Global Research*, published February 4, 2013, at: www.globalresearch.ca/the-pentagon-and-slave-labor-in-u-s-prisons/25376.

Flynn, M. (2018), "Florida Police Framed Three Black Men for Burglaries. One was Deported because of it, Suit Says," *The Washington Post*, See: www.washingtonpost.com/news/morning-mix/wp/2018/09/21/florida-police-worried-about-crime-stats-framed-three-black-men-for-burglaries-one-was-deported-because-of-it-suit-says/?utm_term=.d7f076c14794 accessed 4/15/2019.

Foote, C. L., and C. F. Goetz. (2008), "The Impact of Legalized Abortion on Crime: Comment," *The Quarterly Journal of Economics* 123: 407–423.

Forman, Jr., J. (2018), *Locking Up Our Own: Crime and Punishment in Black America*, New York: Farrar, Straus, and Giroux.

Fox 29 News. (2019), "Report Shows Jaw-dropping Decline in Crime in Camden," *Fox 29*, See: www.fox29.com/news/big-drop-in-crime-in-camden accessed 5/2/2019.

Friedersdorf, C. (2016), "Enforcing the Law is Inherently Violent," *The Atlantic*, See: www.theatlantic.com/politics/archive/2016/06/enforcing-the-law-is-inherently-violent/488828/ accessed 4/23/2019.

Friedersdorf, C. (2017), "The Disappearing Right to Earn a Living," *The Atlantic,* See: www.theatlantic.com/business/archive/2017/11/the-right-to-earn-a-living/546071 accessed 5/1/2019.

Fund, J. (2014), "The United States of SWAT?" *National Review*, See: www.nationalreview.com/2014/04/united-states-swat-john-fund/ accessed 4/17/2019.

Galea, S., A. Hamilton, M. L. Hatzenbuehler, K. Keyes, and M. Uddin. (2015), "The Collateral Damage of Mass Incarceration: Risk of Psychiatric Morbidity among Non-incarcerated Residents of High-Incarceration Neighborhoods," *PubMed-NCBI*, See: www.ncbi.nlm.nih.gov/pubmed/25393200 accessed 4/24/2019.

Garfinkel, I., L. Rainwater, and T. Smeeding. (2010), *Wealth and Welfare States: Is America a Laggard or a Leader?* New York: Oxford University Press.

Gendraau, P., C. Goggin, and F. T. Cullen. (1999), *The Effects of Prison Sentences on Recidivism*, Ottawa: Public Works and Government Services Canada.

Gendreau, P., T. Little, and C. Goggin. (1996), "A Meta-Analysis of Adult Offender Recidivism: What Works!," *Criminology* 34: 575–607.

Gentert, T. (2018), "No Charge, No Conviction—But 956 People Still Lose Stuff to Cops," *Michigan Capitol Confidential*, See: www.michigancapitolconfidential.com/no-charge-no-conviction-but-956-people-still-lose-stuff-to-cops accessed 4/15/2019.

Gleaner Staff (The). (2019), "2018 Murders by Divisions … Rural Parishes Lead Tally," *The Gleaner*, See: http://jamaica-gleaner.com/article/news/20190108/2018-murders-divisions-rural-parishes-lead-tally accessed 5/1/2019.

Goldstein, D. (2015), "Too Old to Commit Crime?" *The Marshall Project*, See: www.the marshallproject.org/2015/03/20/too-old-to-commit-crime accessed 4/24/2019.

Goldstein, R., M. Sances, and H. You. (2018), "Exploitative Revenues, Law Enforcement, and the Quality of Government Service," *Urban Affairs Review*, published August 11, 2018, at: https://doi.org/10.1177/1078087418791775.

Goode, E. (2012), "Stronger Hand for Judges in the 'Bazaar' of Plea Deals," *The New York Times*, See: www.nytimes.com/2012/03/23/us/stronger-hand-for-judges-after-rulings-on-plea-deals.html accessed 5/3/2019.

Gramlich, J. (2016), "Voters' Perceptions of Crime Continue to Conflict with Reality," *Pew Research Center*, retrieved February 15, 2018, from: www.pewresearch.org/fact-tank/2016/11/16/voters-perceptions-of-crime-continue-to-conflict-with-reality/.

Grinberg, E. (2017), "Prison Suicides are on the Rise Nationally and it's Pretty Bad in Massachusetts," *CNN*, See: www.cnn.com/2017/04/19/health/prison-suicides-massa chusetts-trnd/index.html accessed 4/24/2019.

Gruberg, S. (2018), "Trump's Executive Order Rewards Private Prison Campaign Donors," retrieved February 15, 2018, from: www.americanprogress.org/issues/immi gration/news/2018/06/28/452912/trumps-executive-order-rewards-private-prison-campaign-donors/.

Hall, A., and V. Mercier. (2017), "Policing for 'profit,'" in *Rethinking Punishment in the Era of Mass Incarceration*, ed. C. Surprenant. New York: Routledge, pp. 209–224.

Hamilton, K. (2016), "A Big Private Prison Operator May Have Illegally Funded a Trump Super PAC," *Business Insider*, published December 21, 2016, at: www. businessinsider.com/geo-group-may-have-illegally-funded-a-trump-super-pac-2016-12.

Hamilton Project. (2019), "Rates of Drug Use and Sales, by Race; Rates of Drug Related Criminal Justice Measures, by Race," retrieved March 28, from: www.hamiltonproject. org/charts/rates_of_drug_use_and_sales_by_race_rates_of_drug_related_criminal_justice.

Hammurabi. (1910), "The Code of Hammurabi," translated by L. W. King, retrieved September 25, 2017, from: http://avalon.law.yale.edu/ancient/hamframe.asp.

Hardin, R. (2009), *How Do You Know?* Princeton, NJ: Princeton University Press.

Harper, C. C., and S. S. McLanahan. (2004), "Father Absence and Youth Incarceration," *Journal of Research on Adolescence* 14: 369–397.

Harris, A. R., and J. A. W. Shaw. (2000), "Looking for Patterns: Race, Class, and Crime," in *Criminology: A Contemporary Handbook*, ed. J. F. Sheley. Belmont, CA: Wadsworth, pp. 129–163.

Hartig, H., and A. Geiger. (2018), "About Six-in-ten Americans Support Marijuana Legalization," *Pew Research Center*, See: www.pewresearch.org/fact-tank/2018/10/08/americans-support-marijuana-legalization/ accessed 4/23/2019.

Hasnas, J. (2017), "The Problem of Punishment," in *Rethinking Punishment in the Era of Mass Incarceration*, ed. C. Surprenant. New York: Routledge, pp. 15–33.

Haughton, A. (2013), "Social Entrepreneurship: Reducing Crime and Improving the Perception of Police Performance within Developing Countries," *International Journal of Entrepreneurship* 17: 61–76.

Hauslohner, A. (2015), "D.C. Council Rejects Corizon Health Contract after Lobbying Battle," *Washington Post*, published April 14, 2015, at: www.washingtonpost.com/local/dc-politics/dc-council-rejects-corizon-health-contract-after-lobbying-battle/2015/04/14/b784c8e2-e222-11e4-81ea-0649268f729e_story.html.

Hawthorne, M. (2015), "Studies Link Childhood Lead Exposure, Violent Crime," *Chicago Tribune*, See: www.chicagotribune.com/news/ct-lead-poisoning-science-met-20150605-story.html accessed 5/1/2019.

Heinz, F. (2018), "Man Armed with Knives Shot, Killed in Confrontation with Garland Police," *NBCDFW*, See: www.nbcdfw.com/news/local/Garland-Police-Investigate-Officer-Involved-Shooting-487803411.html accessed 4/15/2019.

Heitzeg, N. (2009), "Education or Incarceration: Zero Tolerance Policies and the School to Prison Pipeline," *Forum on Public Policy*, See: https://files.eric.ed.gov/fulltext/EJ870076.pdf accessed 5/1/2019.

Higgins, S. (2016), "Obama's Big Bank 'Slush Fund'," *Washington Examiner*, published January 18, 2016, at: www.washingtonexaminer.com/obamas-big-bank-slush-fund/article/2580431.

Hjalmarsson, R., and M. J. Lindquist. (2016), "The Causal Effect of Military Conscription on Crime and the Labor Market," Working Paper, https://ideas.repec.org/p/hhs/gunwpe/0645.html.

Hohmann, L. (2015), "No-Knock Police Raid Ends in Blazing Tragedy," *WorldNetDaily*, See: www.wnd.com/2015/02/no-knock-police-raid-ends-in-blazing-tragedy/ accessed 4/17/2019.

Holder, S. (2018), "What Happened to Crime in Camden?" *City Lab*, See: www.citylab.com/equity/2018/01/what-happened-to-crime-in-camden/549542/5/2/2019.

Horwitz, S. (2015), "From a First Arrest to a Life Sentence," *The Washington Post*, See: www.washingtonpost.com/sf/national/2015/07/15/from-a-first-arrest-to-a-life-sentence/ accessed 5/1/2019.

Howard, M. (2017), *Unusually Cruel: Prisons, Punishment, and the Real American Exceptionalism*, New York: Oxford University Press.

Huemer, M. (2013), *The Problem of Political Authority*, New York: Palgrave Macmillan.

Husak, D. (2009), *Overcriminalization: The Limits of Criminal Law*, New York: Oxford University Press.

Ibarra, R. (2018), "Crime Rates Plunge in New Jersey, and Bail Reform Advocates are Gloating," *WNYC*, See: www.wnyc.org/story/crime-rates-plunge-new-jersey-giving-bail-reform-advocates-chance-gloat/ accessed 5/3/2019.

Ingraham, C. (2014), "White People are More Likely to Deal Drugs, but Black People are More Likely to Get Arrested for it," *The Washington Post*, See: www.

washingtonpost.com/news/wonk/wp/2014/09/30/white-people-are-more-likely-to-deal-drugs-but-black-people-are-more-likely-to-get-arrested-for-it/ accessed 5/3/2019.

Ingraham, C. (2015), "Law Enforcement Took More Stuff from People than Burglars Did Last Year," *Washington Post*, published November 23, 2015, at: www.washington post.com/news/wonk/wp/2015/11/23/cops-took-more-stuff-from-people-than-burglars-did-last-year/.

Ingraham, C. (2016), "The Feds Have Resumed a Controversial Program that Lets Cops Take Stuff and Keep it," *Washington Post*, published March 28, 2016, at: www.washingtonpost.com/news/wonk/wp/2016/03/28/the-feds-have-resumed-a-controversial-program-that-lets-cops-take-stuff-and-keep-it/.

Innocence Project. (2018), "Man's Burglary Convictions Vacated after He was Already Deported," *Innocence Project*, See: www.innocenceproject.org/mans-burglary-convictions-vacated-after-deported/ accessed 4/15/2019.

Institute for Justice. (1991), "Washington D.C. Hair Braiding," *Institute for Justice*, See: https://ij.org/case/taalib-din-abdul-uqdah-v-district-of-columbia-2/ accessed 5/1/2019.

Institute for Justice. (2014), "IJ Untangles Regulations for Natural Hair Braiders," *Institute for Justice*, See: https://ij.org/issues/economic-liberty/braiding/ accessed 5/1/2019.

Iyengar, S., G. Sood, and Y. Lelkes. (2012), "Affect, Not Ideology: A Social Identity Perspective on Polarization," *Public Opinion Quarterly* 76: 405–431.

Iyengar, S., and S. J. Westwood. (2015), "Fear and Loathing across Party Lines: New Evidence on Group Polarization," *American Journal of Political Science* 59: 690–707.

Jacobson, L. (2018), "Are U.S., Philippines the Only Two Countries with Money Bail?" *Politifact California*, See: www.politifact.com/california/statements/2018/oct/09/gavin-newsom/are-us-philippines-only-two-countries-money-bail/ accessed 5/3/2019.

James, R. (2009), "Sheriff Joe Arpaio," *Time*, retrieved March 28, 2019, at: http://content.time.com/time/nation/article/0,8599,1929920,00.html.

Jarrett, C. (2018), "How Prison Changes People," *British Broadcasting Corporation*, See: www.bbc.com/future/story/20180430-the-unexpected-ways-prison-time-changes-people accessed 4/24/2019.

Jeffery, J. (2015), "U.S., Confidence in Police Lowest in 22 Years," *Gallup*, See: https://news.gallup.com/poll/183704/confidence-police-lowest-years.aspx accessed 4/17/2019.

Jenkins, J., S. Rich, and J. Tate. (2019), "992 People Have Been Shot and Killed by Police in 2018," *The Washington Post*, See: www.washingtonpost.com/graphics/2018/national/police-shootings-2018/?utm_term=.6095119466cf accessed 4/17/2019.

Jethani, S. (2013), "Union of the Snake: How California's Prison Guards Subvert Democracy," *Mic*, published May 14, 2013, at: https://mic.com/articles/41531/union-of-the-snake-how-california-s-prison-guards-subvert-democracy#.aIGaVungs.

Jones, G. (2020), *10% Less Democracy*, Stanford, CA: Stanford University Press.

Jonsson, P. (2006), "After Atlanta Raid Tragedy, New Scrutiny of Police Tactics," *The Christian Science Monitor*, See: www.csmonitor.com/2006/1129/p03s03-ussc.html accessed 4/17/2019.

Joyce, T. (2004), "Did Legalized Abortion Lower Crime?" *Journal of Human Resources* 39: 1–28.

Justice Policy Institute. (2011), "Finding Direction: Expanding Criminal Justice Options by considering Policies of Other Nations," *Justice Policy Institute*, Washington, DC. See: www.justicepolicy.org/uploads/justicepolicy/documents/sentencing.pdf, accessed 9/28/2019.

Justice Policy Institute. (2012), "Executive Summary," *Rethinking the Blues: How we Police in the U.S. and at What Cost*, published May 2012, at: www.justicepolicy.org/uploads/justicepolicy/documents/rethinkingtheblues_executive_summary.pdf.

Kahan, D., E. Peters, E. Cantrell Dawson, and P. Slovic. (2013), "Motivated Numeracy and Enlightened Self-Government," *Behavioral Public Policy* 1: 54–86.

Kahneman, D., P. Slovic, and A. Tversky. (eds.) (1982), *Judgment under Uncertainty: Heuristics and Biases*, New York: Cambridge University Press.

Kaste, M. (2018), "Violent Crime Stays Flat Nationally, Louisiana Still Leads States for Murder," *National Public Radio*, See: www.npr.org/2018/09/25/651521938/violent-crime-stays-flat-nationally-louisiana-still-leads-states-for-murder accessed 4/25/2019.

Kavka, G. (1995), "Why Even Angels Would Need Government," *Social Philosophy and Policy* 12: 1–18.

Kearney, M. S., and B. H. Harris. (2014), "Ten Economic Facts about Crime and Incarceration in the United States," Brookings Institute, Washington, DC. Retrieved September 12, 2018, from: www.brookings.edu/research/ten-economic-facts-about-crime-and-incarceration-in-the-united-states/.

Kennedy, D. (2008), *Deterrence and Crime Prevention: Reconsidering the Prospect of Sanction*, New York: Routledge.

Kight, S. (2018), "The For-profit Bail Bond Industry is at War — And Losing," *AXIOS*, See: www.axios.com/bail-bond-industry-jail-ciminal-justice-california-b9536ae0-5373-4163-9e44-fd9038641264.html accessed 5/3/2019.

King, Jr., M. (1963), "Letter from a Birmingham Jail [King, Jr.]," *African Studies Center-University Of Pennsylvania*, See: www.africa.upenn.edu/Articles_Gen/Letter_Birmingham.html accessed 4/23/2019.

Kleiman, M. (2010), *When Brute Force Fails: How to Have Less Crime and Less Punishment*, Princeton, NJ: Princeton University Press.

Kleiner, M. (2017), "The Influence of Occupational Licensing and Regulation," *IZA World of Labor*, See: https://wol.iza.org/uploads/articles/392/pdfs/the-influence-of-occupational-licensing-and-regulation.pdf accessed 5/3/2019.

Kling, A. (2017), *The Three Languages of Politics*, Washington, DC: Cato Institute.

Kollmann, S. (2018), "The Costliest Choice: Economic Impact of Youth Incarceration," *Community Safety & The Future of Prisons*, Vol. 3 (March 2018), See: www.law.northwestern.edu/legalclinic/cfjc/documents/communitysafetymarch.pdf.

Kramer, M. (2014), *Torture and Moral Integrity: A Philosophical Enquiry*, New York: Oxford University Press.

Laday, J. (2014), "Camden County, Metro Police Union Agree to First Contract since Creation of New Department," *South Jersey Times*, See: www.nj.com/camden/2014/11/camden_county_metro_police_union_agree_to_first_contract_since_creation_of_new_department.html accessed 5/2/2019.

Lane, E. (2019), "New Orleans Ends 2018 with 146 Murders, Fewest in Nearly Half a Century," *Nola.com*, See: www.nola.com/crime/2019/01/new-orleans-ends-2018-with-145-murders-fewest-in-nearly-half-a-century.html accessed 4/25/2019.

Langan, P. (1995), "The Racial Disparity in US Drug Arrests," *Bureau of Justice Statistics (BJS) and US Dept of Justice and Office of Justice Programs and United States of America*.

Langan, P., and L. David (2002), "Recidivism of Prisoners Released in 1994," U.S. Department of Justice, Office of Justice Programs, Bureau of Justice Statistics.

Lappi-Seppälä, T., and M. Lehti. (2015), "Cross-Comparative Perspectives on Global Homicide Trends," *Crime and Justice: A Review of Research: Why Crime Rates Fall, and*

Why They Don't, ed. M. Tonry. Chicago, IL: University of Chicago Press, Vol. 43, pp. 135–230.

Larson, D. (2013), "Why Scandinavian Prisons are Superior," *The Atlantic*, September 13, See: www.theatlantic.com/international/archive/2013/09/why-scandinavian-prisons-are-superior/279949/ accessed 4/25/2019.

Latzer, B. (2013), *The Rise and Fall of Violent Crime in America*, New York: Encounter.

Lee, D. S., and J. McCrary (2005), "Crime, Punishment, and Myopia," *National Bureau of Economic Research*, working paper 11491, Cambridge, MA.

Lehman, C. (2018), "More Cops Means Less Crime, Analysis Shows," *The Washington Free Beacon*, See: https://freebeacon.com/issues/cops-means-less-crime-analysis-shows/ accessed 5/2/2019.

Lenta, P. (2015), "Is Corporal Punishment Torturous?" *Journal of Applied Philosophy*, online first edition, doi:10.1111/jap.12134.

Levitt, S. D. (1998), "Why Do Increased Arrest Rates Appear to Reduce Crime: Deterrence, Incapacitation, or Measurement Error?" *Economic Inquiry* 36: 353–372.

Levitt, S. D. (2004), "Understanding Why Crime Fell in the 1990s: Four Factors that Explain the Decline and Six that Do Not," *Journal of Economic Perspectives* 18: 163–190.

Lin, M. (2009), "More Police, Less Crime: Evidence from US State Data," *International Review of Law and Economics* 29(2): 73–80.

Lind, D., and G. Lopez. (2015), "16 Theories for Why Crime Plummeted in the US," *Vox*, See: www.vox.com/2015/2/13/8032231/crime-drop accessed 4/15/2019.

Lind, D., and G. Lopez. (2016), "The Theory: Lead Exposure Caused Crime, and Lead Abatement Efforts Reduced it," *Vox,* See: www.vox.com/2016/1/14/17991876/crime-drop-murder-lead-exposure-gasoline-environment accessed 5/1/2019.

Littlefield, D. (2016), "How O. J. Simpson Trial Introduced Courts to DNA," *The San Diego Union Tribune*, See: www.sandiegouniontribune.com/sdut-oj-simpson-trial-dna-evidence-fx-2016apr16-story.html accessed 4/23/2019.

Lodge, M., and C. Taber. (2013), *The Rationalizing Voter*, New York: Cambridge University Press.

Lopez, G. (2016), "The War on Drugs, Explained," *Vox*, See: www.vox.com/2016/5/8/18089368/war-on-drugs-marijuana-cocaine-heroin-meth accessed 5/1/2019.

Lorei, C. (2018), "Häufigkeiten von polizeilichem Schusswaffengebrauch," p. 5 of "Statistiken zum polizeilichen Schusswaffengebrauch in Deutschland," See: http://schusswaffeneinsatz.de/Statistiken_files/Statistiken.pdf#page=5 accessed 4/15/2019.

Maldonado, C. (2018a), "New Orleans District Attorney Unearths 249 'DA Subpoenas' Issued over Three Years," *The Lens*, See: https://thelensnola.org/2018/07/09/new-orleans-district-attorney-unearths-249-da-subpoenas-issued-over-three-years/ accessed 4/15/2019.

Maldonado, C. (2018b), "Jefferson Parish DA's Repeated Use of Fake Subpoenas Included One Issued to an 11-year-old," *The Lens*, See: https://thelensnola.org/2018/06/06/jeff-das-repeated-use-of-fake-subpoenas-included-one-issued-to-an-11-year-old/ accessed 4/15/2019.

Manski, C., J. Pepper, and Y. Thomas. (1999), "Assessment of Two Cost-Effectiveness Studies on Cocaine Control Policy," *The National Academies Press*, See: www.nap.edu/read/9441/chapter/5 accessed 4/23/2019.

Marcin, T. (2018), "Nearly 20 Percent of Americans Think Interracial Marriage is 'Morally Wrong,' Poll Finds," *Newsweek*, See: www.newsweek.com/20-percent-america-thinks-interracial-marriage-morally-wrong-poll-finds-845608 accessed 4/23/2019.

Marcius, C., and Fanelli, J. (2018), "Dirty Detective Louis Scarcella insists, 'I've done nothing wrong,' despite sending 13 wrongfully convicted people to jail," *Daily News*, See: www.nydailynews.com/new-york/law-punish-detective-louis-scarcella-dirty-tac tics-article-1.4000501 accessed 9/29/19.

Martin, B., and R. Grattet. (2015), "Alternatives to Incarceration in California," *Public Policy Institute of California*, See: www.ppic.org/publication/alternatives-to-incarcer ation-in-california/ accessed 6/14/2019.

May, C. (2015), "Report: Camden Most Dangerous in the U.S.," *NBC Philadelphia*, See: www.nbcphiladelphia.com/news/local/Local-City-Named-Most-Dangerous-in-US-290907701.html accessed 5/2/2019.

McCabe, S. E., et al. (2007), "Race/Ethnicity and Gender Differences in Drug Use and Abuse among College Students," *Journal of Ethnicity in Substance Abuse* 6: 75–95.

Mcconnaughey, J. (2016), "Eyebrow Threading License Requirements Raise Group's Eyebrow," *Business Insider*, See: www.businessinsider.com/ap-eyebrow-threading-license-requirements-raise-groups-eyebrow-2016-8 accessed 5/1/2019.

McShane, M. (2012), "D.C. Public Schools Grossly Under-Reports Spending," *Huffing-ton Post*, See: www.huffingtonpost.com/michael-mcshane/dc-public-schools-gros sly_b_1638663.html accessed 5/1/2019.

Mello, C. (2018), "More Cops, Less Crime," *Princeton University*, See: www.princeton. edu/~smello/papers/cops.pdf accessed 5/2/2019.

Milanovic, B. (2010), *The Haves and Have Nots*, New York: Basic Books.

Milliken, P. (2010), "Gains: Justice System 'Would Grind to a Halt' without Plea Bar-gains," *The Vindicator*, See: www.vindy.com/news/2010/nov/14/gains-justice-system-8216would-grind-to-/ accessed 5/3/2019.

Mils, E. (2017), "How Much Does it Cost to Send Someone to Prison?" *Marketplace*, See: www.marketplace.org/2017/05/15/world/how-much-does-it-cost-send-someone-prison accessed 5/3/2019.

Miron, J. (1999), "Violence and US Prohibitions of Drugs and Alcohol," *American Law and Economics Review* 1: 78–114.

Moore, D. (2006), "Crime Rate Lower in United States, Canada than in Britain," *Gallup*, See: https://news.gallup.com/poll/21346/crime-rate-lower-united-states-canada-than-britain.aspx accessed 4/17/2019.

Moskos, P. (2011), *In Defense of Flogging*, New York: Basic Books.

Munger, M. (2017), "Government Failure and Market Failure," in *The Routledge Hand-book of Libertarianism*, eds. J. Brennan, B. van der Vossen, and D. Schmidtz. New York: Routledge, pp. 342–357.

Mutz, D. (2006), *Hearing the Other Side*, Cambridge: Cambridge University Press.

Nabone, J. (2008), "Donovan McNabb Turns Ball over Four Times and Does Not Know the Rules in 13-13 Tie with Bengals," *New Jersey Local News*, See: www. nj.com/eagles/index.ssf/2008/11/donovan_mcnabb_turns_ball_over.html accessed 4/23/2019.

Nagin, D. S. (2013), "Deterrence in the Twenty-First Century," in *Crime and Justice: A Review of Research, Vol 42: Crime and Justice in America, 1975–2025*, ed. M. Tonry. Chicago, IL: University of Chicago Press, pp. 199–263.

Naicker, N. (2018), "Is There a Relationship between Lead Exposure and Aggressive Behavior in Shooters?" *National Institute of Health*, See: www.ncbi.nlm.nih.gov/pmc/articles/PMC6068756/ accessed 4/25/2019.

National Association of Criminal Defense Lawyers. (2018), "The Trial Penalty: The Sixth Amendment Right to Trial on the Verge of Extinction and How to Save It," See: www.nacdl.org/trialpenaltyreport/ accessed 5/3/2019.

National Gang Center. (2013), "National Youth Gang Survey Analysis," See: www.natio nalgangcenter.gov/Survey-Analysis/Measuring-the-Extent-of-Gang-Problems accessed 5/1/2019.

National Registry of Exonerations. (2015), "Innocents Who Plead Guilty," *University of Michigan Law*, See: www.law.umich.edu/special/exoneration/Documents/NRE. Guilty.Plea.Article1.pdf accessed 5/3/2019.

Neate, R. (2016), "Welcome to Jail Inc: How Private Companies Make Money off US Prisons," *The Guardian*, published June 16, 2016, at: www.theguardian.com/us-news/ 2016/jun/16/us-prisons-jail-private-healthcare-companies-profit.

Neff, J. (2018), "Petty Charges, Princely Profits," *The Marshall Project*, See: www.themar shallproject.org/2018/07/13/petty-charges-princely-profits accessed 5/3/2019.

New England Historical Society. (2018), "Way More than the Scarlet Letter: Puritan Punishments," *New England Historical Society*, See: www.newenglandhistoricalsociety. com/way-more-than-the-scarlet-letter-puritan-punishments/ accessed 4/23/2019.

Nkomo, P. (2018), "The Association between Environmental Lead Exposure with Aggressive Behavior, and Dimensionality of Direct and Indirect Aggression during Mid-adolescence: Birth to Twenty Plus Cohort," *ScienceDirect*, See: www.sciencedir ect.com/science/article/pii/S0048969717321356 accessed 4/25/2019.

North Carolina State Bar vs. Mike Nifong, Attorney. (2006), See: web.archive.org/web/ 20090327105941/www.ncbar.com/Nifong%20Findings.pdf accessed 4/15/2019.

Nozick, R. (1974), *Anarchy, State, and Utopia*, New York: Basic Books.

O'Donoghue, J. (2017), "Sheriff: Louisiana's Early Release of Prisoners Means Loss of 'The Ones Who Can Work,'" *Times-Picayune*, published October 12, 2017, at: www. nola.com/politics/index.ssf/2017/10/louisiana_good_prisoners.html.

O'Neill, A. (2014), "Speed Trap City Accused of Corruption, Threatened with Extinction," *CNN*, published March 9, 2014, at: www.cnn.com/2014/03/09/us/hamp ton-florida-corruption/.

Open Justice. (2017), "Deaths in Custody from 2008 to 2017," *Open Justice*, See: https:// openjustice.doj.ca.gov/2017/death-in-custody accessed 4/24/2019.

Organisation for Economic Co-operation and Development. (2017), "School Choice and School Vouchers: An OECD Perspective," See: www.oecd.org/education/ School-choice-and-school-vouchers-an-OECD-perspective.pdf accessed 5/3/2019.

Ouss, Am., and M. Stevenson. (2019), "Evaluating the Impacts of Eliminating Prosecu-torial Requests for Cash Bail," *SSRN*, See: https://papers.ssrn.com/sol3/papers.cfm? abstract_id=3335138 accessed 5/3/2019.

Ovalle, D., C. Rabin, and J. Weaver. (2018), "The Chief Wanted Perfect Stats, so Cops Were Told to Pin Crimes on Black People," *Miami Herald*, See: www.miamiherald. com/news/local/crime/article213647764.html accessed 4/15/2019.

Ovalle, D., and J. Weaver. (2018), "For Framing Innocent Black Men, a Florida Police Chief Gets Three Years in Prison," *Miami Herald*, See: www.miamiher ald.com/news/local/community/miami-dade/article222205540.html accessed 4/ 15/2019.

Parker, K. F. (2015), "The African-American Entrepreneur–Crime Drop Relationship: Growing African-American Business Ownership and Declining Youth Violence," *Urban Affairs Review* 51: 751–780.

Parmley, S. (2019), "Two Years Into Bail Reform, Pretrial Detention Much Lower, AOC Report Says," *New Jersey Law Journal*, See: www.law.com/njlawjournal/2019/04/03/two-years-into-bail-reform-pretrial-detention-much-lower-aoc-report-says/?slreturn=20190328122859 accessed 5/3/2019.

Paul, R. (2013), *Government Bullies: How Everyday Americans are Being Harassed, Abused, and Imprisoned by the Feds*, New York: Center Street.

Pavlo, W. (2018), "Are Innocent People Pleading Guilty? A New Report Says Yes," *Forbes*, See: www.forbes.com/sites/walterpavlo/2018/07/31/are-innocent-people-pleading-guilty-a-new-report-says-yes/#67cdec745193 accessed 5/3/2019.

Pease, R. (2012), "Alan Turing: Inquest's Suicide Verdict 'Not Supportable,'" *British Broadcasting Corporation*, See: www.bbc.com/news/science-environment-18561092 accessed 4/23/2019.

Perlstein, M. (2018), "Bail Out: Rape Suspect among 100s of Arrestees Freed from Jail with Help from Mayor's Aide," *WWL-TV*, See: www.wwltv.com/article/news/investigations/bail-out-rape-suspect-among-100s-of-arrestees-freed-from-jail-with-help-from-mayors-aide/289-604934151 accessed 4/24/2019.

Perry, M. (2015), "Milton Friedman Interview from 1991 on America's War on Drugs," *American Enterprise Institution,* See: www.aei.org/publication/milton-friedman-interview-from-1991-on-americas-war-on-drugs/ accessed 4/23/2019.

Pew Research Center. (2017), "The Partisan Divide on Political Values Grows Even Wider," *Pew Research Center U.S. Politics and Policy,* See: www.people-press.org/2017/10/05/5-homosexuality-gender-and-religion/ accessed 4/23/2019.

Pfaff, J. (2017), *Locked In: The True Causes of Mass Incarceration and How to Achieve Real Reform*, New York: Basic Books.

Pitts, L. (2007), "From Living Hell to Living Well: Atlanta Discovers What Works," *The Seattle Times*, See: www.seattletimes.com/opinion/from-living-hell-to-living-well-atlanta-discovers-what-works accessed 5/1/2019.

Possley, M. (2018), "Shawn Williams, the National Registry of Exonerations," See: www.law.umich.edu/special/exoneration/Pages/casedetail.aspx?caseid=5358 accessed 4/15/2019.

Prison Legal News. (1993), "AT&T Exploits Prison Labor," published April 15, 1993, at: www.prisonlegalnews.org/news/1993/apr/15/att-exploits-prison-labor/.

Prison Policy Initiative. (2017a), "States of Incarceration: The Global Context," retrieved August 12, 2018, from: www.prisonpolicy.org/global/.

Prison Policy Initiative. (2017b), "Following the Money of Mass Incarceration," retrieved August 12, 2018, from: www.prisonpolicy.org/reports/money.html.

Prison Policy Initiative. (2019a), "Millions of Children Have Fathers behind Bars," retrieved March 28, from: www.prisonpolicy.org/graphs/childrenfathersinc.html.

Prison Policy Initiative. (2019b), "Mass Incarceration: The Whole Pie 2019," retrieved March 28, from: www.prisonpolicy.org/reports/pie2019.html.

Radford, R. A. (1945), "The Economic Organization of a P.O.W. Camp," *Economica* 12: 189–201.

Rapanut, K. (2018), "Man Shot by Phoenix Police Officer Was Holding Replica Handgun," *azcentral*, See: www.azcentral.com/story/news/local/phoenix-breaking/2018/07/10/man-shot-phoenix-officer-near-seventh-st-greenway-parkway-had-replica-handgun/771902002/ accessed 4/15/2019.

Rasinki, K. A. (1989), "The Effect of Question Wording on Public Support for Government Spending," *Public Opinion Quarterly* 53: 388–394.

Reckdahl, K. (2014), "Mass Incarceration's Collateral Damage: The Children Left Behind," *The Nation*, See: www.thenation.com/article/mass-incarcerations-collateral-damage-children-left-behind/ accessed 4/24/2019.

Rector, R. (2014), "How Welfare Undermines Marriage and What to Do about it," *The Heritage Foundation*, See: www.heritage.org/welfare/report/how-welfare-undermines-marriage-and-what-do-about-it accessed 5/1/2019.

Reilly, R., and S. Knafo (2014), "Law Enforcement Lobby Quietly Tries to Kill Sentencing Reform," *Huffington Post*, published April 3, 2014, at: www.huffingtonpost.com/2014/04/02/sentencing-reform-opposition_n_5065403.html.

Rivers, E. (2017), "Re-entry into Society, or Back to Prison?" *USA Today*, See: www.usatoday.com/story/opinion/policing/reentry/column/2017/12/29/reentry-incarceration-corruption-prison-barriers-recidivism-policing-usa/979903001/ accessed 4/24/2019.

Roberts, A. (2014), "By the Numbers: Guns in America," *CNN*, See: www.cnn.com/2012/08/09/politics/btn-guns-in-america/index.html accessed 4/17/2019.

Rosenberg, A., A. K. Groves, and K. M. Blankenship. (2017), "Comparing Black and White Drug Offenders: Implications for Racial Disparities in Criminal Justice and Reentry Policy and Programming," *Journal of Drug Issues* 47: 132–142.

Roy, Y. (2019), "Lawmakers Targeting Bail, Trial Overhauls, while DAs Say Slow Down," *Newsday*, See: www.newsday.com/news/region-state/new-york-legislature-crime-bills-1.27633785 accessed 5/3/2019.

Sall, D. (2015), "9 Top Reasons for Poverty in the United States," *Life and My Finances,* See: http://lifeandmyfinances.com/2015/11/9-top-reasons-for-poverty-in-the-united-states/ accessed 5/1/2019.

Sances, M., and H. You. (2017), "Who Pays for Government? Representation and Exploitative Revenue Sources," *The Journal of Politics* 79(3): 1090–11094.

Sanderson, S. (2018), "Prosecutor Attributes Spate of Police Shootings in Casper to 'Blaze of Glory Mentality' among Suspects," *Casper Sun Tribune*, See: https://trib.com/news/local/crime-and-courts/prosecutor-attributes-spate-of-police-shootings-in-casper-to-blaze/article_5f6a9ef3-8721-5dc3-b184-b12b048fd13c.html accessed 4/15/2019.

Sawyer, W. (2017), "How Much Do Incarcerated People Earn in Each State?" *Prison Policy Initiative*, published April 10, 2017, at: www.prisonpolicy.org/blog/2017/04/10/wages/.

Schank, K. (2017), "What's in a Name? East Lake Meadows and Little Vietnam," *Atlanta Studies*, See: www.atlantastudies.org/2017/03/16/whats-in-a-name-east-lake-meadows-and-little-vietnam/ accessed 5/1/2019.

Schmidtz, D. (2001), "A Place for Cost-Benefit Analysis," *Philosophical Issues* 11: 148–171.

Schnittker, J., K. Turney, and C. Wildeman. (2012), "Those They Leave Behind: Paternal Incarceration and Maternal Instrumental Support," *Wiley Online Library*, See: https://onlinelibrary.wiley.com/doi/full/10.1111/j.1741-3737.2012.00998.x accessed 4/24/2019.

Schrank, D. (2019), "Murders in Mexico Rise by a Third in 2018 to New Record," *Reuter*, See: www.reuters.com/article/us-mexico-violence/murders-in-mexico-rise-by-a-third-in-2018-to-new-record-idUSKCN1PF27J accessed 4/25/2019.

Shackford, S. (2018), "Police Seized Property of Close to 1,000 People in Michigan— Without Ever Convicting Them of Crimes," *Reason*, See: https://reason.com/2018/07/11/police-seized-property-of-close-to-1000 accessed 4/15/2019.

Shaw, E. (2016), "Where Local Governments are Paying Bills with Police Fines," *Sunlight Foundation*, published September 26, 2016, at: https://sunlightfoundation.com/2016/09/26/where-local-governments-are-paying-the-bills-with-police-fines/.

Sheffield, R., and R. Rector. (2011), "Understanding Poverty in the United States: Surprising Facts about America's Poor," retrieved September 12, 2018, from: www.heritage.org/poverty-and-inequality/report/understanding-poverty-the-united-states-surprising-facts-about.

Shenon, P. (1994), "A Flogging Sentence Brings a Cry of Pain in the U.S.," *The New York Times*, March 16.

Sibilla, N. (2015), "Veteran Loses $60,000 to Police, Despite Lack of Criminal Charges," *Forbes*, published April 16, 2015, at: www.forbes.com/sites/instituteforjustice/2015/04/16/veteran-forfeiture-nebraska/.

Silverglate, H. (2009), *Three Felonies a Day*, New York: Encounter.

Simler, K., and R. Hanson. (2018), *The Elephant in the Brain*, New York: Oxford Universuty Press.

Singer, P. (1989), "All Animals are Equal," in *Environmental Ethics: What Really Matters, What Really Works, 2nd Edition*, ed. D. Schmidtz. Oxford: Oxford University Press, 2011, pp. 49–58.

Siriram, A. (2011), "Pro-legalization Speaker Dominates Debate," *The Brown Daily Herald*, See: www.browndailyherald.com/2011/11/10/prolegalization-speaker-dominates-debate accessed 4/23/2019.

Skarbek, D. (2014), *The Social Order of the Underworld: How Prison Gangs Govern the American Penal System*, New York: Oxford University Press.

Sledge, M. (2018), "'Freedom Fund' Bails Out 100s of New Orleans Defendants, Drawing Praise – And Criticism," *The New Orleans Advocate*, See: www.theadvocate.com/new_orleans/news/courts/article_4b981330-d195-11e8-841f-47fdd1e4ebb6.html accessed 4/24/2019.

Somin, I. (2013), *Democracy and Political Ignorance*, Stanford, CA: Stanford University Press.

State of Hawaii, Department of Attorney General. (2016), "Annual Report of Proceedings under the Hawaii Omnibus Criminal Forfeiture Act," retrieved September 26, 2017, from: http://ag.hawaii.gov/afp/files/2016/04/2014-2015-Proceedings-Under-the-Hawaii-Omnibus-Criminal-Forfeiture-Act.pdf.

State of Louisiana Department of Agriculture & Forestry. (2019), "Louisiana Horticulture Commission," See: www.ldaf.state.la.us/ldaf-programs/horticulture-programs/louisiana-horticulture-commission/ accessed 5/3/2019.

State of New Jersey 216th Legislature. (2014), "An Act Concerning Court Administration, Supplementing Titles 2A and 2B of the New Jersey Statutes, and amending P.L. 1995, c. 325," See: www.njleg.state.nj.us/2014/Bills/PL14/31_.PDF accessed 5/3/2019.

State of New Jersey Judiciary. (2018), "Report to the Governor and the Legislature," *New Jersey Courts*, See: https://njcourts.gov/courts/assets/criminal/2018cjrannual.pdf?c=taP accessed 5/3/2019.

State of New Jersey Office of the Attorney General. (2019), "Application for a Locksmith License," See: www.njconsumeraffairs.gov/fbl/Applications/Application-for-a-Locksmith-License.pdf accessed 5/3/2019.

Statista. (2018), "Number of Reported and Nonnegligent Manslaughter Cases in the United States from 1990 to 2017," See: www.statista.com/statistics/191134/reported-murder-and-nonnegligent-manslaughter-cases-in-the-us-since-1990/ accessed 5/1/2019.

Statista. (2019), "Crime Clearance Rate in the United States in 2017, by Type," See: www.statista.com/statistics/194213/crime-clearance-rate-by-type-in-the-us/ accessed 4/25/2019.

Subramanian, R., R. Delaney, S. Roberts, N. Fishman, and P. McGarry. (2015), "Incarceration's Front Door: The Misuse of Jails in America," See: https://storage.google apis.com/vera-web-assets/downloads/Publications/incarcerations-front-door-the-misuse-of-jails-in-america/legacy_downloads/incarcerations-front-door-report_02. pdf accessed 5/3/2019.

Surprenant, C. (2019), "Are There Alternatives to Mass Incarceration?" *American Public Philosophy Institute*, See: https://appii.org/chris-surprenant-are-there-alternatives-to-mass-incarceration-2/ accessed 4/25/2019.

Svorny, S. (2004), "Licensing Doctors: Do Economists Agree?" *Econ Journal Watch* 1: 279–305.

Swan, R. (2016), "Alameda County Officials to Choose Jail Health Care Provider," *San Francisco Chronicle*, published August 4, 2016, at: www.sfchronicle.com/bayarea/art icle/Alameda-County-officials-to-choose-jail-health-9123755.php.

Taber, C., and E. Young. (2013), "Political Information Processing," *Huddy, Sears, and Levy* 2013: 525–558.

Taibbi, M. (2014), "The NYPD's 'Work-Stoppage' is Surreal," *Rolling Stone*, published December 31, 2014, at: www.rollingstone.com/politics/news/the-nypds-work-stop page-is-surreal-20141231.

Tajfel, H. (1981), *Human Groups and Social Categories*, New York: Cambridge University Press.

Tajfel, H. (1982), *Social Identity and Intergroup Relations*, Cambridge: Cambridge University Press.

Tajfel, H., and J. C. Turner. (1979), "An Integrative Theory of Intergroup Conflict," in *The Social Psychology of Intergroup Relations*, eds. W. G. Austin and S. Worchel. Monterey, CA: Brooks-Cole, 33–47.

Tengs, T., et al. (1995), "Five Hundred Life-Saving Interventions and Their Cost Effectiveness," *Risk Analysis* 15: 369–390.

TheismComics. (2016), "Marijuana Ruins Lives," *Funny Junk*, See: https://funnyjunk. com/Marijuana+ruins+lives/funny-pictures/6129757/ accessed 4/23/2019.

Thorpe, R. (2015), "Perverse Politics: The Persistence of Mass Imprisonment in the 21st Century," *Perspectives on Politics* 13: 618–637.

Toner, C. (2014), "Campaign Booster for Alabama Gov. Bentley was Lobbyist for Corizon, Prison Health Care Contractor Targeted in Lawsuit," *AL.com*, published August 21, 2014, at: www.al.com/news/index.ssf/2014/08/campaign_booster_for_a labama_g.html.

Town of Olla, Louisiana. (2017), "Town of Olla Budget, 2014–2018," published April 28, 2017, at: www.townofolla.com/wp-content/uploads/2014/11/Copy-of-Consolidated-Budget-2016-2017-4.18.17.xlsx.

UNICOR. (2016a), "Federal Prison Industries, Inc., Fiscal Year 2016, Annual Management Report," published November 15, 2016, at: www.unicor.gov/publications/ reports/FY2016_AnnualMgmtReport.pdf.

UNICOR. (2016b), *80 Years of New Beginnings*, retrieved September 28, 2017, from: www.unicor.gov/Publications/Corporate/CATC6500_FINAL_20160114.pdf.

UNICOR. (2017a), "Schedule of Products and Services," retrieved September 27, 2017, from: www.unicor.gov/SOPAlphaList.aspx.

UNICOR. (2017b), "FPI General Overview FAQs," retrieved September 27, 2017, from: www.unicor.gov/FAQ_General.aspx#4.

UNICOR. (2017c), "Contact Center Solutions," retrieved September 27, 2017, from: www.unicor.gov/shopping/ViewCat_m.asp?idCategory=1429&iStore=UNI.

UNICOR. (2017d), "Contract Manufacturing Opportunities," retrieved September 27, 2017, from: www.unicor.gov/PieProgram.aspx.

UNICOR. (2017e), "Fact or Fiction," retrieved September 27, 2017, from: www.unicor.gov/fact_v_fiction.aspx.

United States of America v. $63,530.00 in United States Currency. (2015), "United States Court of Appeals for the Eighth Circuit," filed March 23, 2015, at: http://media.ca8.uscourts.gov/opndir/15/03/141787P.pdf.

United States Sentencing Commission. (2017), "Demographic Differences in Sentencing: An Update to the 2012 *Booker Report*," retrieved March 28, 2019, from: www.ussc.gov/sites/default/files/pdf/research-and-publications/research-publications/2017/20171114_Demographics.pdf.

US Census Bureau. (2018), "Historical Poverty Table 2, 2010 Census," See: www2.census.gov/programs-surveys/cps/tables/time-series/historical-poverty-people/hstpov2.xls accessed 4/15/2019.

US Department of Agriculture (USDA). (2017), "Supplemental Nutritional Assistance Program Participation and Costs," retrieved September 25, 2017, from: https://fns-prod.azureedge.net/sites/default/files/pd/SNAPsummary.pdf.

US Department of Education. (1998), "Median Family Income," See: https://nces.ed.gov/pubs98/yi/yi16.pdf accessed 4/5/2019.

US Department of Justice. (2015), "Asset Forfeiture Program – FY2014 Hawaii," published March 13, 2015, at: www.justice.gov/afp/fy2014-hawaii.

US Department of Justice. (2016), "Phasing Out Our Use of Private Prisons," published August 18, 2016, at: www.justice.gov/archives/opa/blog/phasing-out-our-use-private-prisons.

US Department of Justice. (2017a), "Equitable Sharing Program," retrieved on September 26, 2017, from: www.justice.gov/criminal-afmls/file/817436/download.

US Department of Justice. (2017b), "Asset Forfeiture Program, FY 2017 Performance Budget, Congressional Justification," retrieved on August 12, 2018, from: www.justice.gov/jmd/file/821291/download.

US Department of Justice. (2017c), "Commutations Granted by President Barack Obama (2009–2017)," See: www.justice.gov/pardon/obama-commutations accessed 5/1/2019.

US Department of Justice, Office of the Inspector General. (2016), "Review of the Federal Bureau of Prisons' Monitoring of Contract Prisons," published August 31, 2016, at: https://oig.justice.gov/reports/2016/e1606.pdf.

US Department of Labor. (2010), "Fact Sheet #71: Internship Programs under the Fair Labor Standards Act," published April 2010, retrieved September 27, 2017, from: www.dol.gov/whd/regs/compliance/whdfs71.pdf.

US Federal Bureau of Investigation. (2018), "2017 – Crime in the United States, Violent Crime," See: https://ucr.fbi.gov/crime-in-the-u.s/2017/crime-in-the-u.s.-2017/topic-pages/violent-crime accessed 5/1/2019.

VanNostrand, M. (2013), "New Jersey Jail Population Analysis," See: www.drugpolicy.org/sites/default/files/New_Jersey_Jail_Population_Analysis_March_2013.pdf accessed 5/3/2019.

Vargas, R. (2019), "Cannizzaro Rails against Incarceration Reduction Efforts, Saying They Threaten Pubic Safety," *The Advocate*, See: www.theadvocate.com/new_or leans/news/crime_police/article_52868694-2998-11e9-8c68-7f5ea6a4b208.html accessed 5/3/2019.

Vera Institute. (2016), "Prison Spending in 2015," See: www.vera.org/publications/ price-of-prisons-2015-state-spending-trends/price-of-prisons-2015-state-spending-trends/price-of-prisons-2015-state-spending-trends-prison-spending accessed 4/25/2019.

Verner, B. (2019), "Homicides in the City of St. Louis Strikes 186 in 2018," *5 on your Side*, See: www.ksdk.com/article/news/crime/homicides-in-the-city-of-st-louis-strikes-186-in-2018/63-41609c96-2fe9-4632-a6eb-b48cc3166e8d accessed 4/25/2019.

Wagner, P. (2014), "Incarceration in America: Past and Present: A Panel with Three Leading Scholars," published April 9, 2014, at: www.prisonersofthecensus.org/news/2014/04/09/yale-panel/.

Wagner, P., and B. Rabuy. (2017a), "Following the Money of Mass Incarceration," *Prison Policy Initiative*, published January 25, 2017, at: www.prisonpolicy.org/reports/money.html.

Wagner, P., and B. Rabuy. (2017b), "Mass Incarceration: The Whole Pie 2017," *Prison Policy Initiative*, published March 14, 2017, at: www.prisonpolicy.org/reports/pie2017.html.

Wagner, P., and A. Walsh. (2016), "States of Incarceration: The Global Context 2016," *Prison Policy Initiative*, published June 16, 2016, at: www.prisonpolicy.org/global/2016.html.

Walsh, B., and R. Reilly. (2017), "Jeff Sessions Kills DOJ Settlement Practice that Funded Community Organizations," *Huffington Post*, published June 8, 2017, at: www.huffingtonpost.com/entry/jeff-sessions-kills-doj-settlement-practice-that-funded-community-organizations_us_59371177e4b0aba888b989e4.

Walsh, S. (2013), "All Locked Up," *Philadelphia Inquirer*, published February 7, 2013, at: www.philly.com/philly/news/local/20130207_ALL_LOCKED_UP.html.

Warren, J. (2008), "One in 100: Behind Bars in America 2008," *Pew Center on the States*, See: www.pewtrusts.org/~/media/legacy/uploadedfiles/wwwpewtrustsorg/reports/sentencing_and_corrections/onein100pdf.pdf.

Washington Post. (2018a), "Fatal Force," See: www.washingtonpost.com/graphics/national/police-shootings-2017/ accessed 4/25/2019.

Washington Post. (2018b), "Murder with Impunity," See: www.washingtonpost.com/graphics/2018/investigations/unsolved-homicide-database accessed 4/25/2019.

Washington Post. (2019), "Fatal Force," See: www.washingtonpost.com/graphics/2018/national/police-shootings-2018/ accessed 4/25/2019.

Weaver, J. (2018a), "Haitian Man Served Five Years after Getting Framed. Now, He's Suing Biscayne," *Miami Herald*, See: www.miamiherald.com/latest news/art icle218625710.html accessed 4/15/2019.

Weaver, J. (2018b), "Another Former Biscayne Park Cop is Going to Prison for False Arrests of Black People," *Miami Herald*, See: www.miamiherald.com/news/local/art icle220219750.html accessed 4/15/2019.

Westen, D. (2008), *The Political Brain*, New York: Perseus Books.

Westen, D., P. S. Blagov, K. Harenski, C. Kilts, and S. Hamann. (2006), "The Neural Basis of Motivated Reasoning: An fMRI Study of Emotional Constraints on Political

Judgment During the U.S. Presidential Election of 2004," *The Journal of Cognitive Neuroscience* 18: 1947–1958.

White, G. (2017), "Who Really Makes Money off of Bail Bonds?" *The Atlantic*, See: www.theatlantic.com/business/archive/2017/05/bail-bonds/526542/5/3/2019.

Wikipedia. (2019), "List of Countries by Intentional Homicide Rate," See: https://en.wiki pedia.org/wiki/List_of_countries_by_intentional_homicide_rate accessed 5/1/2019.

Wildeman, C. (2010), "Paternal Incarceration and Children's Physically Aggressive Behaviors: Evidence from the Fragile Families and Child Wellbeing Study," *Oxford Academic*, See: https://academic.oup.com/sf/article-abstract/89/1/285/2235254 accessed 4/24/2019.

Williams, J. (2018), "Cantrell Hints at Compromise on Traffic Cameras, Says School Zone Cameras OK but with Limits," *The New Orleans Advocate*, published on July 7, 2018, at: www.theadvocate.com/new_orleans/news/article_7c9e5c4c-8086-11e8-959e-ff21875d3d46.html.

Williams, P. (2016), "Are Middle Tennessee Policies Profiting Off Drug Trade?" *NewsChannel5*, published April 11, 2016, at: www.newschannel5.com/news/newschannel-5-investi gates/policing-for-profit/are-middle-tennessee-police-profiting-off-drug-trade/.

Winter, C. (2008), "What Do Prisoners Make for Victoria's Secret?" *Mother Jones*, July/ August 2008, retrieved September 27, 2017, from: www.motherjones.com/politics/ 2008/07/what-do-prisoners-make-victorias-secret/.

Yglesias, M. (2019), "The Case for Hiring More Police Officers," *Vox*, See: www.vox. com/policy-and-politics/2019/2/13/18193661/hire-police-officers-crime-criminal-justice-reform-booker-harris accessed 5/2/2019.

Young, A. (2010), "BP Hires Prison Labor to Clean up Spill while Costal Residents Struggle," *The Nation*, published July 21, 2010, at: www.thenation.com/article/bp-hires-prison-labor-clean-spill-while-coastal-residents-struggle/.

Zapotosky, M. (2017), "Justice Department Will Again Use Private Prisons," *Washington Post*, published February 23, 2017, at: www.washingtonpost.com/world/national-security/justice-department-will-again-use-private-prisons/2017/02/23/da395d02-fa0e-11e6-be05-1a3817ac21a5_story.html.

INDEX

CPSIA information can be obtained
at www.ICGtesting.com
Printed in the USA
BVHW042145190521
607779BV00020B/221